LAST STOP BEFORE ANTARCTICA

Society of Biblical Literature

Semeia Studies

Gale A. Yee, General Editor

Editorial Board:
Jione Havea
Tat-Siong Benny Liew
Sarojini Nadar
Jeremy Punt
Erin Runions
Ken Stone
Caroline Vander Stichele
Elaine M. Wainwright

Number 64

LAST STOP BEFORE ANTARCTICA

LAST STOP BEFORE ANTARCTICA

The Bible and Postcolonialism in Australia

Second Edition

by

Roland Boer

Society of Biblical Literature
Atlanta

LAST STOP BEFORE ANTARCTICA

Copyright © 2008 by the Society of Biblical Literature

All rights reserved. No part of this work may be reproduced or transmitted in any form or by any means, electronic or mechanical, including photocopying and recording, or by means of any information storage or retrieval system, except as may be expressly permitted by the 1976 Copyright Act or in writing from the publisher. Requests for permission should be addressed in writing to the Rights and Permissions Office, Society of Biblical Literature, 825 Houston Mill Road, Atlanta, GA 30329 USA.

Library of Congress Cataloging-in-Publication Data

Boer, Roland, 1961–
 Last stop before Antarctica : the Bible and postcolonialism in Australia / by Roland Boer. —2nd ed.
   p. cm. — (Society of Biblical Literature Semeia studies ; no. 64)
 Includes bibliographical references and indexes.
 ISBN: 978-1-58983-348-7 (paper binding : alk. paper)
 1. Bible—Influence. 2. Bible—Use. 3. Bible—Postcolonial criticism. 4. Postcolonialism—Australia. 5. Australia—Religion. I. Title.
 BS538.7.B64 2008
 220.60994—dc22   2008009755

16 15 14 13 12 11 10 09 08   5 4 3 2 1
Printed in the United States of America on acid-free, recycled paper
conforming to ANSI/NISO Z39.48-1992 (R1997) and ISO 9706:1994
standards for paper permanence.

For John Docker

Contents

Preface to the Second Edition ix

Preface to the First Edition xiii

Introduction—Gatecrashing Thanksgiving: Australian Biblical
Studies in the Global Calculus 1

1. Marx, Postcolonialism, and the Bible 23

2. The Decree of the Watchers, or, Other Globalizations 37

3. Explorer Hermeneutics, or Fat Damper and Sweetened Tea 57

4. Home Is Always Elsewhere: Exodus, Exile, and the Howling
   Wilderness Waste 81

5. Green Ants and Gibeonites: B. Wongar, Joshua 9, and Some
   Problems of Postcolonialism 109

6. Dreaming the Logos: On Bible Translation and Language 135

7. Conclusion: (E)Strange Dialectics 161

Bibliography 173

Biblical Index 193

Subject Index 196

Author Index 198

Preface to the Second Edition

Let me begin with a story, before I say a little about what is new and what is the same about this revised edition of *Last Stop Before Antarctica*. A few years ago (in fact, getting close to twenty), I was somewhat reluctantly planning to return to Australia after some years in Canada. With two of my four children born in Canada, with a job offer, and with a sense it was a long, long way to Australia, we said farewell to friends. One of them, Diet Neufeld (now at the University of British Columbia), said, "Well, see you, Roland. When I'm down that way I'll drop in." "Yeah, please do," I replied, "maybe on your way to Antarctica." Needless to say, I have Diet to thank for that first spark that led to the title of the book.

I would prefer not to dwell too much on what I like (the chapter on "Explorer Hermeneutics," for instance) or on what I don't like about the book (apart from some very dense writing, I won't say), since that is a little too much self-indulgence. Instead, I offer a few comments on what is new about the revised edition and then about what has happened with what is now called "postcolonial biblical criticism." Chapter 1, "Marx, Postcolonialism and the Bible" is the major addition. It was published originally in *Biblical Criticism: Interdisciplinary Intersections* (Moore and Segovia 2005) and, with the good graces of T&T Clark, has been republished here. Further, I have been able to correct a few embarrassing spelling errors (especially that of Lancelot Threlkeld), add occasional notes and update the bibliography. Apart from that, I have left the bulk of the chapters alone. Of course, there are some I would write differently now, but that would destroy their integrity and flow of argument.

As for postcolonial biblical criticism, things have changed quite considerably in the decade since I first began writing. At that moment there were one or two books on postcolonialism and the Bible: Sugirtharajah had edited *The Postcolonial Bible* (1998), was in the process of publishing *Asian Biblical Hermeneutics and Postcolonialism* (1999), along with the 1999 issue of *Journal for the Study of the New Testament* (no. 73), and was just embarking on the steady flow of volumes that in many ways now define the field; Laura Donaldson had edited a sole issue of *Semeia* (no. 75 in 1996), from which the "Green

Ants and Gibeonites" chapter is drawn; Jon Berquist had written his *Judaism in Persia's Shadow* (1995), in which he used some postcolonial methods to reconstruct the history of ancient Yehud. Slim pickings indeed! In the last decade there has been a deluge of studies, which I will not delve into here. In fact, I merely refer the reader to Stephen Moore's exhaustive bibliography in his *Empire and Apocalypse* (2006), where he gathers all that has been written on postcolonialism, postcolonial theory, and postcolonial biblical studies. These days we find a whole host of names, such as Fernando Segovia, Judith McKinlay, Musa Dube, Jeremy Punt, Stephen Moore, Kwok Pui-Lan (to name but a very few), sections at international biblical studies meetings and a steady stream of monographs, edited volumes and essays. I have found in my various travels to less than usual haunts (in a conscious decision to avoid those former and present imperial centers), that postcolonial criticism of the Bible is cropping up all over the place—in the study of Christian missions in Greenland, by activists from the Swedish Lutheran Church, by literary critics in Bulgaria for whom "postcolonialism" means "post-communist," in Taiwan and China, Switzerland and on and on. It really is one of those so-called "new" approaches that have caught on in biblical studies. Even old warhorses like Niels Peter Lemche—of the notorious "Copenhagen school" on Israelite history (or the lack thereof)—have taken up postcolonial criticism with some gusto. This revision, then, reappears in an area of study that has changed biblical studies in the last ten years.

Perhaps I should explain what I set out to do when I first began writing the book. I did not attempt to read specific biblical texts in the light of postcolonial criticism. Rather, it seemed to me at the time that we had a curious contradiction: those predisposed to postcolonial criticism in other disciplines continued to ignore the Bible while it was quite obvious that the Bible played a crucial role in the period of colonial conquest and rule—in the hands of missionaries, administrators, Bible translators and whatnot—and continued to be crucial in what has followed, whether we call it postcolonialism or neo-colonialism. So I wanted to offer a small correction to that strange contradiction in wider postcolonial criticism. And since Australia is of course a former colony of the British Empire (some would say that it is now a colony of the U.S.A.), and since Australia was one of the places where postcolonial criticism first emerged (especially with Ashcroft, Griffiths and Tiffin's *The Empire Writes Back* from 1988), it seemed obvious that the focus should be Australia. The trick was to try and raise questions that were much wider than Australia, to use it as a test case, if you will. Whether I have succeeded or not is up to the reader.

Three final points: at the risk of stating the obvious, we need to be aware of two senses of "postcolonial." The first is a temporal one, designating the time after the heyday of classical colonial expansion, subjugation and domination. That was the period, as capitalism was becoming established in Europe, when one European power after another—The Netherlands, Denmark, England (although the English are a bit funny about being called Europeans), France, Italy, Germany and so on—began to conquer lands beyond Europe. In the face of waves of anti-colonial agitation and independence movements, running from the end of the nineteenth century and rising to a crescendo in the twentieth, what is now called the "postcolonial" era began. However, since colonialism is by no means a thing of the past, and since we can easily identify earlier forms of colonialism (the Romans for one), "postcolonial" also refers to a critical way of dealing with those earlier and still contemporary forms of colonialism. It is this wholesale reassessment that really embodies what postcolonial criticism sets out to do, often with the tools provided by various other approaches, including feminism, Marxism, deconstruction and psychoanalysis, among others.

Further, my conclusion to the original book evoked the Seattle protests of November 1999 as a possible model for a new globalized politics. More than one reader of the book found me overly optimistic. But the situation now, after an ongoing series of anticapitalist protests, the U.S. empire stumbling in Iraq, the looming crises of short oil-supplies (the famous "Peak" seemed to pass in 2006 when demand overtook supply), the urgent call by the bulk of the worlds' scientists to do something about global warming, and the way groups like the Fourth International (Trotsky's original organization) are scrambling to provide information and guidance to a large number of young people radicalized by protests throughout the world, of which Seattle was only the beginning, all suggest that a "time of troubles" is upon us. How it may work out is anyone's guess, but it also provides untold opportunities to imagine and plan for something a little better than the rotten system we have.

Lastly, it may seem strange that the revised edition of a book that is largely concerned with the Bible, postcolonialism, and Australia should be published in the United States, the last superpower. But then, the first edition was published in that old and now faded colonial center of England (by Sheffield Academic Press in 2001). The reality is that no press in Australia dares publish an academic book to do with the Bible, let alone theology. One of the paradoxes of postcolonialism, I guess. I am of course profoundly grateful that the Semeia Studies series of the Society of Biblical Literature has enthusiastically agreed to publish this revised edition. I would especially like to thank Gale Yee, Bob Buller, and Leigh Andersen for making it possible.

The Hill, New South Wales
January 2008

Preface to the First Edition

Living on the periphery of the modern world system (Wallerstein), last stop, perhaps, on the way to Antarctica, seems to produce its own curious form of identity scholarship. That is, if I live in a nation-state that was a former colony of one of the European powers, it is in some perverse way assumed that I will be interested in postcolonial theory. It may in fact be read as a default theoretical position: if I am not taken with postcolonial theory, then there is something amiss, I have denied my calling, and I should return to that as soon as possible. All of this I find somewhat frustrating, since my own desire runs against the political assumptions of postcolonial theory—local resistance, alternative identities, and valorization of the peripheral zone over against the center. I am, in other words, an internationalist in the old communist sense, and my desire is to move from the periphery to the center, to be where the action is (if scholarship may be called action). If my desire is but a copy of the constructed wish for the center, and thereby merely reinforces the troubled center-periphery binary, it is also the desire called Marx, the wish to focus on the international scene when so much attention is directed towards the national, regional, local.

Yet (an inevitable dialectical marker) there is something attractive about the peripheral zones in another sense. Strangely, Jeremy Bentham provides a rationale for this sense, in reverse of course. During his long campaign to build his much commented upon panopticon prison (and I will add to the comments in this book), Bentham gathered a number of his tedious letters under the title of *Panopticon Versus New South Wales* (Bentham 1843). By citing numerous newspaper articles and reports on the practice of transporting convicts to New South Wales and then comparing them to a prison in Pennsylvania run on his cherished panopticon model, Bentham argued for the clear benefits—example, reformation, incapacitation (prevention of further offense), compensation, satisfaction, industry, frugality, and economy—of the panopticon. His prison shines as a model of discipline, sobriety, strictness, criminal reform and the impossibility of escape, whereas New South Wales comes through as a place of total and "general depravity" (the first point of Calvinism), of sexual license, lewdness, lack of reformation, and general carousing. All of which was caused by that "universal and incurable" vice of drunkenness (1843: 230). Neither temporal nor spiritual remedies made, according to Bentham, any difference. Even though I am among that one third of Australians that does not have connections with England, Scotland, Wales or Ireland, it takes little reflection to decide where I would rather be.

Contrary to most of my work, which is very much a solitary effort, there are a number of people to thank for their assistance and feedback at different points in this project. Sugi has through his efforts with Sheffield Academic Press provided a forum where the issues of postcolonialism and the Bible may be aired and discussed. Paul Eckert, Tom Webb and Ken Hanson helped me with vital information and feedback on Bible translation in Australia, and Jonathan Nicholls straightened out some of my glaring errors in an early draft of that chapter. Most of the project was researched and written during a Visiting Fellowship at the Humanities Research Centre of the Australian National University in Canberra. It could not have happened without that precious time and space provided for me there. Through the dry heat and occasional rain of a Canberra summer in early 1999, I read and wrote in an increasingly rare place in Australia, a research center. At breakfast I rode into the space provided, eating, talking, reading and writing, and at midnight I rode back to my tent, crawling in to sleep the sleep of the dead. Leena Messina and Misty Cook, the real directors of the center, made my stay very pleasant. Deborah Bird Rose kept me responsible for what I said, and Ann Curthoys provided me with some ideas to ponder. Above all, John Docker was and is a constant companion for talk, reflection, reading and comment.

An earlier, barren and stark, version of chapter 5, "Green Ants and Gibeonites" appeared in *Semeia* 75 (1996): 129–52.

Canberra, ACT
February 1999

Introduction
Gatecrashing Thanksgiving: Australian Biblical Studies in the Global Calculus

In a time span that can only be found in the hyper-market of the present, postcolonialism has established itself in a very short space of time as a vibrant discourse in biblical studies, let alone literary and cultural studies more generally. However, it is not sufficient to seek to understand the Bible in a postcolonial environment, as though it were an orphan seeking a home: it is also necessary to ask questions about both postcolonialism and the Bible in the light of each other. Thus, the underlying theme of this study is the way the intersection of postcolonialism and the Bible problematizes both sides, for neither has postcolonial theory given much thought to the Bible, nor have biblical critics realized the importance of postcolonial criticism for their work.

Biblical studies, however, often functions like Hegel's owl of Minerva, taking to wing in the dusk of the methods it so assiduously appropriates to itself. Indeed, for a method in another discipline it seems that a signal of its shift to comfortable establishment, of the stiffening of the muscles and creaking of the bones, if not obsolescence, is that biblical critics take it up for their own use. Of course, this trades on the very patterns of fashion and product upgrade so characteristic of capitalism more broadly, denying the continued viability of approaches well past their use-by date. And this also conveniently forgets, in a typical moment of repression, that in many respects the very methods appropriated by biblical critics, particularly those from literary and cultural criticism, derive their enabling energy from biblical criticism itself, albeit in a former moment that is no longer with us.[1]

That is to say, the forms of literary criticism established over centuries of interpretation of the Bible, which was the primary literary document for

---

1. For an extended version of this argument, see the introduction to my *Knockin' on Heaven's Door* (Boer 1999, 1–12).

the small clerical group who were literate, eventually fed into the explosion of forms that came with the Renaissance and the rise of capitalism. However, while the *forms*—in key areas such as meaning, hermeneutics, inspiration, classics, canonicity, genre, style and so on—of such approaches derived from biblical criticism, their religious and theological *content* was discarded in that vast campaign of the banishment of superstition from intellectual and social life that came with the Enlightenment. Over time it became possible to use these various secular methods, derived from biblical interpretation, for the study of the Bible, without reference to its religious content or theological claims, something carried out most famously in the grand style of historical criticism. What is of course forgotten in all of this, as with the forgetting of the origins of any socio-economic system, is the enabling function of biblical criticism. To complete the circuit, then, it is not so much that biblical criticism is always late in its appropriation of methods developed elsewhere, but that there is a delay in cashing the checks that all these methods bear, issued and signed by biblical criticism itself, which is now the outcast among the methods to which it gave birth.

If the process I have described all too briefly is somewhat veiled in the usual operation of literary and cultural criticism, it seems to be highly transparent in what goes by the name of postcolonial criticism. That is, not only might it be argued that the Bible had a central role in the various patterns of colonialism, but also that the way in which the Bible has been and is appropriated by both the indigenous colonized and the colonials themselves provides something of a model for postcolonial criticism. In other words, if the various items and issues of postcolonial criticism seem to have a peculiar resonance with the questions associated with the Bible—globalization, the construction of new worlds, Diaspora, identity and translation, to name a few—it is not mere coincidence, for the Bible was crucial not only in the construction of medieval and early modern Europe, but also in the colonial endeavor that saw Europe itself shift from the margin of the global system to its center (see ch. 2). It was, to use another code with which I have a great sympathy, a central item in the ideological construction, language and culture of Europe. This is the sense in which I suggest that the Bible is a hidden factor in postcolonial criticism, insofar as its problematic is colonialism and its aftermath.

Thus, it is somewhat curious—and therefore one of the arguments of this book—to note the absence of the Bible in postcolonial critical work (apart from some notable exceptions with which I will engage in this book), something that stands in stark contrast to its pervasive presence in the production of colonial discourse.

INTRODUCTION

Inevitably, postcolonial theory must negotiate a range of problems that ignite the intellectual passions of a growing group of theorists:[2] the inaugural moments of Frantz Fanon (Moore-Gilbert, Stanton and Maley 1997, 12–15; Gandhi 1998, 17–22); C. L. R. James (1993) and Said's "colonial discourse" (Said 1978; see Moore-Gilbert 1997, 34–73; Moore-Gilbert, Stanton and Maley 1997, 21–27; Gandhi 1998, 64–80); Spivak's deconstruction of the colonial subject and subalternity (Spivak 1988; Moore-Gilbert 1997, 74–113; Moore-Gilbert, Stanton and Maley 1997, 27–32); hybridity, mimicry, translation, and ambiguity (Bhabha 1994; see also Coombes 1994; Moore-Gilbert 1997, 114–151); alternative or subaltern historiography (Chakrabarty 1996; Guha and Spivak 1988; Rajan and Mohanran 1995; Spivak 1988, 197–221); oppositional politics, critical scrutiny, and resistance (Fanon and many others such as Adam and Tiffin 1991; Boehmer 1995; San Juan 1998); the dialectics of difference and identity in global culture (Darby 1998[3]; Spivak 1994; Jameson 1998b); the explosion of indigenous politics and literature (e.g., Devi 1995); globalization, essentialism, and identity (Dussell 1998; Bhabha 1994; Rajan and Mohanran 1995); exile and nomadism (Bhabha 1994; Rajan and Mohrahan 1995; Said 1990); nationalism and postnationalism (Gandhi 1998, 102–40; Paik Nak-Chung 1998; Kapur 1998); and not least feminism (Spivak 1988, 1990, 1996; Gandhi 1998, 81–101). There is also a continual engagement with Marxism and economics more broadly, especially since postcolonial theory, as with so many other critical approaches, finds itself continually dealing with the legacy of Marx (see Ahmad 1992; Moore-Gilbert 1997, 2–3; Hoogvelt 1997, 154–58; Spivak 1988, 77–92 on reproduction, 154–75 on value; Spivak 1990, 95–111 on Marx in general).

In various ways most of these themes are interwoven in the following text, often in a way that problematizes the theme itself. To begin with, there is the peculiarly postmodern dilemma that presents itself to any critical approach: either postcolonial criticism is one of a number of current approaches, often gathered behind the prefix "post," with which it shares certain issues and terms and problems; or it is a distinct break that usurps all of these other approaches, the outsider that storms the field and brings in a new era. Indeed, both of these claims are made, as they are for other overlapping approaches, and Moore-Gilbert (1997) has attempted to deal with such a question by distinguishing between the long history of what may now be named postcolonial

---

2. Some useful surveys must include Gandhi 1998, Loomba 1998, and Moore-Gilbert 1997.

3. Indeed, Darby argues that the earlier interest in Third World literary production has fallen away in postcolonial discussion in favor of theory. He seeks to readdress this with considerations from politics and economics.

criticism (stemming from W. E. B. DuBois and Sol Plaatje at the turn of the twentieth century) and the more recent postcolonial theory, which is characterized by reliance on the French theory of Derrida, Lacan and Foucault through Said, Spivak and Bhabha.[4] This is a salutary effort, except that it is precisely the latter that permits the construction of a tradition of postcolonial criticism in the first place. All the same, it seems to me that a signal of postcolonial theory's (and I do not distinguish between criticism or theory here) status as one other theoretical commodity is the wholesale sharing of terminology with other approaches—such as agency, alterity, appropriation, binarism, discourse, essentialism, globalization, hegemony, marginality, race and so on (see Ashcroft, Griffiths and Tiffin 1998)—and of theorists themselves—Foucault and Gramsci (Said), Lacan (Bhabha), Derrida (Spivak), Marx (e.g., Ahmad, Spivak).

I have delayed the moment of definition since I am inclined not to spend time discussing what postcolonialism might be, assuming that readers will already have opinions on this matter. Yet a few comments may be in order. Arif Dirlik, in a refreshing mode of Marxist demystification that may be instrumental in seeing the overdue return of this practice, identifies three usages of the term: (1) a literal description of conditions in formerly colonial societies that includes formerly third world and some first world political entities (Australia, Canada, and so on); (2) the global condition after colonialism, replacing the term Third World; (3) the discourse on this condition that is informed by epistemological and psychic orientations that are products of those conditions (Dirlik 1997, 54).[5] While one would have expected the first and third items—postcolonialism as a heterogeneous discourse and as a period of socio-economic and cultural history—the surprise is the second item, mediating the other two, somewhere between their concrete and

---

4. Indeed, Moore-Gilbert's agenda is to meet the criticism of the newer postcolonial "theory"—that it is complicit with a neo-colonial world order, it reinscribes the cultural authority of the west, that its modes of cultural analysis are deeply Eurocentric, that its style and language are obscure, and that there are insufficient engagements with class and gender (see 1997, 152–69)—from the older postcolonial "criticism" and to bring the two together.

5. Postcolonialism itself partakes of a deeper pattern of periodization which seems to afflict our thinking. For reasons that need to considered in detail somewhere else, it seems to me that we have two options within our present intellectual and social horizon. The first is to attempt some organization of history into distinct periods which may be identified according to a set of features which mark it off from other periods which will then have their own distinct features. The second option is to argue that history is far too complex to periodize in any meaningful sense. Postcolonialism falls clearly within the orbit of periodization, being in this sense that which comes after the era of (capitalist) colonialism.

abstract opposition. And, despite misgivings by Ella Shohat over the demise of "Third World" as a signifier (1996), it seems to me that postcolonialism is a slogan that usefully indicates the shifts in global economic and political power after 1989 and the absorption of communist Eastern Europe into a capitalist Atlantic. Such a shift is marked in Dirlik's own definition of postcolonialism as the cultural logic of late capitalism, "this time on Third World terrain" (1997, 70). Apart from the echoes of Jameson here—postmodernism as the cultural logic of late capitalism—such a definition also intertwines postmodernism with postcolonialism.

Indeed, in chapter 2 I will argue for an understanding of postcolonialism that cannot avoid postmodernism and for a further understanding of both in terms of a dialectical conjunction between globalization and disintegration, the deeper logic of capitalism itself. This implies a connection between postmodernism and postcolonialism as cultural phenomena (their most common formulation) and as socio-economic developments. In order to make this connection I rely upon a Marxist construction of reality in which the realm of culture, aesthetics and so on, has a necessary but complex relationship with political economics. Rather than proposing a solution, this relationship—normally designated in terms of base and superstructure—states a problem that requires innovative thinking. Yet, what the interlocking of postcolonialism and postmodernism enables is a reverse of the usual relation: that is, it may in fact be argued that postmodernism itself is predicated upon the conditions of postcolonialism, namely, the move of certain third world colonial countries toward independence from their various colonial masters after the Second World War—the last wave, if you like, of decolonization (and then neo-colonialism). In other words, the late arrival of the term *postcolonial* belies the prior socioeconomic status of postcolonialism, which then becomes a condition for the development of postmodern culture as well. What this boils down to is that the two closely related cultural moments of postmodernism and postcolonialism are distinct, spatially determined responses to the vast expansion of global capitalism after 1950.

A definitional discursus like this is not complete without considering the inevitable celebrations and condemnations that a term such as postcolonialism (or postmodernism or globalization or ...) inevitably attracts to itself. While it is salutary to be wary of the ideological mystification that "postcolonialism" may bring, particularly as a mask for neo-colonialism,[6] and to be

---

6. "While admittedly another PC word, 'postcolonialism' is arguably more palatable and less foreign-sounding to skeptical deans than 'Third World Studies.' It also has a less accusatory ring than 'Studies in Neo-colonialism,' say, or 'Fighting Two Colonialisms.' It is more global, and less fuddy-duddy, than 'Commonwealth Studies.' The term borrows,

suspicious of emancipatory expectations generated by the term (most notably Ashcroft, Griffiths, and Tiffin 1989, 38), it is also important to ask why such terms attract approbation and celebration in the first place. What happens here is that the cultural dimensions of postcolonialism bear a positive weight, whereas the economic side is the bogey in all of this. Thus, postcolonial literature, film and art become the focus of intense appreciation, while the political and economic situations of ever more intense capitalist saturation are decried. Yet, it is not really possible to separate culture and economics here so easily, since, as Jameson has argued, the two slide into one another: the celebrated films, for instance, are both enabled and then become part of the global economic system in which such cultural products are bought and sold.

Nevertheless, the disadvantage of such broad-ranging discussions is that the peculiar lilt of the local fades away, as Mishra and Hodge have argued (1993). Although I remain perpetually interested in the global and always read in that light, there are two areas that produce a particular flavor: Australia and the Bible. One of the features of postcolonial criticism that is a distinct legacy of Said is that its major figures derive in some way or another from the "Orient," whether from the Said's paradigmatic Middle East, or Spivak's nonparadigmatic India (Spivak 1984), or Bhabha's Babelian India. Australia is therefore outside this orbit. It is one of a number of white male settler colonies, in distinction from indigenous or "non-white" colonies, or at least places where the European contingent was always a significant but very powerful minority. It belongs, then, to that exclusive club that includes the U.S.A., Canada, and New Zealand, where the attempt to kill the indigenous peoples was most systematically perpetrated. However, despite being, along with Canada and New Zealand, the site for an earlier wave of decolonization in the later nineteenth century, the resulting semi-independent status was established in such a way—framed in a rather hasty and patchwork constitution—as to allow the drive to decolonization to expend itself while keeping Australia firmly tied into British society and political economics. In this context Australia itself became a minor colonial nation in the South Pacific, exercising its paternal care over a number of small islands and Papua New Guinea. In fact, Australia's involvement with the decolonizing moves of the decades following the Second World War lay in Papua New Guinea, which

---

moreover, on the dazzling marketing success of the term *postmodernism*. As the organizing rubric of an emerging field of disciplinary studies and an archive of knowledge, the term *postcolonialism* makes possible the marketing of a whole new generation of panels, articles, books, and courses" (McClintock 1993, 299). See also the misgivings by Shohat 1996 and Brewster 1995, 21–23.

was "granted" independence on September 16, 1975. The decolonized country becomes a colonizer, only to be the target of decolonization itself.

What is significant (and appalling) about the Australian situation is how smoothly a penal settlement with its own subordinate status in relation to the colonial metropolis of London (a dystopian view) should at the same time be understood and understand itself to be a force for colonization over the land and its Aboriginal people (for settlers a "utopian" view, emphasizing wealth and a regenerated social order). The British settlement of 1788 was, in other words, both subject and agent of colonialism, the relations between indigenous peoples and settlers overlaid with the relations between England and the settlers (Fuery 1993, 196). Australia also has a claim to the unique status of beginning its colonial history as a prison, "a gulag for 'excess' victims of the Industrial Revolution," to quote Meaghan Morris, which "went through genocide and ethnocide and gynocide to pioneer hyper-discreet forms of apartheid and race management through genetic engineering" (Morris 1992, 477).

Yet I have reverted to a myth of origins by invoking the founding story of nonindigenous European settlement in Australia. One of the problems with much postcolonial writing is the tendency to lock in the European connection as normative—in Australia it is therefore the English who constitute the postcolonial partner—thereby neglecting, as Sneja Gunew has tirelessly argued, the history of other movements, such as the Afghans, Chinese, and Germans of the nineteenth century or the vast range of migration in the twentieth century. In fact, these other histories constitute something like a third of the population—one of the reasons for my chapter 5 on B. Wongar).

Further, in Australian debates there is a curious split that is generated out of a three-way relation: not only between Aboriginal and settler cultures, but also between these and the imperial centers (and then there is the muted relation between Aborigines and the imperial centers). Who, then, are the colonizers? Settlers/invaders or the imperial centers of Europe?[7] Denied the

---

7. Spivak works away at the problem, without, to my mind, resolving it: "So when you're talking about colonization you are talking about settling a place which was unsettled before, and that brings us to an issue that I've spoken of many times before: the assumption that when the colonizers come to a world, they encounter it as uninscribed earth upon which they write their inscriptions. From that sense when you use the word Australia you are speaking the language of the colonizer, because you have decided that the name of this place is Australia. In fact Australia has no *right* to ignore this, marginalize itself, and feel like a colony. When it calls itself Australia, and when it is defined as you are defining it, that particular segment in fact *is* the colonizer rather than the colonized" (Spivak 1990, 129).

easier opposition between native and colonizer that works so well for someone like Bhabha, debate here divides over whether "postcolonial" applies to the relation between Aboriginal and settler cultures (Gunew in Rajan and Mohanran 1995b, 206), or to settler culture in relation to the old imperial center (Brewster 1995, 20[8]). It seems to me that it is not so much an either/or here but rather that the question of postcolonialism in Australia is precisely this problem, this ambivalence over the multiple layers and relations of Aboriginal, settler and imperial center.

If the Australian, antipodal, location provides a first distinctive feel to postcolonial discourse, then the Bible constitutes a second. Apart from the discussion generated by Edward Said surrounding uses of the Exodus in colonial discourse (Said 1988; see ch. 4) and Homi Bhabha's reflections on the ambiguous appropriation of the "Word" in India (1994, 102–22; see ch. 6), the Bible has by and large been absent from postcolonial theory and criticism. I will let the argument of the book attempt to redress this somewhat. Thus, the second chapter deals with some of the theoretical questions of postcolonialism in relation to biblical studies. It is concerned with the relations between postcolonialism, postmodernism and globalization through the foil of Dan 4, suggesting that globalization is by no means a new way of thinking about the world. With chapter 3 I go on to consider movements that unsettle patterns of domination and identity. Here I focus on the way explorers made use of the Bible in the way they saw Australia and attempted to understand it. Chapter 4 moves on to consider the use and constructions of the biblical motifs of exodus, exile and nomadism in postcolonial theory. Chapter 5 picks up the questions of essentialism and identity, both in regard to the nervousness in the Hebrew Bible over the identity of Israelites (Josh 9) and the difficulties of Aboriginal/European identity. Here I foreground some other postcolonial histories—Serbian-Aboriginal—outside the conventional ones. Finally, in chapter 6 I turn to another category in which identity and travel appear in a different guise—a critical engagement with the translation of the Bible into Australian Aboriginal languages.

The sequence of chapters also follows a trajectory of the colonial critic, from initial theorizing in a study or corner, in a forlorn shack that turns its back to the Antarctic gales, to viewing and attempting to understand the critical landscape, traveling over it, engaging with the indigenes and then seeking to translate into their tongues. At each step, however, this trajectory is undermined, ruptured and broken.

---

8. "Aboriginal people do not produce narratives of post-coloniality or even decolonization" (Brewster 1995, 20).

Australian Biblical Studies in the Global Calculus

The other thing to add is that in Australia we are neither the first nor the third world. (Sneja Gunew, as quoted by Rajan and Mohanram 1995b, 206)

And the first step in such a ruptured narrative, a postcolonial recasting, is that of the practice of biblical studies in Australia. In order to trace this practice in the perennially peripheral zone of Australia, to follow its spoor as it passed by during the night, I want to exploit some images of Australia. These images are in fact clichés of the white settler community in Australia, clichés that provide a rampant misrepresentation of biblical studies in Australia. But is that not the best way to (re)present a history? My three images or clichés are cultural hierarchy, cultural cringe, and the tyranny of distance.

I borrow "cultural hierarchy" from John Docker, who in his turn develops it from Frantz Fanon's "hierarchy of values." It denotes a scaled inferiority in which the indigenous, Aboriginal culture is devalued by the colonial settlers, whose culture is understood to be inferior to the colonial center. Such a scaled approach does not deal sufficiently with either Aboriginal or imperial cultures, lying at either extreme of the scale, but its focus is the central term—white settler culture—which is depicted as a conflictual site, a place of "profound psychological disturbance, at once guilty of enforcing inferiority on others, and haunted by self-doubt and self-contempt before the metropolitan culture's necessary superiority" (Docker 1995, 443). This is ultimately a colonial self-perception, but such a hierarchy continues to characterize the way many intellectuals function: any contributions from Aboriginal or Koori people, from students through to established writers, are measured and often dismissed on the basis of metropolitan-derived academic standards. From the other direction, Australian biblical scholars remain "haunted by self-doubt and self-contempt" before the juggernauts of European and North American biblical studies.

It is only a small step from cultural hierarchy to "cultural cringe"—an almost physical repulsion that bearers of metropolitan or imperial culture feel in the face of anything that champions a distinctly Australian identity or flavor, more often than not in the realm of popular or mass culture. Anything that has a distinctly "ocker" tone, that speaks with a strong drawl, that devotes itself to Australian derivations of country and western or folk music, that plays upon myths of the (male) larrikin or bushman, and that celebrates the focus on sport and leisure becomes an object of sophisticated derision and avoidance. That this also has strong class dimensions—especially in a country that at times lays claim to be a classless society—should not be forgotten. Manifestations of cultural cringe are found with those who place themselves in the upper middle class of Australian society, although even here jingoistic nationalism has made strong inroads. Further, there are those who either visit or migrate to Australia from the decayed colonial centers of Europe, arriving with an assumed superiority of European culture over against the derived colonial culture of Australia. All of this is then reinforced by the popularity of the crassest of Australian television programs, particularly soap operas like "Home and Away" in the late 1980s and 1990s, in the place termed "home" (England) by the majority of an older generation of white settlers. The very shoddiness of the programs reinforces the sense of cultural superiority that is assumed from the European side. Another group for whom cultural cringe has been a determining force is of course the intellectuals who by and large arrived in Australia from Europe for a shorter or longer term (on this, see below). The intellectual dimensions of cultural cringe remain very strong even for contemporary "home grown" intellectuals, since the prestige of publication at a press in Europe or the U.S.A. far outweighs that of an Australian press (where one exists), and the participation at conferences based in the northern hemisphere is far more desirable than those in the Australian region. I must confess my own somewhat unavoidable guilt in expressions of cultural cringe, particularly when theology or biblical studies in Australia lays claim to a nationalistic or patriotic agenda, but I will return to this.

The "tyranny of distance"—a "cliché of Australian pop historiography" (Morris 1988, 165)—is a phrase still encountered at times in the 1990s in Australia. Coined by Geoffrey Blainey in 1966 (see Blainey 1983), the term continues to designate the absence of Europe (and more recently North America) on the visible landscape. Yet it has a double reference: "tyranny of distance" referred not only to the relation between Europe and the coastal cities of Australia, but between those coastal cities and the arid interior, that is, the phrase referred to the size of a largely desert land itself. All the same, today it is usually dredged up in order to be thrown back into the past as a state which no longer holds due to the wonders of travel and communications technology. This maneuver often evokes mixed images and emotions: of recoil at crude and tough conditions at a pioneer station at the edge of the world (last stop, apart from New Zealand perhaps, on the way to the Antarctica), of nostalgia for a time of braver men, of thankfulness for Australia's belated incorporation into media society. For biblical (and other) scholars such a tyranny basically referred to the three months or more it took for passage by boat from Australia to England, Scotland or Wales—the commercial run which ensured Australia's place in the British

Empire.⁹ This meant, of course, that for any scholar traveling "home" in a sabbatical year half of the time was spent in transit. Even if the travel seems to have been two-way, in terms of resources for academic appointments the flow was overwhelmingly from the "old country" to Australian institutions. To be sure, a few journeyed in reverse, invariably not to return as they became comfortable expatriates. Yet the long colonial tradition of academic reproduction in Australia lay in the expectation that boats would continue disgorging scholars, while from the English side a placement in a colony like Australia or Canada might fall into an acceptable academic career pattern. Not that these were all second-rate or even useless, but by and large the better scholars did not choose the colonies, except perhaps some younger scholars out for quick advancement and the chance for some publications before returning home in triumph. In those areas where biblical scholars were required—the training institutes of the various churches—the assumption until the 1960s (and beyond in some cases) was that selection/search committees invariably looked "home" for replacements.

Nevertheless, the imperial legacy was neither resolutely negative nor were biblical scholars always shown the greatest hospitality. In all of the colonial period perhaps the marker of a deeper ambivalence was a predilection for heresy trials against the occasional English and Scottish biblical scholar. Not only was the "churchman" Charles Strong accused of heresy—his Melbourne congregation left the Presbyterians and formed an independent church—but in the 1930s the reasonably well-published New Testament scholar Samuel Angus was accused of heresy, although never finally convicted. His sin was the advocacy of classical Christian liberalism. In a huge time warp that fits better in a science fiction novel, a heresy charge was upheld in 1992 against another New Testament scholar who came from Scotland in 1990 to become the head of St. Andrews College at Sydney University. Although it seemed to be the fundamentalist rump of a continuing Presbyterian Church charging a conventionally liberal Peter Cameron, the language of anti-colonialism ran strongly in the whole procedure.

A number of other factors influence the ideological makeup of academics in Australia, apart from (yet structurally related to) those which are integral to their situation in regard to class (relations of production) and political economics (mode of production). Among the former should be included a relative absence of intellectual stimulus and lack of academic resources (both closely tied in with tyrannical distance), the relatively small number of aca-

---

9. The subversive note to all of this is that for the sizeable Catholic population, mostly Irish, the academic center was the "Greg" in Rome.

demics as a whole (especially biblical scholars among whom potential job movements are often known well in advance), a wide antiintellectualism in Australian society in response to which intellectuals prefer to travel incognito in transit from one safe house to another, and a virtual absence of the pressure to publish, particularly within the seminary or college system. What the peripheral status of Australian scholarship produces is a simultaneous freedom from the extraordinary expectations of the academic systems of the Atlantic and a claustrophobia that closes down the possibilities of scholarship, a blinkering into a cowered state. However, what is interesting to note here is a patchwork professionalization and "Americanization" of academic life (to borrow a term from Ahmad in regard to India [Ahmad, 278–81]), in which the pressure for higher degrees, conference hunting and professional publication is beginning to make inroads into biblical and theological studies, although there are plenty of academics who hold onto the older tradition of being of service to the church before being intellectuals and scholars. These elements should be related to the nature of institutional life, in which the various churches and the state have often arranged compromise deals in both funding and control (most recently the state funded Australian Catholic University, but also state allowances for students at the various theological colleges) and where the universities have overwhelmingly been run by the state, flirting occasionally with the old "queen," theology, and more recently religious studies. Yet even in the newer religious studies programs which cling to the edge of existence biblical scholars struggle to find a place, except perhaps under cover, researching in biblical studies while teaching in other areas of religious studies.

If cultural hierarchy, cultural cringe and the tyranny of distance go some way towards characterizing the ideological context for biblical scholarship in Australia, then I want to suggest that there have been, until and into the postmodern/postcolonial era, three major possibilities for the pursuit of biblical studies—emulation, nationalism and positive unoriginality. For (biblical) scholars in places outside the super states the dominant option in the past has been emulation of the work done in the metropolitan centers from which those scholars inevitably came (for Australia this was for so long England and Scotland, although replaced by Dublin for Roman Catholic scholars), much like the classic colonial gentleman who imitates the colonial center. The intensity of the drive to emulate metropolitan scholarship seems inversely related to the distance from the metropolitan centers: emulation seemed to be the appropriate response to the tyranny of distance. Those disgorged by the boats mentioned earlier worked hard to emulate the scholarship and teaching of their own source, thereby attempting to erase their colonial presence in any teaching or writing they might undertake. Part of this of course was due to the training those scholars received before arriving in Australia, and in fact, it is only in the last two generations that biblical scholars have trained in Australia, or returned after study and work overseas. This is a rather ambivalent change, since although there is an increasing trend to Australian born incumbents who have completed Australian degrees, the pressure remains for intending scholars to procure graduate degrees in North America or the U.K. and then return to take up posts in Australia itself, if they are not in the meantime drawn into the academic market place of these larger metropolitan centers. The paradox here is that with an increasing trend to a complete Australian cycle of academic life there is an simultaneous increase in insularity, with distinct marks of lack of international contact.

The change toward Australian bred biblical scholars has, however, led to the flowering of the second option I noted above—nationalism—although it has had a sporadic existence alongside the stronger tendency to emulation. Although stemming politically and socially from the 1890s—the drive towards semi-independent status in relation to the colonial power of Britain resulted in the compromise deal of the federated Australian commonwealth of 1901—and finding more recent life with the failed drive to become a Republic by 2001,[10] the nationalist option presents a curious bind for biblical scholarship. For many scholars it seems to be the only way to avoid what is increasingly regarded as the undesirable practice of metropolitan emulation, of the encroachment of the global system of scholarly dominance. By "nationalist" I refer to intense interest in "contextual" issues, in that which has a uniquely Australian feel to it, all of which is most often expressed in terms of Australian publishing, scholars, appointment, and content, but it rarely includes Aboriginal discourses and mostly assumes that the adjective "Australian" is an unambiguous term in itself. The connections between this move in (biblical) scholarship and the opposition between globalization and disintegration that I will explore in chapter 2 in regard to Australia's own (post)colonial history should not be missed, but there are some interesting twists within a nationalist emphasis. To begin with, the distinctness of Australian forms of academic produce is often presented as a resistance to "American" influence, specifically that of the U.S.A. The feeling here is that the truly global cultural forces are those which stem from the U.S.A.—most notably in Hollywood films, television programming, McDonald's, Coke, Pepsi, and so on. Yet the resistance to these all too persistent influences is often cast in Anglophile terms, assert-

---

10. In a curious twist, postcolonialism is somehow connected with republicanism in Australia: it is seen both as a casting free from Britain and as a moment for Aboriginal "reconciliation" (see Gunew in Rajan and Mohanran 1995b, 208).

ing those values which were the hallmark of emulation of the metropolitan centers. One final twist here is that the issues of scholarly value often operate with the canonical, metropolitan assumptions of the metropolitan centers themselves: thus, success depends upon showing such centers that something good can in fact come out of Australia, despite contrary expectations.

Yet the increasing assertion of a national identity is part of the dynamic of globalization itself: the desire to be distinct is generated in response to the inexorable drive to economic and cultural uniformity. And then in the very response to globalization, at the point where one feels a genuine oppositional move has been made, globalization shows through even more strongly. I am thinking here of the way particular ethnic, local and national quirks become the stuff of global fashion and interest—Australian accents and films, Aboriginal art and literature, to name a few more notable examples. The key term here that is closely related to the national but generates its own logic is the "exotic," a term redolent with older colonial associations. The attraction is that there is something distinctly South East Asian or South Pacific about Australia and its location, yet its dominant culture is western and language English—something both familiar and strange. (This "exotic" status operates a little like certain forms of global tourism which may be defined by the internally contradictory need to avoid being touristy by seeking precisely those areas not frequented by [too many] tourists.) Thus, biblical studies in Australia may be said to be truly "national" when it digs deep into that which is distinct or exotic about the place itself. As a colonial construct, the exotic appeal is what drew at least some scholars to Australian appointments in the first place, and then kept them there for a lifetime of work. And it seems that Australia's exotic status may pay some postcolonial dividends, with its very distance and poverty of intellectual life being that which attracts those who have traditionally had a surfeit of accessibility and intellectual stimulus. All of this points finally to the deeply conflicted yet relentless logic of a globalization which inevitably absorbs the very particularities of a local situation: one by one the local quirks and oddities are put on public display where they quickly lose their exotic status and become humdrum.

A third option—positive unoriginality—has played an ambiguous role in biblical scholarship in this part of the world.[11] In using the phrase "positive unoriginality" I want to designate the troubled place of modernism (as both a term within biblical scholarship and as a designation of a cultural period) on

---

11. There are close connections with mimicry and mockery: colonial discourse seeks to produce compliant subjects who mimic the colonial source, yet mockery is never far away (see Ashcroft, Griffiths, and Tiffin 1998, 13).

the Australian scene. As Meaghan Morris has argued (1990, 10–11), modernism in Australia, at least in the realms of architecture and cultural theory, has rarely been driven by slogans of the *novum*—innovation, originality, future, rupture, unknown, and so on. Whatever was "modern" was understood "as a *known history*, something which has *already happened elsewhere*, and which is to be reproduced, mechanically or otherwise, with a local content" (Morris 1990, 11). The introduction of modernism, then, was more a case of catching up with metropolitan centers in a perpetual time lag, and by the time they arrived there was a distinctly archaic feel to modernist cultural artifacts. And biblical studies shows this up in a rather remarkable fashion, modernist or liberal methods of biblical study arriving late and with considerable suspicion in the person of Samuel Angus, Professor of New Testament at the Presbyterian Theological Hall at Sydney University in the earlier part of the twentieth century. Vilified and idolized in his lifetime, the near martyr status granted Angus after his death ensured that the modernist currents of biblical and theological scholarship from the turn of the century that he embodied carried on within sections of the Protestant churches well into the 1960s and 1970s. But this is not the only use of "positive unoriginality': here my debts are to a study of the film *Crocodile Dundee* by Meaghan Morris. The film is for Morris "a post-*colonial* comedy of survival" (Morris 1988, 244), enabled by a clever positioning in relation to the American film market and Hollywood itself. Neither original nor mere copy, the film pursues a "positive unoriginality," a process of copying which persistently alters the "original" so that it comes out the worse for the imitation (e.g., Davy Crockett is the worse for the comparison). But the activity is reciprocal, since the various items of Australia's own ideological makeup undergo a similar process of belittlement—the bushman, Aboriginality, the outback, mateship, larrikinism, masculinism.

The most appealing dimension of this sort of positive unoriginality (Bhabha would call it mimicry) lies in the disavowal of the need to take the international currents of biblical scholarship with complete seriousness. What counts in the end are a good beer and a few jokes, and anyone who takes things too seriously is either a nerd or a dag. Such a positive unoriginality means not only a process of what Marxists would call demystification—the need continually to call the bluff on reactionary and conservative ideological formations (in other words, crap detection)—but also an appropriation of whatever methodological means are provided on the global theoretical market (this is the "unoriginal" bit) and the use of such methods for more intense studies of biblical texts in conjunction with local textual artifacts (this is the "positive" bit). The models I would suggest here are those of Sreten Bozic and Mudrooroo Narogin (see ch. 5). Both have slippery and uncertain identities (most debate has in fact focused, not unexpectedly, on questions of authenticity and identity). Mudrooroo, African American and Nyoongah Aboriginal, brings about a conjunction between Aboriginal forms and content and those of European and Indian background (Mudrooroo Narogin Nyoongah 1979; 1983; 1987; 1991; 1992; 1993). Sreten Bozic, a Serbian immigrant, amateur anthropological field worker, and writer of an astounding series of poems, short stories and novels,—especially the "nuclear trilogy" of *Walg* (1986), *Karan* (1986), and *Gabo Djara* (1988)— writes as the Aboriginal, Banumbir Wongar, at times as a woman. Not only is each novel is a "site of contestation between European and Aboriginal narratives" (Connor and Matthews 1989, 719) and between genders, but each one also problematizes the status of such distinctions. What appeals to me about their work is a certain antipodality: instead of the mimicry of colonial masters by the indigenes, here we have alternative migrants—African American and Serbian, mimicking the natives.

Yet it would seem that the distinct nature of any area, or of any local tradition, mode of interpretation or group of scholars is enabled by the means made available internationally by the globalization of academic life. Thus, for instance, Meaghan Morris, Australia's foremost cultural critic, deals with Australian popular culture in terms of French and American theories of culture which are no longer particularly French or American but transnational. From biblical and theological studies comes the example of *Freedom and Entrapment*, a collection of essays on Australian feminism and theology edited by the Melbourne New Testament scholar Dorothy Lee, as well as Maryanne Confoy and Joan Nowotny, but with a foreword by Elisabeth Schüssler Fiorenza. The tension I have been pursuing comes out most sharply in the paper, "Not Yet Tiddas," by Anne Pattel-Gray, an Aboriginal activist and religious thinker about whom the Romanian born Fiorenza writes in proper postcolonial form. For Schüssler Fiorenza, an Aboriginal woman writing on theology from Australia is precisely where the future for biblical studies, the academy, and the church lies. Yet in order to make her intervention in the relatively small scene of Australian religious and theological feminism, Pattel-Gray makes use of the developments in womanist work in North America, appropriating in her turn its racial and class dimensions for an Australian situation.

Indeed, it would be possible to push the seeds of this contradiction back into colonialism proper, when many of the trajectories, such as Christianity itself, were set on their way to end up in the distinctive cultural, theological and biblical contributions from places outside the former metropolitan centers (see the Asian examples in Sugirtharajah 1993, 58–63) For biblical studies all of this means not merely an appropriation by a relentlessly globalizing scholarship but also the chance to adapt to a "critical regionalism" (the phrase is from architecture; see Frampton) the tools of postmodern and postcolonial discourse in order to provide interpretations from the local situation which begin, homeopathically, to resist and undermine the logic of those instruments.

Antipodality, or Gatecrashing Thanksgiving

Gramsci has now become an alibi for not being Marxist. (Spivak 1990, 142)

What Marxism really has to offer is global systems. I think that the most powerful thing Marxism in the Third World can offer is crisis theory (Spivak 1990, 138).

Thus far I have been guilty of an elision all too common in postcolonial criticism, namely, the elision of the global and the local, taking a particular situation (in my case biblical studies in Australia) as in some way paradigmatic for the global condition (again, of biblical studies). The binary is less than helpful here, for the two poles are of course inseparably connected with, indeed constitutive of (as I will argue in chapter 2), each other, but in ways that need to be rethought. I have made a start in this by attempting to situate Australian biblical studies—a curiously hybrid and minimal exercise, with nothing much to show for itself—within the global, colonial and postcolonial structures of biblical studies. Further, it seems to me that the particular issues of the Bible in (post)colonial Australia have distinct resonances with and turn around some of the same questions as those that appear elsewhere. But this is then a mark of chronically global nature of all those minor, local concerns we felt, or perhaps hoped, were distinct.

So, it seems to me that a consideration of biblical studies in Australia, a distinctly local concern in many ways, is able to provide a particular perspective on the global practice of biblical studies. In order to do so I want to invoke a term with a long and somewhat checkered history—antipodality. A term from classical Greece, used through the Middle Ages and then reappearing with more derogatory associations during the period of capitalist imperialism, the Antipodes refers literally to those lands—Australia, or Terra Australis, the Southern Land, New Zealand, the Pacific Islands and so on—where the inhabitants have their feet opposite to Europeans, where they walk upside-down, contrary to correct way of walking and then of being itself (see further Ryan 1996, 105–12). This antithetical way of characterizing the other side of the globe carried through in the first descriptions of Australia, its flora, fauna and people, by Europeans. Platypi, kangaroos, marsupial dogs, eucalyptus trees that regenerated from their roots rather than seeds, even the seasons themselves—all of them making European category mistakes—became objects that reinforced the antipodality of the country.

Antipodality has of course been used in a range of other ways, not least of which is the appropriation of the term to signify a more positive difference and distinctness. My use here, however, has a distinctly political bent that trades on the opposition of the term itself. Given that the imperialism which led to the European invasion and settlement of Australia—as a prison, it must be remembered (indeed convicts were sent to Australia for almost one hundred years, from 1787 to 1868 [Hughes 1996])—was part of the expansion of capitalism and the subsequent competition between European states for global dominance, then the political antipodality in which I am interested is a distinctly Marxist one. This is not to say that Australia should be cast as a worker's paradise (see Buckley and Wheelwright 1988), nor that communism has had huge successes here (even though Fred Paterson was elected twice to the Queensland Parliament from the Red North [Fitzgerald 1997]), nor that the prospects for socialism are any better in Australia than elsewhere; rather, I am suggesting that antipodality may give an Australian inflection to Marxism itself, particularly in the light of the global reality of capitalism at the turn of the millennium. Further, it seems to me that any discussion of postcolonialism without a serious engagement with Marxist thought and practice will remain awash in the terms and categories of liberalism, the ideological justification of capitalism.

But how might this be realized in biblical studies? Biblical studies is itself a subset of religion, which belongs to the superstructure of the totality of society, sharing that space with art, culture, philosophy, politics, and ideology (although this latter term is all-encompassing); it is then dependent upon the economic forms and social relations of that society, yet it may also anticipate possible future forms of social and economic organization. Biblical studies has an ambiguous role in all of this, since the Bible has played a constitutive role in the development of "western" culture, which itself has moved through the Roman Empire and feudal Europe into capitalism, where Christianity seems to have foundered and taken on a more marginalized status.

With this model in mind, there are, it seems to me, two possibilities for the ways postcolonial biblical studies may disrupt conventional or metropolitan ways of studying the Bible. The first owes its debts to the important work of Chantal Mouffe and Ernesto Laclau, *Hegemony and Socialist Strategy*. In their efforts to think through the political implications of poststructuralism and a more encompassing postmodernism, they theorize concerning the profoundly postmodern development of a host of small political pressure groups, normally designated with the term "micropolitics" and engaging in political practices that no longer follow older class lines. Mouffe and Laclau also want to reshape Gramsci's notion of hegemony, and they do so by developing an anti-essentialist ideological framework for this new micropolitics, whose various groups will eventually move into alliances based on their drive for a radical equality. Although there are some problems in losing the Marxist base for such equality—the universalization of wage labor and of the commodity form (see Jameson 1991, 319)—it seems to me that there is some initial promise for the possibilities of postcolonial biblical studies. Of course, I would like to recover the role of class which begins to disappear in the work of Mouffe and Laclau, since the danger of much reflection about the new social movements relies on the idea that the older class politics have dissipated in the new dispensation (rather, the older configurations of class and politics have been redistributed with the new global reorganization of capital and its technologies). Yet, as Jameson reminds the persevering reader, all of these groups of the micro-political arena, including those newly identified, owe their "ultimate systemic condition of possibility" (1991, 325) to late capitalism. It is within this context that any alternative possibilities for postcolonial forms of biblical criticism must situate themselves, although I am sufficiently a Marxist to hold that the very possibility of overturning a dominant system comes in part from the logic of that system itself. I write "in part," since not all the processes of breakdown are the result of internal contradictions; some oppositional currents may come from "outside" the economic system and threaten to disrupt its desire for business as usual. This seems particularly pertinent to micro-groups within postcolonialism, who remain both constitutive of postmodern capitalism as such and yet come from "beyond" to challenge such an economic system. This may be the place for Aboriginal contributions to biblical studies, or indigenous possibilities in other parts of the globe, although I want to avoid the dangers of both "idealization" and "appropriation" that David Spurr has identified as basic to the colonial agenda (see especially Spurr 1993, 28–42, 125–40). In the end I am not sure that anything can come any longer from "outside" late capitalism, so that any forms of resistance, in which indigenous people are sure to play a part, need to come from elsewhere. Biblical critics may be identified as yet another political and social grouping in the micro-political territory of late capitalism, yet an oppositional stand from biblical critics in postcolonial situations would seem to be possible only within the dynamic of capitalism itself.

However, even the suggestions of Mouffe and Laclau do not seem to me to go far enough, particularly with the peculiarly ineffectual nature of much small group politics—insofar as one's desire is for permanent radical change. It seems to me that a better direction is charted in the work of Aijaz

Ahmad,[12] who articulates a distinct place for a Marxist postcolonial praxis. It is not so much the devastating critique of third-worldism, or the three worlds theory as such, nor his clarifications of Marx's writings on India or the question of Indian literature, or his problematic critical engagements with the work of Fredric Jameson, Edward Said (on this conflict see Moore-Gilbert 1997, 14–20; George 1996, 106–7), and Salman Rushdie, that I want to focus on here, but rather the argument that the only viable form of political and social opposition in this present world comes from socialism. This of course identifies Aijaz as a relatively orthodox Marxist, but it also signals something about India itself that is often forgotten in the heavily European focus of much Marxist work, namely, the long experience of Marxist government within a secular, democratic state. I am thinking here of the viability of the Marxist governments of Kerala and West Bengal that have provided a pattern of economic and social reform that has ensured them a firm electoral base over many years. The difference, in comparison to western Europe, North America, and countries such as Australia, is that the experience of elected government has provided a practical political base for significant theoretical reflection.

It is from this context that Aijaz sounds most strongly the old Marxist argument that in the present historical conjunction—global capitalism—the only coherent alternative remains socialism. Moving from the point that the great majority of former colonial countries cannot make the transition to a fully fledged capitalism of the European type, since they have no external, imperial, resources to exploit, he argues:

> This structural inability of capitalism to provide for the vast majority of the populations which it has sucked into its own dominion constitutes the basic, incurable flaw in the system as a whole.... Negation of this contradiction can come only from outside the terms of this system as such, because the backwardness of the backward capitalist countries, hence the poverty of the majority of the world's population, cannot be undone except through a complete redistribution of wealth and an altogether different structuring of productions and consumptions on a global scale, among classes, regions, countries and continents of the world. Socialism is the determinate name for this negation of capitalism's fundamental, systemic contradictions and cruelties. (316)

---

12. By comparison, San Juan's work, while admirable for its polemic and advocacy of Marxist insurrection, too quickly treats all postcolonial theory as imperialist, trenchantly opposing it on political grounds.

And the primary object of socialist resistance is precisely those backward economic formations that have been colonized and are now belatedly included in full-blown capitalism only to be denied inclusion. This is where, it seems to me, the oppositional dimensions of postcolonialism may be found. It is also a viable way of answering Dirlik's challenge that "postcolonial" discourse effectively blocks out and erases, through its periodizing logic and rewriting of history, the revolutionary pasts of the many places from which it emerges and about which it speaks (Dirlik 1997, 163–85). However, if we follow Dirlik and name the "postcolonial" as also "postrevolutionary" then it indicates an urgent need to recover the viability of such revolutionary pasts.

All the same, I am not sure that Ahmad or Dirlik have tracked Marx's logic to its conclusion, for Marx argued that the greatest contradictions of capitalism are to be found in its most advanced (and therefore decayed) centers. Thus, while the oppositional, antipodal, possibilities of postcolonial spaces must be developed to the full, any lasting change must be enacted not merely in the peripheral bungalows but also in the glistening, marble rooms, soft leather chairs and plate glass views of power.[13] In the end, or course, there is nothing outside capitalism, so that any opposition must be generated out of the contradictions inherent within it. Dussell identifies three contradictions, or, what he terms "limits': the chewing up of a global ecology; superfluous human labor, the destruction of living labor and the attendant poverty; and the impossibility of completely subsuming those on the periphery (Dussell 1998, 19–21). Indeed, Dussell locates the possibilities of an end of capitalism in this periphery.

Yet what is remarkable about this essay is the way it replaces a Eurocentric discourse (Europe as the center from which modernity spread forth) into a planetary one: that is, before the rise of capitalism and modernity Europe was distinctly peripheral and the imaginary, ideological center of the globe was toward India. Thus, travelers and "explorers" set out eastward towards India, whether Vasco da Gama or Columbus from Europe, or the Chinese in a westward direction. It is only with colonization and capitalism, fuelled by the money of the "new world" that Spain and then Holland effect a slow shift of the center to Europe. Or, to put it in oceanic terms, the flow was from the Indian Ocean to the Atlantic, which now, in the postmodern moment includes North America. With Japan, China and the west coast of North America now rivaling cross Atlantic trade, it may be the Pacific that claims the next dominance. And it is precisely these places, these global centers, in

---

13. Leslie Sklair is more skeptical about the possibilities of global organization and opposition (1998), although she cites only the labor movement and uses word-of-mouth information without any discussion of examples and situations.

which any viable change beyond capitalism will take place. For, in the same way that the dominance of the imperial centers was established and continues to be maintained by drawing in the best global talent from outside, sucking the greatest minds, artists, musicians, sports people and finance experts into a vast vortex, so also the oppositional possibilities Ahmad envisages need to be exploited to the full in the overdeveloped places of Europe, North America and Japan. In other words, the local, postcolonial struggles function as a precursor, a model, for global opposition: "This is a period in which the counterpart to multinational capitalism and its organization of global relations has to be, on the part of the left and a progressive culture, an internationalization as well" (Jameson and Paik 1996, 367).

As for biblical studies in all of this, I want to pick up Fredric Jameson's suggestion that culture—of which biblical studies is a part (and in the construction of "western" culture it has played a constitutive role)—may also be *anticipatory* as well as determined by economic formations, that the superstructure may provide a glimpse of better possibilities. What is required then is the development and improvement of a Marxist or socialist culture, of the discussion, debate and reflection on Marxism within the context of capitalism itself (of which Marxism remains the most potent interpreter), as well as the production of art, literature, film, music and so on that is properly oppositional, and a full Marxist criticism that may interpret all that has gone before. And that anticipatory culture needs very much to be an international one, alongside a reinvented global socialism, a rethought global class consciousness, a global network of intellectuals, and so on. It is to the ongoing construction of such a culture that biblical criticism may contribute, so that it may be a vital part of the cultural and ideological arrangement of whatever it is that will follow the demise of capitalism. It seems to me that the most (or should I say "the only"?) viable mode of destabilizing, disrupting and finally replacing hegemonic, imperial, biblical scholarship is one that seeks to be part of the construction of a culture that anticipates the end of the capitalist social and economic organization that is part and parcel of such a hegemony.

This is, then, what I mean by "gatecrashing thanksgiving," since Marx always argued that any lasting socialism or communism would arise out of the most advanced capitalist places. A vast feast of consumption, it is an item ideologically crucial to capitalism itself (through the use of a myth of precapitalist origins). A religious/civil feast, derived from harvest celebrations and a reconstructed tradition of the first pilgrims with their biblical focus and vision of their move to North America, but now a crucial item in the ideological self-perception—family, simplicity and especially consumption—of the most developed, purest, and therefore most decayed and rancid, capitalist center in the world, it is an appropriate feast to gatecrash.

1
Marx, Postcolonialism, and the Bible

> I have frequently had the feeling that I am one of the few Marxists left.
> (Jameson 1988, 347)

My argument is relatively straightforward: the almost complete absence of Marxism in biblical postcolonial criticism is a legacy of the wider zone of postcolonial theory itself that has been all too keen to dump Marx. But I also want to show how the gradual forgetting of Marx in postcolonialism and postcolonial theory has distinct ramifications for the engagements with postcolonial theory by biblical critics. So, after outlining the way postcolonial theory has forgotten its own history, a history in which Marxism was the key factor, I select two biblical critics working with postcolonial theory in order not only to make the obvious point about the absence of Marx, but also to indicate some of the shortfalls such an absence generates. Finally, I pick up the work of Ernst Bloch in order to locate a more political version of Bakhtin's widely influential dialogic criticism.

Left Out: Marx and Postcolonial Theory

Postcolonial theory, understood as a particular method that arose in the late 1980s and is employed in academic circles for interpreting cultural products, especially those of the era of European colonialism, seems to have forgotten two crucial dimensions of the possibility of its existence: history and Marxism.[1] One might grant that Marxism has somehow slipped out of the picture, but history? Is not postcolonial theory very much concerned with rereading the history, art, texts, and practices of European colonialism and its

---

1. The first part of the argument that follows is an expanded version of one that I first developed in the introduction to a *Semeia* volume on postcolonial theory (Boer 2001b).

aftermath? Postcolonial theory's concern is therefore postcolonialism itself, whether we hyphenate the word in a more periodizing frame of mind or not. However, this is not the history that concerns me here: I write of the history of the theory itself, of postcolonial theory.

The rapid emergence of postcolonial theory with the work of Edward Said, Gayatri Spivak, and Homi Bhabha has effaced the long path that led to this theory. It seems to me that this obliteration has taken place not so much through a willful neglect on the part of this triumvirate and their various followers, as through the process of reinterpreting the older theorists, the precursors to postcolonial theory. Thus, Bhabha gives extensive attention to Frantz Fanon, and Spivak identifies Marx as one of her inspirations. Others have fallen by the wayside, such as W. E. B. DuBois and Sol Plaatje at the turn of the century, although the former has been taken up by African American critics such as Cornell West. Bart Moore-Gilbert (1997) usefully reminds us of this longer critical history by distinguishing between postcolonial theory—that which we have now after Said, Spivak, and Bhabha—and postcolonial criticism—the longer history of the critique of colonialism. In fact, as I will argue in a moment, we need to go back to Marx and Lenin for the origins of this kind of criticism. The catch with Moore-Gilbert's distinction, however, is that the very notion of a tradition of *post*colonial criticism relies upon the more recent development of a postcolonial theory. That is to say, the idea of a history of this intellectual and political project seems to be enabled by the subsequent theory, which generates its own history. In this case the history itself—which happened without a distinct identifier such as "postcolonial"—does seem to vanish before the other history of postcolonial theory, which boils down to a version of *creatio ex nihilo*. What is needed, then, is a strategy for recovering this alternative history that simultaneously deals with the historical constructions of postcolonial theory.

To state what is in many respects the obvious: Marx and then Lenin first developed a critical approach to what they variously called colonialism and imperialism. If Marx traced the way capitalism for its very survival had to expand, to "grow" (still very much the benchmark of economic success) beyond the confines of Europe and conquer ever new colonial spaces, Lenin, especially in *Imperialism, the Highest Stage of Capitalism* (1950), developed an analysis of imperialism, or imperial capitalism, as the most advanced stage of capitalism up until that point. From a Leninist perspective, both "world wars" were conflicts between the European imperial powers, vying for global dominance, the struggle coming to head in the competition for the conquest of ever more territories throughout the globe. After Lenin the systematic theorization and critique of capitalist expansion, including colonialism, took place in the Marxist tradition. Key figures of earlier postcolonial criticism, following Moore-Gilbert's classification, such as Frantz Fanon, W. E. B. DuBois and C. L. R. James were all Marxist critics of colonialism. Apart from the analysis of colonialism, there were two other vital parts of their work: the study of literature and other cultural products from their own locations and a distinct level of political involvement. For instance, C. L. R. James was not only intensely interested in the role of cricket as both a colonial and anticolonial cultural force, but he was also a central figure in the process towards independence in the West Indies.

Given this history, which I have sketched far too briefly and haphazardly, why is it that the Marxist dimension of postcolonial theory has been lost? Through a simultaneous process of transformation that systematically detached various key aspects of Marxist theory from Marxism itself and then negated their political potential. The process began with Edward Said's use of Antonio Gramsci's notion of hegemony.

Two-edged, the theory speaks both of the necessary combination of consent and force, and the complex patterns whereby a dominant ideological position is maintained and overthrown (see Gramsci 1971, 268, 328, 348, 365, 370, 376). As far as the necessary link between consent and force is concerned, Gramsci argues that a dominant hegemony works by articulating and spreading a specific set of cultural assumptions, beliefs, ways of living and so on that are assumed to be "normal," accepted by people as the universally valid way of living. Here intellectuals, the "organizers" of ideology, culture, philosophy, religion, law and politics are central to the idea and operation of hegemony. Hegemony runs deeply through any social and political formation, for the structures of knowledge and values, the filters through which society acquires form and meaning, are precisely those that are constructed and maintained by the leading class or party.

But hegemony is both a tool of analysis and of revolution. This means that any force for change must brook no rivals, no possibilities of oppositional hegemony in the construction of the new state. Consent must be at one with the use of force, the two sides of hegemony. Religion thereby forms a crucial component of consent, falling under the rubric of intellectual and moral leadership (*direzione*). Domination or coercion (*dominio*), especially over against antagonistic groups, is the inescapable obverse. By contrast, those with which the leading group in is alliance and association work together by consent: "The supremacy of a social group is manifested in two ways: as "domination" and as "intellectual and moral leadership." A social group is dominant over those antagonistic groups it wants to "liquidate" or to subdue even with armed force, and it is leading with respect to those groups that are associated or allied with it" (Gramsci, quoted in Fontana 1993, 141).

In the period of colonialism such hegemony involved wholesale ideological work, ranging from racial theory, through military action and the production of belief in the superiority of the imperial center to Said's well-known "orientalism" (Said 1978). But Said linked this in problematic fashion to Foucault's work on power, specifically the dispersed, capillary forms of power that never reside in the named and expected seats of power. One can see the connection—dispersed power and a threatened hegemony—but Foucault was not a Marxist, despite being a student of Althusser and a political activist. The absence of other categories crucial to hegemony, such as class, class conflict and the central role of political economics,[2] meant that the notion of hegemony was orphaned, drifting away from the conceptual context in which it made sense. So the first step in watering down the Marxist heritage in postcolonial theory was made.

Even though Gayatri Spivak claims Marxism as part of her own theoretical and political position, it was her translation of Derrida's *Of Grammatology* (1980), and especially the long and difficult introduction that she wrote, which brought deconstruction into the mix of what was becoming postcolonial theory. The subsequent appearance of *In Other Worlds* (1988) reinforced the prominence of Derridean deconstruction, along with Gramsci and Foucault via Said, as one of the theoretical strands available for critics wanting to forge a new approach. In its much-vaunted refusal of method, in the careful attention to the details of the text in question, in the perpetual discovery of the way texts face an incoherence that both subverts and structures the text itself, deconstruction became a useful tool in reading for the other voices, those excluded and marginalized by the dominant discourses of the European colonial powers. But a Derridean Marx—taking for a moment Spivak's effort to combine deconstruction, Marxism and feminism seriously—is a strange Marx indeed, looking more like a slightly left-of-center liberal, as Derrida's own *Specters of Marx* (1994) showed only too well.

The final step in the banishment of Marx from postcolonial theory came with Homi Bhabha's work, especially *The Location of Culture* (1994),

---

2. How long has it been since the economy was itself a political domain? At first glance, it seems that economics is precisely the domain of politics. Do not the various governments and political parties in the so-called "democracies" vie with each other for the best means to facilitate economic growth, generate jobs and maintain consumer confidence? But there is never a question posed at to the type of economics that might be best. In their various ways, the governments and political parties assume that capitalism is a given, that it is not a domain of political contestation, that a political party cannot in fact say that capitalism is inimical to the well-being of the population, and act accordingly.

which introduced Lacanian psychoanalysis along with a demarxified Mikhail Bakhtin into the reading of colonial texts that range from the Bible in India to a de-fanged Frantz Fanon. Although he has become a model for so many postcolonial critics, one is never sure whether the looping and idiosyncratic style and the misreadings of Lacan are all designed to turn Lacan against himself, or whether Bhabha is covering other tracks. As more than one radical critic first mesmerized by Bhabha has found out to her or his dismay, Bhabha is a solid bourgeois writer for whom liberalism is the only possible ideological position (witness his later art and literary criticism). But with Bhabha, Lacanian psychoanalysis and Bakhtin's dialogic reading strategy became part of the contradictory hybrid of postcolonial theory, and now, along with hegemony and deconstruction, terms such as mimicry, hybridity and border crossing became the keys to reinterpreting the texts of colonial encounters.

So, postcolonial theory sets one looking for the wealth of subversive material that remains buried and forgotten, such as indigenous literary resistance, unexpected or unwanted appropriations of the colonizer's cultural tools, or even counterhegemonic moments in canonical texts. Rather than the overwhelming dominance of European colonial culture, myriad moments of resistance, negotiation and alternative uses that slid out of the colonizer's grasp become the focus of one's attention. While this is an immensely fruitful and necessary task, to the point of constructing an alternative narrative or history, I still want to ask: What next, after the resistance has been located, after the text deconstructs, after the Real has been glimpsed? Is this the kind of work that begins to make sense of the anticolonial movements and wars of independence, or do these acts of alternative agency remain ultimately futile, absorbed into the dominant system? Is postcolonial criticism caught in a fruitful but limiting methodological mix?

However, by the time postcolonial theory achieved something of an identity and maturity, the Marxist heritage of postcolonial theory had vanished, and even Gramsci appeared less of a Marxist and more of a postcolonial critic *avant la lettre*. I am tempted to make a Lacanian point (especially in light of Bhabha's appropriation of Lacan) and suggest that the forgetting of Marx is necessary for the constitution of postcolonial criticism: in light of the enabling role of Marxism in postcolonial theory, that theory can only exist by excluding that which keeps it functioning. What is outside the system provides the glue that keeps the system running. Yet, rather than a somewhat irritated tracing of this gradual forgetting, one of the agendas for subsequent work in postcolonial theory, it seems to me, is a recovery of this tradition that has been "left out," as Andrew Milner argues in relation to the history of cultural studies.

Where's Marx? Postcolonial Biblical Studies

It should come as no surprise, then, that one is more likely to come across Groucho or Harpo Marx in the writings of biblical critics who have taken up postcolonial theory, or indeed, postcolonial critics who have written about the Bible. And those biblical critics who do work with Marxism, such as Norman Gottwald (1985, 1992, 1993, 1999), Gale Yee (1995, 1999, 2003), Ron Simkins (1999), and Richard Horsley (1999, 2001, 2002), notwithstanding his guarded essay in *The Postcolonial Bible* (Horsley 1998), tend to cluster in the domain of the social sciences rather than, say, ideological or literary criticism, although David Jobling (1991, 1992a, 1992b, 1998) and I have made contributions in this area (Boer 1996a, 1997, 2003). Only Gerald West and I have sought the links between Marxism and postcolonial criticism (see West 1999; Boer 2001a as well as this book).

Apart from West's work and my own, in the increasing number of works that are beginning to appear in what might be called postcolonial biblical studies, I can find references to Said, Spivak and Bhabha, and less often to Bakhtin. But neither Gramsci nor Marx rate a mention. At times, these works rightly stress the absence of considerations of the Bible in postcolonial studies, given its crucial role in European colonial expansion (see Boer 2001b, Sugirtharajah 2002). But, rather than survey the growing amount of postcolonial biblical studies, what I want to do here is take a sample of these works and see what happens methodologically. I cannot go past R. S. Sugirtharajah's texts, especially *The Bible and the Third World* (2001) and *Postcolonial Criticism and Biblical Studies* (2002). Along with Sugirtharajah's central work, I also want to include an Australian example, namely, Mark Brett's *Genesis: Procreation and the Politics of Identity* (2000).

Sugirtharajah has been the most voluminous writer in this area, but what interests me are his various and scattered methodological reflections. Thus, in the closing pages of *The Bible and the Third World* he produces the standard material on the development of postcolonial theory, listing the obligatory three (Said, Spivak, and Bhabha), but especially Said's *Orientalism* (1978). His recitation is a little gentler than that of the Marxist, Arif Dirlik. Thus, over against Sugirtharajah's "Utilizing the space offered by the Western academy in the 1980s…," I prefer Dirlik: "'When exactly … does the "postcolonial" begin?' queries Ella Shohat in a discussion of the subject. Misreading this question deliberately, I will supply here an answer that is only partially facetious: 'When Third world intellectuals have arrived in First World academe'" (Dirlik 1997, 52).

Marx himself appears but twice, once in the tension between the "mutually incompatible critical categories" (Sugirtharajah 2001, 246) of Marxism and poststructuralism, and the other in a criticism of liberation theology's use of Marx: "Marx's dialectical materialism failed to perceive the potentiality for revolution in religion" (Sugirtharajah 2001, 264). That he pairs Marx up with Karl Barth—as the "two Karls"—is as convenient a dismissal as might be found (Barth could not find room for revelation in religion). And that is it as far as Marx is concerned.

We don't need to look far to find the implications for sidestepping Marx on the way to his own definition. Sugirtharajah suggests three historical conditions for the emergence of postcolonial criticism: the failure of socialism, the rise of global capitalism and the market economy, which resulted in the disruption of both metropolitan and village economies, and the loss of political momentum among Third World countries (see Sugirtharajah 2001, 247). While we may grant the first point—although the failure of "actually existing socialism"[3] might be a better description—the second I find most astounding. Did global capitalism and the market economy first arise with the revolutions in the former communist countries of Eastern Europe? This would date global capitalism from the years 1989–1990; I suspect it has been around for a little longer than that. And the metropolitan and village economies were very much integrated in the intricate systems of capitalism well before then. What is wanting here is an analysis that takes into account the mutations in capitalism, which may be analyzed in the terms of Hardt and Negri as an acephalous "empire" in which there is no central power (Hardt and Negri 2000), or in terms of the regulation school, with the financialization of the market and the emergence of "regimes of accumulation" (Boyer 1990).

However, there is another narrative operating in this three-fold historical periodization, and that is the demise of Marxism itself. Each of the points may read as alternative versions of this same story: Marxism is finished, in terms of the political economics of nation-states, as the source of opposition to capitalism itself, and as the only viable political option for many Third World countries. In its place comes postcolonialism, on which the hope of the future rests. Or, to put it in Arif Dirlik's terms, the term "postcolonial," through its alternative periodization, effectively erases the revolutionary pasts of the places from which it emerges and about which it speaks (Dirlik 1997, 163–85). The postcolonial may therefore also be described as the "postrevolutionary." And so it becomes possible to read Itumeleng Mosala's explicitly Marxist biblical criticism of the book of Esther (Mosala 1992) as postcolonial

---

3. The paradox of "actually existing socialism" is that this has never "actually" existed, the states that did and do operate with socialism being a halfway house, a glimmer of socialism that fell short.

instead: Vashti's model of revolt becomes an agenda for multiculturalism in which diasporic communities can both celebrate their ethnic identities and embrace the cultural heritage of their new homes.

And yet postcolonialism, at least in Sugirtharajah's formulation, shares with Marxism the combination of theory and practice, or praxis; it is, in other words, a method that comes out of and entails a distinct political practice, like feminism or gay and lesbian criticism. "The task of postcolonialism is ensuring that the needs and aspirations of the exploited are catered to, rather than being merely an interesting and engaging avenue of inquiry" (Sugirtharajah 2001, 275). No comment here on the intellectual as vanishing mediator, the one who speaks and writes on behalf of others, or "caters" for them, from a place of privilege while erasing his presence in the process (see Boer 2001b).

In the end, Sugirtharajah would like to find the source of such a theoretical politics in the Third World. Marxism, then, is but one of many Eurocentric approaches with which Sugirtharajah wishes to dispense. He makes little, if nothing, of Lacanian psychoanalysis, or of Derridean deconstruction, or even of dialogic readings that came by way of Bakhtin—all of them central to much postcolonial theory. Instead, unlike "other critical categories which are in vogue today, postcolonialism's original incarnation was in the form of imaginative literature, in the writings of Indians, Africans and Latin Americans" (Sugirtharajah 2001, 272; see also 1998c, 91–94).[4] Indeed, Sugirtharajah's great contribution to postcolonial theory and biblical studies is to show how deeply the Bible was enmeshed in both colonialism and the myriad ways in which it was appropriated, re-interpreted and resisted. The breadth of his survey is stunning, running all the way from the Peshitta to contemporary vernacular hermeneutics, from Tertullian to Ananda Coomaraswamy (see Sugirtharajah 1998b, 16–18; 1998c; 2001; 2002). I can also understand the political need for such a move, but I wonder at the absence of any sense of a dialectical relation between colonizer and colonized. In the conclusion to this book I will argue that the possibilities of anticolonialism and postcolonialism came, in part at least, from the contradictory nature of European imperialism, providing colonized peoples with the physical, economic and conceptual tools—individual subjectivity and agency, collective identity in a nation-state, racial and ethnic identity—that made anticolonialism possible in the first place.

---

4. Further: "I define postcolonial criticism as a textual and praxological practice initially undertaken by people who were once part of the British, European and American Empires, but now have some sort of territorial freedom while continuing to live with burdens from the past and enduring newer forms of economic and cultural neo-colonialism" (Sugirtharajah 2001, 246).

Instead of the encyclopedic range of Sugirtharajah's work, preferring synoptic sweeps over the field, Mark Brett's *Genesis* book tacks close by the biblical scroll of the same name. The contrasts runs in other directions as well: instead of the Third World intellectual in the old colonial center, Brett works on the colonial fringe, an uneasy and ambivalent Australian with white settler background. As for the book itself, he puts forward a pluralist approach to methods, a "contest of methods" that I take as a slightly milder version of Paul Ricoeur's conflict of interpretations. Postmodernism, nonconformist Protestantism (Baptists), historical study (especially that of Kenneth Hoglund 1992), the narrative poetics of Alter and Sternberg, pragmatic and structuralist linguistics (especially of Saussure), anthropology, particularly of a structuralist bent, Pike's linguistics, deconstruction, and of course postcolonial theory all come together in Brett's approach. However, as he points out, his reading strategy is "inspired especially by postcolonial theory" (2000, 5), and the issue that draws him in is the tension between social structures and individual agency. Hence the significant place accorded to anthropology, and the long defense of intention, broken down into explicit and indirect communicative intention, as well as motive.

Agency is of course crucial for postcolonial theory, and Brett cites both Mary Douglas on Numbers (1993) and the work of James Scott on covert resistance (1990). But he relies most heavily on Homi Bhabha "in assuming that some kind of agency is necessary in any resistance to a dominant culture" (Brett 2000, 23). Indeed, Bhabha provides Brett with the means for distinguishing between a deconstruction of free-play and libertarian pessimism and that of postcolonialism, where the agency of resistance comes from a "hybrid inter-subjectivity" (Brett 2000, 23). Not necessarily aware of its own work, such an inter-subjectivity brings together both Israelite and non-Israelite materials in contesting colonial power in the Persian period.

What we have, then, is a postcolonial deconstruction—described most fully as a "subversive and artful hybridity" (Brett 2000, 23)—that comes through Homi Bhabha rather than Gayatri Spivak. But the methodological spoor that Brett tracks in Bhabha is not that of Lacan but of Mikhail Bakhtin. There is but one reference to Bakhtin's *The Dialogic Imagination* (1981), and yet Brett's description of intentional hybridity may as well have come from this book: "intentional hybridity is a blending of two or more voices, without compositional boundaries being evident, such that the voices combine into an unstable chorale—sometimes speaking univocally, but more often juxtaposing alternative points of view such that the authority of the dominant voice is put into question" (Brett 2000, 22). The vast difference is that whereas Brett, following Bhabha, postulates a distinct redactor responsible for the undermining voice, Bakhtin saw such "voices" emerging in the writings of a single author. There was no need for more than one writer to speak with more than one voice.

We are a long way from Marx, which is entirely Mark Brett's prerogative, although Slavoj Žižek does make a brief entry on the question of ideology (Brett 2000, 21). The connection is oblique, although not as much as the one that swirls around Bakhtin himself. Whether or not Bakhtin was Vološinov is perhaps not as relevant here as the debate itself—was Bakhtin the guardedly innocuous *nom-de-plume* of a more political Vološinov, or was Vološinov the cover for Bakhtin's critical Marxism? For it was only when Bakhtin was freed from the troublesome shackles of Marxism, with all the associations of Soviet orthodoxy and the robot-like subservience to the Great Cause, that he could be taken up in the Western academy as a dissident liberal within the enemy ranks (hence Bhabha's great liking for Bakhtin). This is not to say that Bakhtin's dialogic readings are not political, for in the end we find him favoring the quiet subversive voice, the one that speaks not too loudly for fear of reprisal, a covert textual whisper here and there.

So, in the case of Genesis, Brett identifies a tension or conflict between a voice that expresses an ethnocentric, exclusivist position concerned with the dominance of one group over another (males, priests, genealogically pure Judahites over everyone else), and a voice that quietly and subtly opposes this position, urging instead an inclusivist approach that does not operate by means of domination. The hypothesis he wants to test is that such a conflict took place in the Persian period (537–331 B.C.E.) under Persian governors. The debate is in fact between the position represented in Ezra and Nehemiah and the one he finds in Genesis. But it is more than this, for the dominant position of Genesis is similar to the one we find in Ezra and Nehemiah. It is only the quieter, subversive voice of Genesis that challenges this, an editor working carefully through the material of Genesis in order to make his point, always seeking to avoid the heavy hand of the censors.

Now, there are specific political reasons and implications of such an argument for both the particular and general contexts in which Brett works: the use of texts such as Genesis within the churches on issues ranging from gay and lesbian involvement to indigenous rights, and the wider national debates over refugees, terrorism, and the inability of the Australian government of the time to understand what "justice" means in relation to Aboriginal peoples. In these contexts, I stand by Mark Brett's positions over against the forces of reaction. And yet, the way he reads for the dialogic voices in Genesis may also be understood, if we take a more Marxist line, as the normal function of ruling-class ideology, which is precisely to manage the range of objections and criticisms directed at it so as to be better rulers by offering what appears to be a more comprehensive approach that does not stifle debate. This means that the tensions and problems Brett finds represented in the text are not so much ones of dominating and subversive voices but different positions within a ruling class situation. For it is interesting that Brett spends little time with the notion of a Priestly editor, passing over that debate in a couple of pages. The exclusion is symptomatic, to my mind, for most of the scholarship that stresses the Persian era for texts like Genesis indicates that the only viable class or class fraction that could have done any editing of texts would have been priestly scribes. This means that—given Brett's wish to locate Genesis within a particular historical debate—a more comprehensive hypothesis is that here we have a dialogue between priests or priestly groups.

Disinterring Ernst Bloch

However, rather than dismiss Bakhtin and even Bhabha as bourgeois critics, I want to suggest a different line, one that takes account of the importance of Ernst Bloch and recasts the dialogic relation in class terms. Apart from the fascinating narrative of Bloch's critical legacy—passing through liberation theology to become a key figure in utopian studies (see Moylan 1997)—he provides a distinctly Marxist version of the strategy that Brett applies to Genesis. And it is not that we need to plunder Bloch's work for the possibilities they might contain for biblical studies, for Bloch is one of those extraordinary Marxists who wrote a book on the Bible—*Atheism in Christianity* (1972)—as well as finding it one of the great sources for *The Principle of Hope* (1995).

The key feature Bloch wishes to introduce into biblical criticism—this in the 1950s and 1960s—is the category of class, since the Bible, he suggests, is very much a text of both those who labor and those who live off that surplus labor and do none themselves. In all its variety and contradictions, there are stories in the Bible that have become homely in the smallest of peasant households, but also those used by the overlords and religious professionals. And it is not just that such class differences indicate a different reading strategy, different assumptions about the various narratives, poetry, and statements: the texts themselves tend in either direction, their content and form speaking with a double voice, one that is and is not folly for the rich and powerful. The Bible is then a text riven with class conflict: not a conflict that may be read in terms of bourgeoisie and proletariat alone but in terms of the basic Marxist category of class difference, however that may be articulated historically, between oppressors and oppressed, rulers and ruled.

The litmus for such a method of reading—which is very much part of Bloch's famous utopian hermeneutics—is the conflict between the Reformer Luther and the peasant leader Thomas Müntzer. While the former could invoke Paul and the cross of Christ as the lot of all, the latter called upon the exodus and the Bible's anger "against the Ahabs and Nimrods" (Bloch 1972, 23). But the deepest affinity of the Bible, despite its "adaptability to select master-ideologies" (Bloch 1972, 24), is to ordinary, uneducated people who took the stories as their stories, something the clergy and rulers could not do.

For what Bloch seeks to do in *Atheism in Christianity* is to uncover both the way in which ruling class ideologies have been imposed on the text and to examine the patterns and strategies of subversive slave talk. The interlacings, overlays, and myriad complexities of such materials require readings that are attentive to the subtle shifts and changes that have taken place. Thus, Bloch is not interested in submissive varieties of slave talk (and so the Psalms do not appear), but rather texts whose subversive voice is either early or late, of the first strata or at some later stage of usage. The one that survives is the masked text: "it wears its mask, rather, from below, and wears it freely, as a first form of alienation, a characteristic change of ground" (Bloch 1972, 14). Such texts have a double function, a "sly irony," appearing to appease the rulers while openly criticizing and lampooning them. "Men often spoke in parables, saying one thing and meaning another; praising the prince and praising the gallows to prove it" (Bloch 1972, 15).

As an example of the complexity of such readings, Bloch offers an interpretation of Korah's rebellion in Num 16, a text that as it is now speaks of a priestly rebellion, centering on the issue of ritual and incense, which is crushed through divine intervention. As the story stands, it is an account of a "premature palace revolution" (Bloch 1972, 80) within the priestly upper class, but what catches Bloch's attention is the way the revolt is dealt with: God opens the ground, which swallows them up as an example to anyone else who would rebel, who would burn incense before the Lord. This is not a God of war, waging a fight for survival, but a God of "white-guard terror" (Bloch 1972, 80), one who emerges from the redactor's pen. For Bloch, an echo of political rebellion reverberates through the text. Not only does the punishment itself signal this, but the perpetual recurrence of the Israelites' grumbling throughout the chapter indicates for Bloch a subversive, rebellious, anti-Yahweh voice that has been turned into something else—the sign of disobedience and recalcitrance on the part of the people themselves.

The dialogic reading strategy is similar to that of Bakhtin, Bhabha, and Brett, but the Marxist in Bloch leads in another direction, seeking the traces of subversion and rebellion in class and economic terms. In Bloch's hands such biblical detective work becomes a political tool, the various traditions and layers of the Bible full of politics and economics. Although he finds major elements at the ideological center of the Bible, especially the exodus and the Apocalypse, he assumes that by and large the dominant textual traditions are those of official power, priestly establishment and institutions—the ones who write, copy, and preserve texts. But also the ones who impose ideas, political and economic domination, and negative representations of the people. It is here that Bloch locates the alternatives, the possibility of opposing the hierocratic system of control and oppression. So, he focuses on the murmuring of the people against Moses, the trenchant prophetic critique of political economics, the early forms of Christianity rejected and persecuted by the early church, such as gnostics, Ophites and so on, who championed the serpent in the garden, saw the God of the Hebrew Bible as an evil power, a demiurge who sought to ensnare human beings within this world. These things indicate for Bloch a healthy revolutionary force or tradition in the Bible. All of this leads Bloch to posit a distinct, although highly diverse, thread, potentially revolutionary, antiruling class, antipowerful, antiwealth, that appears in many different guises throughout the Bible. And this stands over against the texts of the oppressor, in which Baal and Yahweh become one, where the literary elites work tirelessly as ideologues for the ruling class.

However, Bloch's effort to locate a continuous thread echoes in many respects Brett's effort to find a coherent alternative voice in Genesis. In both cases there is a failure of dialogic or dialectical nerve, for properly subversive voices—those of women, the economically abused and exploited, outsiders and heretics—are inevitably piecemeal and fragmentary, with no necessary coherence, if they get any chance of appearing at all. For in the Bible it is hard enough for a subversive voice to be heard, particularly in a document that is itself the product of a scribal elite working in a profoundly patriarchal society and culture. Bloch is more enthusiastic than I am in finding such voices, but he is determined to locate what it is that fed the burning revolutionary spirits of Münzer and company. I cannot but help wonder whether the truly subversive voices have not been entirely effaced from the text, although Bloch would argue that such an effacement is never complete, that traces are always left behind, but above all that there is more there when you know how and where to look, especially in those myths that have later been papered over with more acceptable ideological positions.

Bloch is well aware of the complexities, layers, varying voices to be found in the Bible, and I would agree that a dialectical reading is able to deal with such contradictory complexity better than any other approach. However, what is needed is an even more sophisticated dialectical reading that accounts even better for the twists, fold backs, curious alliances, and changing oppositions of the text, one that reads back and forth between the ideological, social, and economic contradictions that are inevitably found there.

2

The Decree of the Watchers,
or, Other Globalizations

[T]here is something daring and speculative, unprotected, in the approach of scholars and theorists to this unclassifiable topic. (Jameson 1998, xi)

Discussions of globalization, whether in biblical studies, theology, or academic disciplines more generally, tend to suffer three deficiencies: an ethical stance for or against, an absence of dialectical thinking, and an assumption that whatever we are experiencing now is unique, distinct. Insofar as globalization is both an economic and a cultural phenomenon, it is useful to bring out of the cellar some other dusty and forgotten efforts to conceptualize a global situation, such as those in the Bible (especially apocalyptic) or the notion of a global, catholic, church. As for the unceasing urge to invoke ethical categories in response to globalization (as also with postcolonialism and postmodernism), it seems to me that a decent dose of dialectical thinking is called for, as it is for understanding globalization itself (whose dialectical opposite then becomes disintegration).

One of the things that makes a topic such as this interesting—why globalization? and why now?—is that at the moment when it seemed as though no one was capable any longer of thinking about global tendencies, when a conceptual block had lodged itself firmly and apparently permanently, there begins a rash of studies of what is now labeled globalization. I would hazard a guess that what makes it so urgent is in part the new situation in which we find ourselves after the apparent end of the communist bloc in Europe (which may then be understood as the material form of the conceptual bloc), but what is interesting (to follow a methodological suggestion of Jameson and Macherey) is not only the way the new situation enables some of this reflection but also how it sets inexorable limits to precisely how we think about it. Further, the terms I am using function as ideological constructs, each in their own way assisting and hindering any efforts to make sense of our own social and political location. They are, to use a term of Derrida and Jameson, ideologemes, those minimal units or building blocks of thought with which we structure our understanding of the social world. What is interesting about ideologemes is that the ultimate purpose of locating and analyzing them is to decode their social, historical, and theoretical content or message, to identify what contradiction or tension in political economics they seek to address and resolve. Thus, not only will I be making use of the terms *globalization, postcolonialism*, and *postmodernism* in my discussion, but I will also be on the lookout for the various messages they emit about themselves.

Globalizations

> Upon my bed this is what I saw;
> there was a tree at the center of the earth,
> and its height was great.
> The tree grew great and strong,
> its top reached to heaven,
> and it was visible to the ends of the whole earth.
> Its foliage was beautiful,
> its fruit abundant,
> and it provided food for all.
> The animals of the field found shade under it,
> the birds of the air nested in its branches,
> and from it all living beings were fed.
> (Dan 4:7–9/10–12)

For anyone who has spent some time in peripheral zones, psychologically, socially, or globally, whether in madness, a tent, a humpy, or the Antipodes, the pull of the center becomes ever stronger. Yet imagining the global is by no means a recent invention. Thus, in order to skew contemporary deliberations on globalization, I want to introduce a relative outsider—the hoary biblical text of Daniel—to this rather intimate circle. Apart from preventing the dangers of inbreeding (a lantern jaw here, a dim wit there), my methodological debts here are to Brecht's estrangement effect (*Verfremdungseffekt*) or the Russian formalists' defamiliarization (Shklovsky's *ostranenie*), for my analysis of Dan 4 functions as a strategy of indirection, a looking awry or askance in order to see the whole question of globalization more clearly. One part of such a strategy is that the biblical text serves the useful function of relativizing or periodizing the contemporary outbreak of discussions of globalization, among which my own must then be counted.

Before turning to what seems to me to be the most persuasive and comprehensive way of dealing with globalization, it is interesting to note that there is a wide disciplinary awareness, almost an apocalyptic feel, sometimes a desperate assertion, that the globalization we have now is distinct. Economics, to begin with, seems to be vitally concerned with the question. So, for Cowhey and Aronson, globalization means "that the leading firms rely on foreign markets, on production and competitive assets (such as access to research and development) in other countries, and on global networks (such as the global payments network shared by the leading banks) to accomplish their fundamental business objectives" (1993, 14). One finds, apart from the textbooks (Gill and Law 1988; Salvatore 1993), that many are concerned with the dynamics of the new economic situation, whether in terms of economics itself (O'Brien 1992; Dicken 1992), the important relation between economics and the state (Bell and Head 1994; Cerny 1994; Cowhey and Aronson 1993; Helleiner 1994; Picciotto 1990), or the specific areas of economics such as labor (Van Liemt 1992), automobiles (Cowhey and Aronson 1993, 91–124), semiconductors, electronics, and telecommunications (Cowhey and Aronson 1993, 125–214; Warf 1989), and multinational or translational companies themselves (Kirby 1989; Ohmae 1990; Miyoshi 1996). Others debate in an ethical turn the possible benefits and drawbacks of a globalized economic system, whether it is possible to make it work better by dealing adequately with questions of poverty, unemployment, and environment (e.g., Miller 1995), or whether the new forms of capitalism are essentially baleful (Bello 1994). The interest in the economic forms of globalization is found in both the political right and the left (see the special issue of *Review of Radical Political Economics* produced in conjunction with *Capital and Class* [Radice et al.]).

Economists are not averse to seeking broader ways to describe a term with such a strong economic odor: thus, for Hoogvelt globalization, having won out over against some unwieldy and ugly competitors such as internationalization and transnationalization, designates the "ever-intensifying networks of cross-border human interaction" (1997, 114). Beyond economics—although from a Marxist perspective it is significant that the weight of research seems to lie here and with literary and cultural studies—the discussion of globalization has crept into the deliberations of anthropology (Stolcke 1995), psychology (Sampson 1989), sociology and military studies (Dandeker 1994; Moran 1990, for whom the associated dependence on foreign military technology is a security threat), geography (Warf 1989), urban and rural planning (Afshar 1994), public administration (Davies, Greenwood, and Robins 1995), the study of sport (Harvey and Houle 1994; Houlihan 1994; Maguire 1993), sociology (Sklair 1991), and religion (Beyer 1994; Robertson 1987). Closer to my own methodological home, the ferment in literary studies includes globalization as one of a constellation of issues, whether consideration of the book industry

(Kitson 1989), the new category of global writers (Robbins 1982–83), or, most extensively, in the notion of postcolonialism itself.

Returning to the model that is the most comprehensive in the light of these studies—and staying with the economic for a few more moments—I would suggest that globalization under capitalism is quite simply the worldwide dominance of capital in all areas of life, or to use Jameson's appropriation of Ernest Mandel, the purest form of capitalism thus far: "capitalism today is a purer form of capitalism than the very uneven situation about which Marx wrote and there is a way therefore in which the ideal model of *Capital* may correspond better to our situation than it did to that of the nineteenth-century British and continental one" (Jameson and Paik 1996, 352). I am of course following a Marxist model, one that informs the approach of Williams and Chrisman to postcolonialism as well. For them, modern colonialism, "the conquest and direct control of other people's lands," may be understood as a particular phase of capitalist globalization—which they term imperialism—that is the spread of the "capitalist mode of production, its penetration of previously non-capitalist regions of the world, and destruction of pre- or non-capitalist forms of social organisation" (Williams and Chrisman 1994, 2). This in turn owes its formulation to the monumental work of Immanuel Wallerstein and "world-systems theory," in which the Marxist emphasis on the primacy of economic forces finds one of its fullest expressions (Wallerstein 1983). Indeed, before the 1990s, there were only two areas in which globalization had been thought about systematically: international relations theorists, who saw the nation-state as a global actor; and the world-system theory work of Wallerstein and his followers, in which the economic is dominant (see Giddens 1990, 63–78). In the end, both need to be thought through the eyes of the other, as Giddens attempts to do: the nation-state through capital and capital through the nation-state. Yet even this leaves out a crucial third term—disintegration—that I will consider below.

As far as capital itself is concerned, its globalization is the result of the inherent need for expansion or "growth," the term that has become a marker of economic success. Capital, or rather, to avoid personification, those who deal in capital, have a distinct interest in expanding capitalism around the globe. This "interest" must be understood as the strong form of a wish fulfillment, since expansion is necessary for the very survival and reproduction of capitalism. By "expansion" I mean not only the continual geographical spread of capitalism (now into Eastern Europe, China, and so on) but also in the extension of existing markets through the continual generation of new products and areas for consumption, as well as the division of existing products into ever more subgroups. (One need only think of the recent proliferation of the types of specialist shoes: dress, casual, running, baseball, cricket, cross-training, basketball, field hockey, and so on.) This second type of expansion may alternatively be understood as the oft-noted need to increase the tempo of the pattern of product upgrade, replacement, and obsolescence, most remarkable now for its pure speed in the computer industry. It is here that Virilio's study (1977) of the necessary role of ever-increasing speed within capitalism extends Marx's perception of the continual revolution of capitalist production and social relations:

> The bourgeoisie cannot exist without constantly revolutionizing the instruments of production, and thereby the relations of production, and with them the whole relations of society. Conservation of the old modes of production in unaltered form was, on the contrary, the first condition of existence for all earlier industrial classes. Constant revolutionizing of production, uninterrupted disturbance of all social conditions, everlasting uncertainty and agitation distinguish the bourgeois epoch from all earlier ones. All fixed, fast-frozen relations, with their train of ancient and venerable prejudices and opinions are swept away, all new-formed ones become antiquated before they can ossify. All that is solid melts into air, all that is holy is profaned, and man is at last compelled to face with sober senses his real conditions of life and his relations with his kind. (Marx and Engels 1967, 83)

Two objections to this understanding of globalization need to be met. First, and more easily, the old charge of reduction of all forms of existence—political, social, intellectual, religious, cultural—to the economic (thus Beyer 1994, 21 regarding Wallerstein's work) may be countered by the observation that the notion of mode of production includes all of these areas in its ambit. It thus serves to expand analysis rather than reduce. A second objection is that this model does not account sufficiently for the more recent move to globalization that is felt by many to be unique. However, the Marxist model quite usefully reminds us that globalization may not be so unique or recent: instead, the expansionist processes of capital that have gradually fallen into place over the last five hundred years are finally coming to fruition (see Shohat and Stam 1996, 151–52). Indeed, Stuart Hall makes the useful point that, in the case of imperial nations, the search for global dominion was crucial to their very formation. Globalization therefore has a much longer history (Hall 1997, 173). At the same time, the idea of a leap or jump into a new phase is not to be discounted, although I prefer to speak of this in terms of a permutation in the capitalist mode of production rather than, for instance, the relationship of *Gemeinschaft* and *Gesellschaft* structures, or the shift from stratified differentiation to functional differentiation (see Beyer 1994, 26–41), or the move into a postindustrial society (see M. Rose 1991, 21–39), or an American globalization (Hall 1997, 178).

Yet if the solitude of contemporary globalization is broken down by thinking about the *longue durée* of capitalism and its earlier efforts to realize and conceptualize globalization, then a text like that of Dan 4, coming as it does from a context more than fifteen hundred years earlier than the beginnings of capitalism, will relativize globalization even further. What our postcolonial critic finds, turning with some relief from the pile of economic and cultural theory to the shelf on biblical studies—although the covers on these books have curled and warped in the humidity and heat—is a distinct image of globalization straight out of the apocalyptic imagination of the Hebrew Bible: the world tree in Dan 4.

The text itself is riven with some intriguing contradictions—between first-person and third-person narrative, between tree and animal images, between the epistolary beginning and the dream interpretation/fulfillment (in fact, the layering of the whole chapter), and between the Masoretic Text and the various Greek versions, particularly Theodotion and Old Greek—which it would be interesting to pursue in another context.[1] However, here I will somewhat peremptorily locate only a couple of features of this text that are important for my own larger discussion: the world tree and the wider intersections with nature, and the dominion of the King of Heaven (*melek hashamayim*). I am, in other words, coming at the text at the level of the ideological, in search of the various constructs of reality that inform the ways individuals—whether authors, readers, interpreters, or characters themselves—shape their own place in the larger whole.

The first item in such an ideological construct is the tree, which is rather blatantly an image of globalization (the Septuagint pushes beyond the globe and into the universe, for there the tree's "top drew near to heaven and its trunk to the clouds, filling that which was under heaven; the sun and the moon dwelt in it and lighted the whole earth" [4:8, Ziegler 1968]). The tree—the initial reference for Lacocque (1979, 73–74, 77–8; see also Coxon 1986) with the appropriate debts to Eliade—has in Dan 4 the features of the world tree as *axis mundi*, an aspect it shares with the sacred or primal mountain, holy rock or tower, those items in other words that function in the mythology of particular groups in order to locate (in the widest sense of the term) themselves in relation to the cosmos. Now while all of this may be ideological in the sense I have outlined, it is also very much indebted to an archetypal read-

---

1. The book of Daniel has its own tensions, not least of which are the differences between the stories of Dan 1–6 and the visions of Dan 7–12, the relationship between the Hebrew and Aramaic parts, and between these parts and the various Greek translations. In my consideration of Dan 4 I have consulted the representative commentaries of Collins (1993), Goldingay (1989), Lacocque (1979), and Montgomery (1927).

ing of the text, not that there is anything necessarily undesirable about such an approach, especially since it gives access to a range of comparative material outside Dan 4. Thus, apart from similar uses of the tree in the Hebrew Bible—the two major parallels are from Ezek 17 and 31, but to be added are Ezek 19:10–14, Isa 10:33–11:1, and the tree of life in Gen 2–3—its usage in the ancient Near East was quite common, although commentators restrict their mutually echoing listings to those stories in which trees form part of the dreams of rulers.[2]

If I follow the archetypal path it would be possible to include the tower of hubris (Babel) and the holy mountains of Sinai/Horeb/Zion, yet my point may be made if I restrict myself to the tree and the other major manifestation of nature in Dan 4, namely, the animal imagery that overlaps that of the tree in 4:12/15 and then dominates 4:13–14/16–17. In Daniel's interpretation of the dream—allowing for a few moments some interpretive insight to Daniel and following the *mise en abyme* of my own interpretive act in the text itself—the pivot that holds together both tree and animal imagery is of course Nebuchadnezzar (4:15–24/19–27). King and emperor, Nebuchadnezzar connects with the other examples from the ancient Near East, for those stories relate the world tree and the ruler that makes David Jobling's arguments in regard to Ps 72 relevant (1992b).

In the part of this study that interests me on this occasion, Jobling argues for the integral role of nature in the imperial ideology of the ancient Near East, for Jobling finds the ruler crucial to the ideological construction of plenty, understood in terms of fertility, produce, agricultural labor, and imperial wealth. Yet what influences me particularly here is the way this idea of plenty relates to nature, for in the "perpetual motion machine" of royal legitimation in Ps 72:1–7—that is, the king is a pivot, an ideological "point de capiton," to evoke Zizek, in the way people understood the world—Jobling sees a parallel between the theme of royal justice leading to *shalom* among the people with the theme of rain leading to natural *shalom* for the earth. That is, the human and natural worlds intersect with the king: the king's activity and existence are part of the natural order. The despot and all that the despot stands for is "natural," or, to avoid a later language of realism, is ordained by the gods in the appropriate mythologies.

Yet there is a final twist in all of this, for the whole relationship works the other way as well, since the despots through their symbiosis with nature

---

2. There is the Mede Astyages with his dream that a vine grew from his daughter's womb to cover Asia, Xerxes' olive branch crown from which branches spread out to cover the earth, and the prayer of Nabonidus, from Qumran, where Babylon appears as a speaking tree (see Collins 1993, 223–24; Lacocque 1979, 77; Montgomery 1927, 228).

also affect if not control nature through their own activities. Thus, the king himself is a motor for the system as a whole. It is this final interaction that is important for an understanding of the natural images—tree and animal—in Dan 4: the king is part of nature, as tree or animal, but then also controls nature (the tree, after all, is an allegory of empire). In Daniel there is no claim on behalf of the Israelite king that Jobling traces in Ps 72: it is rather concerned with the imperial figure himself, Nebuchadnezzar (the desire of commentators to see Nabonidus behind the depiction here makes no difference to my point).

Thus far I have suggested that the key image of globalization in Dan 4, the tree, grafts the king or despot onto nature in a way that makes the association perfectly natural. In fact, the tree is the king, who is then himself as large as the globe itself, a sort of vast earthy body that encompasses everything. Yet despite this direct reference to the despot in Dan 4 (Nebuchadnezzar) I would suggest that this is not the end of the representational terminus, the long tap root seeking another connection. Here I need to break away from the interpretive guidelines of the text and look beyond the boundaries of Daniel's interpretation (the tree is the king). It is not so much that the despot is the allegorical reference point but that the interaction of tree and despot I have already noted functions as a trace or figuration of empire, or, more correctly, of mode of production. Without going into the detail that I have produced elsewhere (Boer 1996a, 176–82), the despot—and my usage of this term is quite deliberate—in the ancient Near East is a crucial figure in what is known as the tributary or Asiatic mode of production, whose economic, social, and ideological systems turned on the need for a large, centralized bureaucracy, exacting tribute (by tax farming or military means) from an amorphous and necessarily far flung (due to the smallness of individual tributes) collection of agriculturally based subject groups. It is here that the issue of globalization resurfaces as a more conscious item, since my suggestion is that the various ideological presentations of globalization are parts of the larger realm of modes of production.

What of nature? Apart from the more general observation that those who live under various modes of production tend to forget that their particular situation is historically contingent, it seems that the close connection between nature and the despot was a crucial feature of the Asiatic mode of production. It is precisely from those societies operating under an Asiatic mode of production that the creation myth as political myth arises without any consciousness that politics and nature are distinct areas. Yet I have left out a final term that appears in Dan 4 and serves to bind despot and nature together, namely, the role of the deity. This role is in fact taken more directly by the *'irin*, the "watchers" or the "vigilants," as Montgomery deftly translates, who perform not only the task of universal sentinels but also carry out any of the interaction between the human and heavenly worlds (see further Collins 1993, 224-25; Montgomery 1927, 231-32). Where the deity does participate more actively in events it is normally as creator of the natural, social, political, and economic world, but also as despotic forebear (I am thinking here of *Enuma Elish*). While it is not always clear where the distinction might be made between current ruler and deity, in Dan 4 the relationship is set in up terms of a contest or conflict between Nebuchadnezzar and Yahweh—much like two despots vying for greater power—with Yahweh not unexpectedly coming out on top as supreme ruler and "King of Heaven."

The image of the imperial tree in Dan 4 thus provides a useful counterpoint to contemporary discussions of globalization, forcing us not to assume too much about the uniqueness of our own awareness and discussions of globalization. What is the difference, in other words, between our own notions of globalization and those of Dan 4, or, more broadly, those expressed in the sheer temporal and spatial range of the apocalyptic literature of this period? For one, the subsuming of everything within nature in Dan 4 stands out sharply from the distinct absence of nature, except as an absence, as something to be defended, in contemporary representations of globalization. Yet capitalism, as David Harvey has argued in a striking essay (1998), constructs its own natural order that then depends on capitalist flows of money to continue. In fact, each mode of production, and each form of globalization that goes with it, creates a system of nature upon which both rely. Of course, the contradictions within such systems are often concerned precisely with nature and the earth as a whole.

On the other hand, the very effort to produce a global image, and the associated ideological construction of the globe through tree, king, nature, and society in Dan 4—a construction whose complexity I have attempted to trace above—should make us a little more wary about the uniqueness of this particular moment of globalization. In the end, the difference between the Asiatic mode of production represented in Dan 4 and present-day capitalism comes down to a difference in modes of production. This rather abstract concept is able to include within its orbit everything from the minute formal shifts in a particular text to economic history: thus the globalizing image presented by Dan 4 may be expanded and connected with political, social, economic, and cultural dimensions of the same mode of production. In doing so—as I have done in part above—the feeling of familiarity or contemporaneity for any reader with an eye open for globalization begins to dissipate before the chilling difference and distance of the text's wider connections.

Destruction Versus Disintegration

I continued looking, in the visions of my head as I lay in bed, and there was a holy watcher, coming down from heaven. He cried aloud and said:

Cut down the tree and chop off its branches;
strip off its foliage and scatter its fruit.
Let the animals flee from beneath it
and the birds from its branches.
But leave its stump and roots in the ground,
with a band of iron and bronze,
in the tender grass of the field.
Let him be bathed with the dew of heaven,
and let his lot be with the animals of the field
in the grass of the earth.
Let his mind be changed from that of a human,
and let the mind of an animal be given to him.
And let seven times pass over him.
The sentence is rendered by decree of the watchers,
the decision is given by order of the holy ones,
in order that all who live may know
that the Most High is sovereign over the kingdom of mortals;
he gives it to whom he will
and sets over it the lowliest of human beings.
(Daniel 4:10–14/13–17)

But there is another part of this discussion, through which Identity and Difference may be traced. It is also important to make a distinction between culture and ideology on the one hand and economics on the other. They have been looped together up until now, and in many ways they cannot be untangled, but it does help, every so now and then, to realize that a text such as Daniel, or even a discussion such as this one, is distinct from the economic conditions under which it exists.

What else, then, is Dan 4 on about? Once again I will restrict my discussion to the image, or ideological item, of the world tree in Dan 4. The despotic conflict between Yahweh and Nebuchadnezzar—which is a crucial indicator of the text's ultimate referent—is sparked to violence in the tree itself. What is interesting here is the terminology (4:11/14): in a string of imperatives, the tree is cut down (*goddu 'ilana'*) and dismembered (*weqatsitsu 'anefohi*: cut off its branches), its fruit and foliage shaken off (*'attaru*) and dispersed (*uvaddaru*), and the dependent animals flee (*tenud*). The overwhelming image is one of destruction and dispersal: the tree is destroyed and its various parts scattered (a section is, of course, left to be restored later).

Closely connected with this is Nebuchadnezzar's transition into an animal psyche, or lycanthropy (4:13/16), which opens up a host of interesting questions regarding the (dis)continuity between animals and human beings in this text, relations of inferiority and superiority, "the visceral fear of animality in the Book of Daniel" (Lacocque 1979, 86), and depictions of and assumptions regarding the psyche as such. As I will show in a few moments, this focus on destruction and the animal psyche is quite distinct from the disintegration characteristic of our present moment, yet one cannot help but notice the foliage bursting through this text, the reversion of the king's coat to fur, the claws, paws, and slit pupils. Destruction of the order can only be posited in the same terms as its construction, namely, the code of nature. The linchpin of the natural and human orders, its corner stone, is absorbed by a nature he no longer influences. Nevertheless, this does not mean that there is no longer a despot at the helm, one to ensure the peace and fertility of the natural and social realms, for the true despot here is Yahweh, the one who defeats Nebuchadnezzar and puts him in his brutish place. In other words, Nebuchadnezzar, the global tree, is destroyed and dispersed at the hands of another despot (Yahweh).

Yet there is a further level to this text that explicates the whole issue of destruction: the conflict between Yahweh and Nebuchadnezzar might initially be understood as a figure for despotic relations as such. To pursue this further I would suggest (rather arbitrarily, since all of this needs more detailed analysis) that the opposition of globalization and destruction I have isolated from Dan 4 is a trace or figure of economic relations themselves. What I mean is that economic relations under the Asiatic mode of production rely on both an impression/idea of global extent and control—particularly via the intersection with nature—and a pattern of repeated military enforcement of the payment of a tribute that is fundamental for the system's reproduction. In the latter case destruction is a crucial element not only of interdespotic relations but also of relations between the central bureaucracy and the tribute-paying satellites. The monotonous appearances in the texts of the Hebrew Bible, from Kings to Daniel and through to the New Testament, of troops from one empire after another, each army with the task of ensuring tribute or destroying the town or city in question if it refused to comply, should provide narrative reinforcement at least to my proposal. The occasional dispersal of peoples by more vigorous imperial administrations indicates the place of dispersal alongside destruction.

There are two qualifications to this broad picture. First, the tree in Dan 4 is not utterly destroyed; a stump and a root remain, bound with a band of iron and bronze. Although no explicit reason is given in the text, there is at least the possibility of new life from the stump, a situation that is quite appropriate for the area of economic relations, since an utterly destroyed subject is no longer able to pay tribute to the victor (just as Nebuchadnezzar pays tribute to Yahweh, so satellite states pay tribute to the despot). Second, the assumption of a uniform Asiatic mode of production is not particularly valid, given the assumption that, while one mode of production may be dominant, others may have a residual or emerging presence at any one historical juncture. The signal in Dan 4 of at least one other mode of production must lie with the "Watcher," for, as Lacocque points out, there is a significant shift from the messenger delivering the word of Yahweh ("thus says Yahweh") to the messengers presenting their own message without a word from Yahweh as such. Thus, in Dan 4:11–14/14–17 the words are those of the Watcher; although they may be understood to come from Yahweh, this is not explicit by any means. The Watcher takes the initiative with the message rather than passing on that of Yahweh. I seems to me that what we have here is a narrative appearance of the fundamental change brought about by the Hellenistic world of the Roman Empire: the economic and social necessity of slaves in what is known as an ancient or slave-based mode of production. That slaves not only mediate social and economic relations but take a vital initiative in these relations is essential to such a mode of production.

To sum up: alongside the bushy code of nature in which globalization is represented (the king is a global tree), the other side of this ideological construction is the destruction and subjugation of tributary peoples. Here Yahweh destroys the power of the other despot, Nebuchadnezzar, in order to make him subservient (Dan 4:14/17).

Is there an echo of this pattern—what might be cast in terms of an opposition between globalization and destruction—in the ideological construction of contemporary globalization? At first sight, the related item of dispersal at least finds some reverberations, for what is particularly interesting about the plethora of discussions of globalization is its conjunction, at least temporally, with the whole development that may be characterized as a profound suspicion of discourses of totalization and the advocating of difference, heterogeneity, multitudinous singularities. For Dirlik (1996, 23–28) this is what constitutes the growth of the category of the "local": micro-groups, Vietnam guerrillas, feminism, ecology groups, the end of metanarratives, and so on. I would add decentering or the splintering of the individual subject, sexual ambivalence (queer theory), the importance of pastiche and/or parody in place of distinct styles, the infinite dispersal of power in society and politics, the collapse of high culture into mass culture and the total commodification of culture as such, the end of the great master narratives of history (including the Christian and Marxist master narratives), and consequently the recovery and development of micro-histories and counternarratives of groups formerly marginalized (women, indigenous peoples, gays and lesbians, racially and economically oppressed groups, and so on).

Indeed, the global/local opposition has become one of the working contradictions of postcolonial theory, although there has been little effort to think it through further than an ethical and/or political binary. For what I miss in most of the discussion of globalization and localization—whether in economics (e.g., Ruccio 1991; Hoksbergen 1994; Van Raaij 1993; Parpart 1993; Brown 1991) or cultural theory (Wilson and Dissanayake 1996; Jameson and Miyoshi 1998)—is not only an intersection of the two discourses but also a properly dialectical approach to the whole question. What Dan 4 may indicate is that globalization, in both its economic and cultural forms, relies on some form of opposite for its very production.

There has indeed been some reflection on the interdependence of the global and the local. For instance, some sociological studies show an interest in how the various ethnic, cultural, political, and social units might operate under and indeed be constitutive of globalization (Beyer 1994, 45–68). Other manifestations of a concern with particularism and fragments appear in the realms of economics, such as J. Morris's "global localization" (1991) or Amin's "polycentrism" (1990), and sociology, such as Regan's concern with privacy in the context of global communications (1993) or Beyer on globalization and privatization (1994, 70–77).

The issue for all of these types of studies may be subsumed under the philosophical category of the part and the whole.[3] In fact, the remainder of my discussion shifts to a more philosophical level, for here the deeper fragmentary logic of capitalist globalization may be found. Let me replace "localization" with the philosophical term *reification*, which is more generally known as *commodification*. Both terms have a venerable Hegelian Marxist pedigree, finding their first expression in Hegel's *Phenomenology of Spirit* (1977) in the famous section on master and slave, where the relationship between the two is mediated by a "thing,"[4] and then subsequently

---

3. Another philosophical, if not theological, debate which has some bearing here is that between the universal and the particular. This has of course been cast in terms different from the present situation, most significantly under the signature of Plato's forms and then theologically in terms of God and the world. The globalization-fragmentation opposition forms a somewhat distinct permutation on this tradition of thought, having a family resemblance yet shifting the opposition out of philosophy and theology and into the realm of sociology and political economics.

4. "The lord is the consciousness that exists *for itself*, but no longer merely the Notion of such a consciousness. Rather, it is a consciousness existing *for itself* which is mediated

developed by Marx and then Georg Lukács. Although the term "reification" (*Verdinglichung/Versachlichung*) is found in Marx's work (Marx 1973, 160; 1976, 209, 1052–60), Lukács developed it into a more systematic philosophical concept by combining Marx's notion of fetishism with Max Weber's idea of rationalization (see Marx 1976, 163–77; Lukács 1971, 83–222; Jameson 1981, 62–63). Etymologically, reification means the transformation of a living being into a lifeless thing (*res facere*). More comprehensively, reification may be described as a swapping of roles and therefore of power: relations between human beings take on the nature of relations between things or objects (specifically commodities), while the relations between material objects are invested with the quality and power of human and social relations, all of which obscures social processes but transforms objects into spiritual and glamorous entities, into "fetishes" (see Marx 1976, 163–77). Reification, in other words, deals with the relations of production, yet it also extends to the relations between human beings and nature and the self-understanding of humans.

A second part of the reification process is fragmentation: emphasized in particular by Jameson, the important economic process here is the division of labor and Taylorization (breaking up production into the smallest and most efficient units). However, this goes well beyond the economic into social, psychological, institutional, even sensual realms of existence, as well as the separation of public and private, poetic and political, consumer and producer. Further, reification and fragmentation operate in the long term at an increasing pace and with an increasing reach, so that it is no longer possible to think in nonreified forms: even those passionately held beliefs in the possibility of avoiding commodification and reification are themselves reified (which then applies to the whole area of the interpretation of texts).

Finally, the increasingly rapid splintering of reification takes place side by side with the contradictory trend toward totalization or globalization. It cannot be overemphasized that the drive to globalization is dialectically related to reification: the greater the totality, the more forces work to break up the elements into ever-smaller parts; the greater the reification,

---

with itself through another consciousness, i.e., through a consciousness whose nature it is to be bound up with an existence that is independent, or thinghood (*Dingheit*) in general. The lord puts himself into relation with both of these moments, to a *thing* as such, the object of desire, and to the consciousness for which thinghood is the essential characteristic.... The lord relates himself mediately to the bondsman through being [a thing] that is independent, for it is just this which holds the bondsman in bondage; it is his chain from which he could not break free in the struggle, thus proving himself to be dependent, to possess his independence in thinghood" (Hegel 1977, 115).

the more newer unities are developed. As capitalism dominates more and more of the globe, it transforms everything into commodities, it reifies all relations; yet capitalism is unable to globalize without that reification and commodification it sets under way. On a micro-level this may seen in the way government money is crucial for even the remotest Aboriginal communities in central Australia, in the way they play a role in the wider capitalist economy and ideology. On a macro-level the inclusion of countries in a global economic network has the dialectically opposed effect of generating greater demands for the autonomy of ever-smaller units, whether they are ethnic, geographical, religious, or linguistic, as with Quebec in the context of the North American Free Trade Deal, or the states of the former Yugoslavia, Czechoslovakia, and the U.S.S.R. in a united Europe, or the desire for a republic in Australia, or the drive for the autonomy of Scotland, Wales, Northern Ireland, and even Cornwall in the United Kingdom. The greater impetus to the political autonomy and recovery of language and culture by indigenous peoples must also be understood in the light of a globalizing process that includes these indigenous groups as well. Similarly, the local expressions of opposition to capitalism—indeed, the only major ones now that the communist states have dissipated in eastern Europe—are those of religious and ethnic fundamentalisms. No longer bound by the nation-state, its former unit of contraction, capitalism is able to expand unchecked, and "the reaction to this boundless expansion which threatens to sweep away every particular self-identity are 'postmodern' fundamentalisms as the violent 'contraction' of social life into its religious-ethnic roots" (Žižek 1996, 27).[5] That the nation-state may have a greater role to play is posited by Jameson (1998a; 1998b; see also Paik Nak-Chung 1998; Kapur 1998, 193), who sees it as the crucial third term of a triple dialectic: the global and local are articulated through the national, which now takes on new and unknown forms.[6]

---

5. A related though distinct example of all of this comes from the study by Naficy of Turkish film. He identifies an opposition between the claustrophobic and transworld/agoraphobic, the claustrophobic here figured by suitcases, buses, cages, prisons, barns, TV sets—the phobic partners of agoraphobes. Claustrophobia is created also through closed-shot compositions, tight physical spaces, barriers within the *mise-en-scène*, shots that impedes vision and access, lighting that creates a mood of constriction and blocked vision (Naficy 1996).

6. Wilson and Dissanayake also find some space for the nation-state: "Globalization, paradoxically, has led to a strengthening of local ties, allegiances and identity politics within different nation-state formations" (1996, 5).

In the end, the basic reality to which all of this applies is that of transnational capitalism, in which there is an ever-greater reification in the form of the commodity. I am, in fact, indebted to Henri Lefebvre for this insight in his wonderful book *The Production of Space* (1994). Lefebvre predicted when he first wrote the book in 1974 that global capital would be fractured from within by enduring ties to religion, place, city, country, and class. This dialectic is the "principle contradiction" of late capital, and it is to be found "[b]etween the capacity to conceive of and treat space on a global (or worldwide) scale on the one hand, and its fragmentation of procedures and processes, all fragmentary themselves, on the other" (1994, 355).[7]

Thus, just as the globalization I tracked in Dan 4 is determined by despotic conflict and destruction, so also globalization within capitalism cannot do without reification and disintegration at all levels. At the same time, the formal identity between these two very different economic and cultural systems flips over to difference when the contents of destruction and disintegration are dissected and spread out for inspection.

The Problem of Ethics

> The theoretical challenge, however, is to avoid the twin pitfalls of euphoria and melancholy. (Shohat and Stam 1996, 146)

Despite Shohat and Stam's argument (1996, 145–46) that there is little to be gained from either an enthusiastic celebration or a furrowed disapproval of globalization, it seems as though a host of critics want to do just that. Apart from the enthusiasts of both economic and cultural (that is, media) globalization, the form of condemnation on which I want to focus is that which identifies the disintegrated local and particular as a site for resistance, for this casts the global as something to be overcome and the local with

---

7. Similarly, Hetata writes: "The movement toward a global culture might seem to be contradicted by the other movement toward cultural division, fragmentation, and strife. My contention is that there is no real contradiction" (Hetata 1998, 282–83). Hetata, however, sees this in terms of a divide and conquer strategy: fragmented power at the bottom means easier global power at the top. A different perspective is provided by Featherstone (1996, 64), who sees impossible blends of homogenization and fragmentation, globalization versus localization, universalism versus particularism, without being able to theorize them except in terms of Appadurai's overlapping, disjunctive realms of people, technology, finance, media and ideas (1993). The globe is for Featherstone not really that globalized: global culture is a series of heaps, congeries, aggregates of cultural particularities juxtaposed on the same field.

a positive aura, a halo even. A sample from the Wilson and Dissanayake anthology is indicative: Miyoshi (1996) wants to oppose transnational companies while outlining their development; Mitchell (1996) reads for local resistance while noting the complexities and impurities of such resistance (in her example of Vancouver it is often middle class and racist); although Polan (1996) notes the inevitability of the way globalism shapes localism, she laments the loss of the local and the ability to work oppositions in her reading of films such as *Mr. Baseball* and *Iron Maze* in the context of the Pittsburgh steel revival; Wilson (1996), with his cyberpunk language and style, tracks films as well, focusing in the end on Hawaiian efforts at cultural resistance; and even though Dirlik (1996, 32–35) sees local identity and resistance as generated out of the global, the local is still something worth fighting for. Elsewhere JanMohamed and Lloyd (1997) argue for a plurality of minority voices, literatures, and discourse against a monolithic majority. The list might go on indefinitely. Each item on it would push for some type of change that begins with and values what is peripheral and marginal.

In order to register my skepticism about such possibilities, it might be worth returning to Dan 4 for a moment, for this text too may be read as oppositional. It is not so much that it wants to oppose Yahweh but that the representation of Yahweh as some bejeweled potentate, as a thundering super-despot, all amour, fiery eyes, and bulging gut, functions as a response, an imaginary resolution to a social situation (to echo Lévi-Strauss), which is that of imperial domination over Israel by Persia. The textual, imaginary dominance of this dreadfully marginal deity, against the imperial despot himself, is that which constitutes the great contradiction, and power, of this text. Yet no matter how much it opposes, undermines, usurps power at a cultural level, the situation itself is there, whether one likes it or not. In the same way that the oriental despot of the Asiatic mode of production is an unavoidable part of the economic and social world of this text, so also the global and the local, globalization and reification, are part of this one. In fact, Jameson's distinction between cultural (media, communicational technology) and economic forms of globalization has been central to my discussion here, and it is worth noting that in this light both levels may be seen as positive and negative. Culturally there can be either a postmodern celebration of difference and diversity, of cultural variety and multiculturalism, or one may offer a lament for the spread of global American mass culture; economically, one can curse transnational capitalism and the destruction of local forms, or trumpet the richness of the free market as the most basic expression of human nature. To indicate how mixed the ethical assessments can be, it is worth remembering that global corporations are as interested in the local and value it as highly as the many opposition groups who fight to protect the local zones from those same transnationals (see Dirlik 1997, 72–73).

Rather than worrying about its ethical status, it might be better to understand globalization. Thus, in a fascinating suggestion regarding the global/local opposition I have tailed, and especially the attempt to locate oppositional movement, Jameson notes the first signs of an international class struggle: "What emerges worldwide are then patterns of negative and positive exchanges which resemble those of class relations and struggles within the nation-state, even though … they do not (yet) define themselves in that way and currently remain fixed and thematized at the level of the spatial and the geopolitical" (1998a, xii[8]). Indeed, for Jameson an antagonistic definition is what globalization requires: "I propose to 'define' globalization as an untotalizable totality which intensifies binary relations between its parts—mostly nations, but also regions and groups, which, however, continue to articulate themselves on the model of 'national identities' (rather than in terms of social class, for example)." These conflictual relations are symbolic ones, cultural, although "such symbolic transmission requires the preexistence of economic and communicational channels and preestablished circuits" (Jameson 1998a, xii).

In concluding this section I would suggest that the intense dialectical opposition between globalization and fragmentation is characteristic, alongside the more obligatory depthlessness and loss of affect, of the particular historical moment that goes by the title of postmodernism. This of course makes the connection between culture, aesthetics, and economics for which Fredric Jameson is well known, yet to my knowledge Jameson does not come at it in this way. I should qualify my discussion thus far with the self-realization that in many respects the opposition of globalization and disintegration is an ideal and highly abstract one, as is the notion of mode of production. As I noted earlier, they are ideologemes, or ideological units (along with postmodernism) with their own particular messages. An initial aspect of those messages lies in the dialectical conjunction of globalization and disintegration, for there is an insistence, in making this connection, on a Marxist model of making sense of the real, over against the only other great and viable model of liberalism, in which there is both the idea that the seeds of a liberal world lie in the origins of time and move from there on a gradual path of improve-

---

8. In a more formal explication of this question, Sklair (1998, 299–301) attempts to identify the features of a new transnational capitalist class with four major fractions: transnational executives and their local affiliates; globalizing state bureaucrats; globalizing politicians and professionals; consumerist elites (merchants, media).

ment, and the belief that the liberal ideological construct is part of the natural order (for instance, competition is part of nature).

Finally, although the particular form and intensity of reification and fragmentation has a frenzied quality not found in earlier eras, like globalization it is by no means distinct, for the disintegration of older certainties and stabilities has been remarked upon since Marx (see Lears 1980). It is, in other words, as old as the five-hundred-year history of capitalism itself.

3
Explorer Hermeneutics,
or Fat Damper and Sweetened Tea

We celebrated the day [Easter] with a luncheon of *fat* damper and *sweetened* tea. (Leichhardt 1847, 190)

After having celebrated Whit-Sunday with a double allowance of fat cake and sweetened tea ... (Leichhardt 1847, 252)

Having completed this last morsel, I occupied myself for a little with my journal, then read a few chapters in the New Testament, and having fulfilled these duties, I felt myself as contented and cheerful, as I had ever been in the most fortunate moments of my life. (Grey 1841, 2:60).

With the global survey complete, from a high window overlooking this water planet, it is time to descend the stairs and take to the road, to follow the tracks of the "explorers" of Australia, people, mostly men, who traversed a country full of distance and Aboriginal people, pretending that they were the first to "discover" the vast stretches of Australia: Mitchell in New South Wales, Sturt in both New South Wales and South Australia, Eyre in South Australia, Leichhardt in Queenland, Stuart across the center, and Giles through the deserts of South and Western Australia. It is an endless trek of perpetual wandering, tracing, tailing, trailing, although now it can be done via the tracks themselves as well as the explorers' journals, which were formative in the construction of how the land and its people were and are viewed, in the construction of "Australia" itself. Those texts yield some distinct surprises, particularly in the way the Bible permeates them in so many ways, ranging from explicit biblical references to what might be termed a biblical imaginary, a construct of perception that rendered the foreign, antipodean Australian land, flora, fauna, and people in terms that were comprehensible, that is, in biblical terms. The evangelical Grey is perhaps the most obvious, citing distinct moments of biblical study and reading, or at least he writes that he did so:

> It may be asked, if, during such a trying period, I did not seek from religion that consolation which it is sure to afford? My answer is, - Yes; and I farther feel assured that but for the support I derived from prayer and frequent perusal and meditation of the Scriptures, I should never have been able to have borne myself in such a manner as to have maintained discipline and confidence amongst the rest of the party: nor in all my sufferings did I ever lose the consolation derived from a firm reliance upon the goodness of providence. (Grey 1841, 1:381)

To be sure, this was not a solitary occurrence, avid Bible student that he was:

> The safety of the whole party now depended upon my forming a prompt and efficient plan of operations, and seeing it carried out with energy and perseverance. As soon as I was out of sight of Mr. Smith and Coles, I sat down upon the shore, to reflect upon our present position.... I determined not to decide hastily between these plans, and in order more fully to compose my mind, I sat down and read a few chapters in the Bible. (Grey 1841, 1:393-94)

Out of the half dozen major texts—journals, crucial not only in the gathering of scientific information in a haphazard way but also for the burgeoning travel and tourist literature—a number of items in what might be termed explorer hermeneutics emerge. None of them more than amateur students of the Bible, although Eyre was the son of a clergyman, they thereby produced some striking signals not only of the way the Bible influenced their modes of perception but also of how the Bible itself was read and understood. Despite their differences, there are some common motifs that appear in their scribblings, particularly the notion of the call, divine strength, relief from trouble (especially the finding of water), antiquarian evidence, particularly with reference to the indigenous people met at nearly every step of the way, and then the providential, all-surveying, all-knowing eye (what used to be known as the gaze). And in all of this the overwhelming reference, despite Mr. Grey's reading of the New Testament, is the Hebrew Bible.

Implicit Israelites

Ernest Giles, least orthodox out of them all and thereby at the other pole from Grey, gives voice to a sense of calling to the explorer vocation. Giles indulges in theological and philosophical reflection, including gentle questions on orthodox Christian ideas such as the nature of heaven (1889, 1:237-8; see also 1889, 2:118-9). All of this takes place when he is under fever, but it is not clear whether this is a strategy to avoid theological censorship, the fever of his later writing, of the trip itself, of reflection and thought, of.... Yet Giles writes that he felt divinely appointed, called, anointed even, to the task: a heavenly choir with angelic harps sings—echoes of the shepherds at Christmas and a prophetic calling: "Be bold of heart, be strong of will, for unto thee by God is given, to roam the desert paths of earth, and thence explore the fields of heaven. Be bold of heart, be strong of will, and naught on earth shall lay thee low" (1889, 2:155).

To support such a notion of calling, that most ideologically suspicious of theological categories, the sense of strength from "Providence," the "Creator," the "Almighty" (rarely, if ever, "God") pervaded the ideological construction of the world of the explorers. They felt clearly that God was guiding them and keeping them out of danger (at least, those who were not killed or who died of thirst, hunger, or exposure, as nearly every expedition experienced). The devout Grey is a model of pious strength:

> It is only those who go forth into perils and dangers, amidst which human foresight and strength can but little avail, and who find themselves, day after day, protected by an unseen influence, and ever and again snatched from the very jaws of destruction, by a power which is not of this world, who can at all times estimate the knowledge of one's own weakness and littleness, and the firm reliance and trust upon the goodness of the Creator which the human breast is capable of feeling. Like all other lessons which are of great and lasting benefit to man, this one must be learnt amidst much sorrowing and woe; but, having learnt it, it is but the sweeter from the pain and toil which are undergone in the acquisition. (Grey 1841, 1:381)

For Grey, a perfect reliance on "the goodness of God" and "the merits of our Redeemer" is a "sure refuge and certain source of consolation" (Grey 1841, 1:394). The Scriptures themselves provide him with a sense of resignation and contentment at his present fate, sure as he is that his Redeemer will either rescue him or have him die by starvation.[1]

---

1. "By the influence these [Bible readings] imparted, I became perfectly contented and resigned to our apparently wretched condition, and, again rising up, pursued my path along the beach to the party. It may here be remarked by some that these statements of my attending to religious duties are irrelevant to the subject, but in such an opinion I cannot at all coincide. In detailing the sufferings we underwent, it is necessary to relate the means by which those sufferings were alleviated; and after having, in the midst of perils and misfortunes, received the greatest consolation from religion, I should be ungrateful to my Maker not to acknowledge this, and should ill perform my duty to my fellow men, did I not bear testimony to the fact, that under all the weightier sorrows and sufferings that our frail nature is liable to, a perfect reliance upon the goodness of God, and the merits of our Redeemer, will be found a sure refuge and certain source of consolation" (Grey 1841, 1:393–94).

Giles, in his characteristic way, uses the Bible while shifting the emphasis to human initiative. Thus when talking of the burden of leading the other people on his journey and the strain it induced after their 325-mile trek without water across the desert by camel, writes "I gathered some support from a proverb of Solomon: 'If thou faint in the day of adversity, thy strength is small'" (1889, 2:155).

Apart from a general sense of calling and of divine providence and strength, there is a distinct evocation of divine assistance in moments that were felt to be rescues from imminent death—inevitably associated with the finding of water (and the subsequent destruction of Aboriginal water supplies as the horses and, for Giles, camels, were watered). There is a repeated focus on water, a struggle to locate that which seems to keep the many tribes whom they meet alive, their campfires at night indicating not only their presence but also the fact that they seemed to know where the water was (see Eyre's reflections: 1845, 1:351). Indeed, all the explorers obsess about water. Grey runs short within minutes of landing on the West Coast, being totally unprepared (1841, 1:69–71).

Giles, traveling completely blind—despite the presence of Aborigines about him—through some of the most arid territory in the world, identifies thirst as "that dire affliction that besets the wanderer in the Australian wilds" (Giles 1889, 1:75) and then connects Providence and water closely with each other: "It is in circumstances only such as we had lately been placed in that the utter hopelessness of all human efforts is truly felt, and it is when relieved from such a situation that the hand of a directing and beneficent Being appears most plainly discernible, fulfiling those gracious promises which he has made, to hear them that call upon him in the day of trouble" (Giles 1889, 1:365; see also 1889, 2:120). The footnote to this then quotes Isa 41:17, 18; 43:19.[2] In general Giles, despite his lack of orthodoxy, is "[s]incerely grateful to the Almighty for having guided us through so many difficulties, and for the inexpressible relief afforded to us when so much was needed, but so little expected" (1889, 2:69). And this after his Aboriginal "boys" (see below) had killed his overseer and he had been left all but stranded in the desert before coming upon the whaler, Mississippi.

---

2. "When the poor and needy seek water, and there is none, and their tongue is parched with thirst, I the Lord will answer them, I the God of Israel will not forsake them. I will open up rivers on the bare heights, and fountains in the midst of the valleys; I will make the wilderness a pool of water, and the dry land springs of water" (Isa 41:17–18). "I am about to do a new thing; now it springs forth, do you not perceive it? I will make a way in the wilderness and rivers in the desert" (Isa 43:19).

Charles Sturt, evangelical Anglican with a divine mission to explore Australia, also feels that it is Providence that has protected him and his party on so many occasions from calamity, neglecting to mention the stupidity that got him into the situations from which Providence was then obliged, good Christian gentleman that he was, to rescue him: "Something more powerful, than human foresight or human prudence [of which he seemed to be singularly lacking], appeared to avert the calamities and dangers with which I and my companions were so frequently threatened; and had it not been for the guidance and protection we received from the Providence of that good and all-wise Being to whose care we committed ourselves, we should, ere this, have ceased to rank among the number of His earthly creatures" (Sturt 1833, 2:6).

Ironically, Leichhardt, who disappeared into the desert never to be seen again, writes that "an Almighty Protector had not only allowed us to escape [privation] hitherto but had even supplied us with an abundance" (Leichhardt 1847, 235). Indeed, Leichhardt opens up another window on the explorers, for whom Providence was not always so kind, nor did they always feel so much in the good register of the Almighty Protector. Thus, Giles found himself identifying with Pharaoh during the plagues of Egypt: when afflicted by ants, mosquitoes, and flies, he wonders why Moses had not thought of these plagues. Indeed, he would delight in a cool, watery plague of frogs.[3]

John McDouall Stuart, succumbing to scurvy on the long trek from Adelaide to the Gulf of Carpentaria (despite the many Aborigines he met on the way who were remarkably free of scurvy), invokes the Almighty to help him: "I feel myself getting weaker and weaker every day. I hope that the Almighty will have compassion on me, and soon send me some relief. He is the only one who can do it—my only friend" (Stuart 1865, 454). Passages such as these in fact provide some relief in the staccato, frenetic journals of Stuart. They are as frantic as his five major journeys in rapid succession, attempting to cross the continent from north to south, and as his subsequent devotion to alcohol. Nothing embellishes his journals, including revision (unlike Giles's flourishes), and all he is concerned with are water, the horses, food, illness, continually hostile natives, and the direction of the fucking wind. Even when he is in the depths of despair, evoking the biblical psalms of complaint or laments and riddled with disease, these concerns may still be found: "What a miserable life mine is now! I get no rest night nor day from this terrible gnawing pain; the nights are too long, and the days are too long, and I am so weak

---

3. "Whatever could have obfuscated the brains of Moses, when he omitted to inflict Pharaoh with such exquisite tortures as ants, I cannot imagine" (Giles 1889, 1:236; see also 310).

that I am hardly able to move about the camp. I am truly wretched. When will this cease? Wind, south-east" (Stuart 1865, 453). It seems as though "my friend," the "Almighty," has deserted him; the wind had not.

Apart from points of experiential contact with the Bible, the explorers made a very different use of these texts. They became a resource for comparison with Aboriginal culture and behavior. Yet the comparison was quite specific, antiquarian, seeking to present Aboriginal people as ancient as those civilizations felt to be represented in the Hebrew Bible.[4] The most extensive antiquarian use of the Hebrew Bible is found with Thomas Mitchell, surveyor-general of New South Wales, who systematically grids the Aborigines he meets and knows with the Bible, alongside other ancient sources. For instance, after the narrative description of mourning by Aboriginal women and their singing, he quotes Pope's *Ilian*, Homer, and Jer 9:17, 18: "Call for the mourning women that they may come, and let them make haste, and take up a wailing for us, that our eyes may run down with tears, and our eyelids gush out with water" (Mitchell 1839, 1:118–19). All of this functions as proof that such practices once existed in other, ancient places, sucking back the Aborigines in question into a similar time frame.

Once there, a swarm of other practices see them more at home in the Hebrew Bible and among its peoples. This is the case with other burial customs, such as cutting for mourning, especially about the head. The reference here is to Jer 48:37 (via the cryptic citing of "Harmer" [Mitchell 1839, 2:346]), although the Jeremiah text actually refers to the shaving of head and beard and the cutting of hands, rather than the head. A little slippage, but the connection is made, this time with mourning Moabites in an oracle against them.

So also with the use of burial mounds. Mitchell notes their use along the Darling after the ravages of smallpox, a burial practice comparable to the Bedouin Arabs of Mount Carmel. A string of biblical texts are then referred to but not quoted. "See also," he writes, "2 Kings xxiii. 16—1 Kings xiii. 2 and Isaiah xxii. 15–17" (Mitchell 1839, 1:254). The curious thing here is that it is really only the last text that refers to tombs on a height, for the others speak of sacrificial practices on the "high places," apparently understood by Mitchell as sepulchers rather than altars (unless human sacrifice is meant, but even this is not quite the same thing as burial).

The dead return, as it were, a little later, where, after narrating the finding of some graves in which there was evidence of occupation of the tomb,

---

4. Ryan (1996, 136) argues that this is an orientalist move, following Said's delineation of the term. In part this is the case, but I think the ancient biblical trope has other functions as well.

Mitchell writes in a note: "Isaiah lxv. 4. *Who remain among the graves*. 'The old Hebrews are charged by the prophet Isaiah with *remaining among the graves and lodging in the monuments*.'—See *Lewis's Origines Hebraeae*, vol. iii. p. 381" (Mitchell 1839, 2:105). Apparently the understanding is that a close relative remains with the body until it is decayed. Here the text of Lewis (no further references are provided for this half-identified piece) is used to interpret the biblical text, although the text itself comes as part of a condemnation of the practices of the rebellious Israelites, which include sacrificing in gardens, offering incense on bricks, eating swine's flesh, and abominable broths (Isa 64:3–4). Sinful Israelites maybe, but still Israelites.

Apart from burial and the treatment of the dead, there is the use of smoke signals on mountaintops in order to send messages. Mitchell notes: "This mode of communicating intelligence of sudden danger, so invariably practised by the natives of Australia, seems quite in conformity with the customs of early ages as mentioned in Scripture [Jer 6:1]. 'O ye children of Benjamin, gather yourselves to flee out of the midst of Jerusalem, *and set up a sign of fire in Beth-haccerem*: for evil appeareth out of the north, and great destruction'" (1939, 1:129). Indeed, there is a hint of an unconscious enrollment of the Aborigines in the ranks of the amorphous and disparate numbers of Israel itself.

The web tying the natives in with ancient Israel strengthens with comparisons relating to bodily ornaments, reverence for elders, cooking, magical stones, hunting methods, housing, and the carrying of children. Thus, the wearing of a bracelet of corded hair as a sign of royalty links the Aborigines in with 2 Sam 1:10,[5] again via Harmer's ready reference to "Oriental practice" (Mitchell 1839, 1:265). The authority of old men and women, characteristic among Aborigines Mitchell meets, sees them obeying the command of Lev 19:32[6] (Mitchell 1839, 2:346). The specific cooking reference is to the use of hard clay mounds instead of stones, regarding which Mitchell quotes the Hebrew Bible again: "'And Jacob said unto his brethren, Gather stones: and they took stones, and made a heap, and they did eat there upon the heap.' Genesis xxxi. 46" (Mitchell 1839, 2:81). Of course, even though the particular Aborigines Mitchell meets use hard clay, this is in replacement of the more usual stones, as well as a patriarchal approach to cooking and a covenant meal between Jacob and Laban in the biblical text. Stones are also at issue in relation to "magical" practice and reverence. Writing that the natives carry

---

5. Here the reference to the "armlet that was on his arm" is that of King Saul's, claimed to have been taken from a slain Saul in the words of the Amalekite produced in this text.

6. "You shall rise before the aged, and defer to the old; and you shall fear your God: I am Yahweh."

crystals of quartz and other shining stones that are highly valued, especially the "coradjes" or "priests," Mitchell refers to Gen 28:18, which, in the midst of the story of Jacob's overnight stop and dream at what was named Bethel, speaks of his taking the stone on which he had put his head, setting it up as a pillar, and anointing it.

As for hunting methods, particularly the use of spears, axes and nets, Mitchell invokes the enigmatic Isaiah once again, in a note: "Isaiah xxiv. 17.—*Fear, and the pit, and the snare, are upon thee*" (Mitchell 1839, 2:153). Ever full of the trivia Mitchell is seeking, Harmer comes to the rescue in relation to a poetic that renders judgment on the whole earth, no less: "These images are taken from the different methods of hunting and taking wild beasts, which were anciently in use. The snare or toils were a series of nets, enclosing, at first, a great space of ground, in which the wild beats were known to be; and drawn in by degrees into a narrower compass, till they were at last closely shut up and entangled in them." Having cited Harmer, Mitchell himself closes, in the shadow of this authority, with "This is precisely the method adopted by the Australian natives at present for the same or similar purposes" (Mitchell 1839, 2:154).

Even the housing made and used by Aborigines has its connection with the Israelite Feast of Booths, at least the practice of making and living in the huts themselves. Indeed, it is their "mode of life, as exhibited in the temporary huts made of boughs, bark, or grass" that may be compared not only to the Arabs but ultimately the command of Nehemiah to the Israelites (or, more specifically, the Judeans), after the "return" from Babylon and the "reestablishment" of Judah, recited in Neh 8:15[7] (Mitchell 1839, 2:343).

Finally, in a whole series of Aboriginal-Israelite links, including mourning and burial practices, smoke signals, bodily ornaments, reverence for elders, cooking, magical stones, hunting methods, housing—in short, a collection of key social features—there is the mode of carrying children: "We trace a further resemblance between this rude people and the orientals, in their common method of carrying children on their shoulders; and the sketch of Turandurey with Ballandella so mounted affords the best illustration of a passage of Scripture, which has very much puzzled commentators." The note quotes Isa 49:22[8] (Mitchell 1839, 2:347).

---

7. "Go out to the hills and bring branches of olive, myrtle, palm, and other leafy trees to make booths [*succoth*], as it is written."

8. "Thus says the Lord God: I will soon lift up my hand to the nations, and raise my signal to the peoples; and they shall bring your sons in their bosom, and your daughters shall be carried on their shoulders."

The only exception to the resolute focus on the Hebrew Bible appears in Mitchell's discussion of what he calls rituals of repulsion. After a spear was pointed at one of the party and a green twig at Mitchell, "He [an Aboriginal] and the boy then threw dust at us, in a clever way, with their toes. These various expressions of hostility and defiance, were too intelligible to be mistaken" (1839, 1:245–46). A footnote then connects this with "the early history of mankind," specifically the Hebrews. So "King David and his host met with a similar reception at Bahurim.—'And as David and his men went by the way, Shimei went along on the hill's side over against him, and cursed as he went, and threw stones at him, *and cast dust.*' 2 Sam. xvi. 13. So also we read in Acts xxii. 23, 'They cried out, and cast off their clothes, *and threw dust into the air.*'" Wider comparisons to rituals of repulsion are made to the "Turks," "Oriental customs," and Num 12:14, but what interests me is the sole New Testament reference in the explorer texts, depicting the response of the Jews in Jerusalem to Paul's sermon in the temple. Indeed, this text traces its way through into Eyre's journal, published some two years after Mitchell's, although not referring to it. Eyre narrates a stand off, produced through Eyre's overseer kidnapping a woman for a couple of days to find out about "water": "yet they had established themselves in the close proximity of our encampment [at a depot], and repeatedly exhibited signs of defiance, such as throwing dust into the air, shouting, and threatening with their weapons." He footnotes the same text, Acts 22:23 (Eyre 1841, 1:83).[9]

This turn to Eyre indicates that Mitchell is not alone in this use of the Bible, especially in a way that makes the Aborigines implicit Israelites (or Jews, in the case of the Acts passage). Eyre, for instance, casts himself in terms of Saul and the natives as David, during the long pursuit of the former by the latter in 1 Sam 21–30: while doing meteorological observations he finds that he has lost a horizon glass, a piece of canvas, spade, parcel of horse shoes, axe, tin dish, ropes, grubbing hoe, and other smaller things left outside the tent. He then reflects how close the natives had come under cover of night. They must have seen him lie on the ground, he reflects, to read the stars and then write by candle in his tent. "The only wonder with me was that they had not speared me, as they could scarcely have been intimidated by my individual presence" (Eyre 1845, 1:143; compare 1 Sam 26:8–9) They can come so close to him, like David to Saul in the camp, yet they design not to kill him, although the effect was almost the same, for "[t]hey had, however, in their

---

9. One other New Testament exception is found with Sturt, but there is no direct biblical reference here. He casts himself in messianic terms, finding in one diseased Aboriginal camp that "the lame had managed to hobble along, and the blind were equally anxious to touch us" (Sturt 1833, 2:135).

turn, produced as great an effect upon me, and had at least deprived me of one night's sleep" (1845, 1:144).

Grey also comes to the party. He speaks, for instance, of manna, but his signified is somewhat skewed in a characteristic nineteenth-century scientific reading. For the manna found on the trees resembles, he feels, the medicinal stuff prevalent in Europe, although in Australia it is mottled red or brown, firm, and sweet (Grey 1841, 2:273). And in another part, after describing a cave painting of an extraordinary figure with a yellow headdress, he writes in a note: "This figure brings to mind the description of the Prophet Ezekiel: -'Men pourtrayed upon the wall, the images of the Chaldeans pourtrayed in vermillion, girded with girdles upon their loins, exceeding in dyed attire upon their heads, all of them princes to look to, after the manner of the Babylonians of Chaldees, the land of their nativity.' - Chap. XXIII. 14, 15" (Grey 1841, 1:215). Then he relates how the naming of children from some circumstance connected with their birth is a custom "prevalent equally amongst the most ancient nations of whom any records are preserved, and the modern Australians." Evidence comes in the form of Gen 30:11, "'And Leah said, A troop cometh, and she called his name Gad;' &c. &c. &c." (Grey 1841, 2:343).

Indeed, it is both Mitchell and Grey who make explicit the identification I have been tracing, one negatively, the other less so. For until now I have tailed what has been an unconscious element in a more deliberately antiquarian, archaicizing move by the explorers, who sought to link the Aborigines with the earliest human beings and thereby place them lower on the evolutionary scale, closer to animals. Yet the unconscious has a habit of surfacing. So Mitchell speaks of an Aboriginal face with "features decidedly Jewish, having a thin aquiline nose, and a very piercing eye, as intent on mischief, as if it had belonged to Satan himself" (Mitchell 1839, 1:270). If this identification is demonic and Jewish, Grey sees them in a much better light. Although subincision is a practice he finds unique,[10] it is circumcision that makes the Aborigines, and others who practice, purer and more faithful children of Moses:

> The injunctions contained in Deuteronomy, ch. xxiii, ver. 12, and 13, are literally fulfilled by the natives in several parts of the continent. In addition to my own testimony on this point, I will refer to "Wilson's Voyage round the

---

10. Assuming the greater ability of those who know Latin to handle the reference, as well as the politeness of avoiding direct reference in English, he describes it as "*Finditus usque ad urethram à parte infera penis*," noting that "This extraordinary and inexplicable custom must have a great tendency to prevent the rapid increase of the population; and its adoption may perhaps be a wise ordination of Providence, for that purpose, in a country of so desert and arid a character as that which these people occupy" (Grey 1841, 1:213).

World," p. 165, where he states, "They are cleanly in their manners, and, in some respects, superior to the Europeans, fulfiling the injunction of Moses in the twelfth and thirteenth verses of the twenty-third chapter of Deuteronomy...." They also conform strictly to the injunctions in Leviticus, ch. xv. ver. 19. (Grey 1841, 2:344; see also Leichhardt 1847, 413–47)

Yet it is not just Aborigines who seem to become Israelites in these texts, for the explorers themselves have a tendency at odd times to go native, for survival if nothing else. The curious Eyre, infamous for his brutal repression of a mutiny in the West Indies after his time in Australia, begins to use native names to things and places, rather than the exclusively English names normally provided in the frenzy of Adamic naming, such as Yeer-kumban-kauwe (Eyre 1841, 1:284). He starts to dig for water like natives and describes its procuration from a tree root (1:350–51). But Eyre is notable for raising issues of dispossession and for his calls, paternalistic to be sure, for an inquiry and means to prevent the abuse and decline of Aborigines. In contrast to Sturt, who sees them as scarce, diseased, starving, animal-like cannibals (Sturt 1833, 1:114; also 2:222), Eyre concludes that our presence in the land is an act of intrusion and aggression, that Aborigines cannot comprehend the English presence, the taking of the land and ignorance of their laws. He feels their violent reactions perfectly justified (Eyre 1841, 1:163–172). Even theological justification for rapid Aboriginal death and decline is criticized:

> It is most lamentable to think that the progress and prosperity of one race should conduce to the downfall and decay of another; it is still more so to observe the apathy and indifference with which this result is contemplated by mankind in general, and which leads to no investigation being made as to the cause of this desolating influence, or if it is, terminates, to use the language of the Count Stzelecki, "in the inquiry, like an inquest of the one race upon the corpse of the other, ending for the most part with the verdict of 'died by the visitation of God.'" (Eyre 1841, 1:x)[11]

A Providential Eye?

One final item of explorer hermeneutics that comes through in these journals is the most elite of the senses that have been separated out from the amorphous territory of human perception, namely, sight. Here the discussion moves into wider theological zones than the biblical texts alone, yet the issue

---

11. Even Mitchell describes "my friends," the Dharuks, as the "first inhabitants" who are "deprived of the liberty which they formerly enjoyed." He also sees the inevitable march forward of what he feels is a superior civilization (Mitchell 1839, 1:10).

of sight, the eye, the eyeball with its nervous wiring that reaches back to the brain, is crucial for the hermeneutics in which I am engaged. For the way the explorers saw Australia (the subtitle of Simon Ryan's book that is so important for this section) is not only influential for the way they read the Bible but is also determined by a certain biblical or theological imaginary, a way of constructing the seen in terms of a framework in which theological and biblical categories were fundamental.

But let me begin with the gaze and its problems.[12] The mention of "gaze" (or now the more favored "eye") will activate a whole area of cultural criticism, ranging from gender and its construction in film theory, through Freud's scopophilia and Foucault's work on the panopticon, to an increasing interest in the role of the gaze in postcolonial criticism. In fact, the particular department of the gaze that interests me here is the colonial gaze, the "cartographic eye," as Simon Ryan has dubbed it.

Read some more and make it relevant: my interlocutors here are Michel Foucault, particularly his well-known "panopticism," a term he derives from Jeremy Bentham's panopticon, a prison in which the prisoners may be seen without seeing their centralized warder and in which the warder sees but cannot be seen. Following Bentham's suggestions for its use in education, industry, hospitals, and so on, Foucault traces a transition to panopticism, which, along with the suburban home, family car, weekend sport, deodorant, and heterosexuality, has become a necessary marker of everyday bourgeois life—a surveillance of life rather than the feudal policing of death (modeled by public executions). Apart from Foucault and Bentham, there is the strong influence of David Spurr's *Rhetoric of Empire* (1993), especially his discussion of "surveillance" as a colonial discourse. Finally, in Simon Ryan's *The Cartographic Eye* (1996) there is the sustained study of the various discourses by which the European explorers of Australia constructed Australia and its people as a place for narrative possession.

The motif that binds these different theoretical sources together is the look from the height, the view from the mountain, the elevated and enlarged eye that roves and controls, the phallic eye that winks its seminal influ-

---

12. There is a general question—obviously pertinent to this chapter but also much wider—that perpetually bothers me in all the contemporary perusal of the visual. It is a sort of class identification of the senses, a hierarchy in which sight, hearing, and speech, once they have been separated off from one another, attain a higher status than touch or smell. Indeed, sight may now be in a class of its own, and if it is by sight that the panopticon was supposed to work, then seeing is the sense most closely tied in with the bourgeoisie at this historical juncture. That the early explorers of Australia relied primarily on sight only reinforces my point.

ence over tracts of the earth's surface. Thus, Bentham's jailer looks over the prisoners from the central tower, Foucault's panopticism operates from the privileged central place, Spurr's journalists survey foreign lands from hotels, helicopters, or heights, Ryan's explorers seek out rise after rise to gain strategic (and scenic—but are they not one?) and descriptive advantage, and God himself, or rather, Providence, provides the ultimate perspective. In the words of Mitchell: "the visible possibility of overlooking the country from any eminence, is refreshing at all times, but to an explorer it is everything" (Mitchell 1848, 157–58).

Yet what drew me to these texts in the first place is a curious conjunction of Foucault, Bentham, and Australia, all around the infamous panopticon. Despite my profound ambivalence about Australia (Do I not always wish to draw closer to the global "center"?), I remain intrigued by any passing connections, moments when others speak about it. So it is with Jeremy Bentham and the panopticon, for in a work—itself a couple of long letters published together and then later appearing in the Collected Works—entitled *Panopticon versus New South Wales* (Bentham 1843), he argues at laborious length against transportation and in favor of his dearly beloved panopticon prison. Bentham—whom Marx called "the arch-Philistine … that soberly pedantic and heavy-footed oracle of the 'common sense' of the nineteenth century bourgeoisie intelligence" (Marx 1976, 758)—spent two decades or more of his time and money drawing up plans for a prison, factory, school, or asylum in which a central tower enabled surveillance of a series of individual cells. While the observer is able to see the inmates, they are not able to see the observer. Further, each cell is lit by a window on the other side of the surveillance window so that the warder can see each inmate, as in a theater. The power of the panopticon—the all-seeing device—is not that the jailer actually observes all the time, but that he or she is able to do so. The inmates do not know when the jailer, or teacher, or doctor, or, more recently, surveillance camera, is looking, but the knowledge that they may be doing so is as good as if they were.[13] In short, surveillance becomes reflexive, the inmates becoming their own warders: the inmates are "caught up in a power situation of which they are themselves the bearers" (Foucault 1979, 201).

Comparing the prison built on panopticon principles in Pennsylvania with transportation to New South Wales, Bentham, not unexpectedly, finds the prison wins on the counts of using the convicts as an example, refor-

---

13. "[T]he greater chance there is, of a given person's being at a given time actually under inspection, the more strong will be the persuasion— the more *intense*, if I may say so, the *feeling*, he has of his being so" (Bentham 1995, 44).

mation, incapacitation or the prevention of further offense, deterrence to escapes, compensation, and economy. His prison leads to industry, frugality, and sobriety rather than general depravity, drunkenness, and debauchery. One may be forgiven for thinking that Bentham is in fact advocating New South Wales, especially since transportation went ahead while Bentham failed to have his prison built in England.

However, in a dialectical twist, Michel Foucault suggests that it was in fact the panopticon, or its principle, that won out. In *Discipline and Punish* (1979) Foucault digs up, as it were, the transition from power over death to power over life; the slide from public executions to prison timetables (to recall once again the well-known opening to this book); the rotting away of public, overtly violent, and highly ritualistic forms of power and the new growth of covert violence, surveillance, and systematic control; the vast and gore-stained transition from the feudal lords and kings to the modern bourgeois state of capitalism, with its institutions of discipline—prison, school, hospital, asylum, and factory. Bentham himself presented the panopticon as a widely applicable and cheap idea.[14]

The panopticon becomes panopticism, the telltale mark of new arrangements of power: "What would you say, if by the gradual adoption and diversified application of this single principle, you should see a new scene of things spread itself over the face of civilized society?" (Bentham 1995, 95) For Foucault the panopticon is a signal of a seismic shift in systems of power: as part of the slow, conflict-ridden move from feudalism to capitalism, the operation of power slides from public and exemplary forms to subtle forms of observance and observation. Bentham himself was a strong campaigner for the abolition of capital and corporal punishment, as well as universal suffrage and the secret ballot. Yet these show the internal contradiction of the new arrangements of power: while the principle was one of egalitarianism (what will later be seen as the fundamental equality of everyone as a consumer), the very structures of bourgeois society ensured that such a society was anything but egalitarian, that it was structurally and hierarchically in favor of the middle class. In other words (and to move beyond Foucault to Jameson),

---

14. The panopticon for Bentham is not merely a prison, as his elaborate title suggests: "Panopticon; or, The Inspection-House: Containing the Idea of a New Principle of Construction Applicable to Any Sort of Establishment, in Which Persons of Any Description Are To Be Kept under Inspection; and in Particular to Penitentiary Houses, Prisons, Poor-Houses, Lazarettos, Houses of Industry, Manufactories, Hospitals, Work-Houses, Mad-Houses, and Schools" (Bentham 1995, 29). Bentham, half in jest, even suggests it as a way to preserve the virginity of "young damsels," by transferring them to a strict inspection-school (1995, 90).

whereas the rhetoric of the bourgeois revolution was one of the liberty and equality of all people, the middle class positioned itself so that when the checks came to be cashed, when the peasants and the newly formed working class demanded their cut, the bourgeoisie used its newfound strength to avoid paying its debts to precisely those who had helped it win in the first place (the 1848 revolutionary movements in Europe constitute the moment of this shift). The egalitarian drive was unable to be realized. So Foucault:

> Historically, the process by which the bourgeoisie became in the course of the eighteenth century the politically dominant class was masked by the establishment of an explicit, coded and formally egalitarian juridical framework, made possible by the organization of a parliamentary, representative régime. But the development and generalization of disciplinary mechanisms constituted the other, dark side of these processes. The general juridical form that guaranteed a system of rights that were egalitarian in principle was supported by these tiny, everyday, physical mechanisms, by all those systems of micro-power that are essentially non-egalitarian and asymmetrical that we call the disciplines.... The contract may have been regarded as the ideal foundation of law and political power, panopticism constituted the technique, universally widespread, of coercion. (Foucault 1979, 222)

Panopticism does not "stick out," as it were: in contrast to the power of kings and lords, it works its way into the very flesh of social interaction. It is, for Foucault, "capillary," entering into the smallest extremities of the social body.

However, what Foucault does not draw out is that the panopticon is a profoundly theological idea. In a remarkable introduction to *The Panopticon Writings* (Bentham 1995), Miran Bošovič (1995) shows how the panopticon may best be seen as a transmutation of the idea of God into particular, bourgeois, and utilitarian forms. In a reading that connects Bentham's theory of fictions with his panopticon writings, Bošovič argues that the production of the panopticon is the production of God. Even though Bentham exempts God from the category of nonentities, in which are included ghosts, the bane of Bentham's life, God of course is precisely such a nonentity.[15] The key

---

15. A conclusion Bentham allows in an extraordinary footnote. After discussing, in the main text, that God is a supreme superhuman entity—"sanctioned by revelation; sanctioned by the religion of Jesus as delivered by the apostle Paul"—and that, since no one has seen God, God must be an inferential real entity, Bentham then notes: "Should there be any person who, incapable of drawing those influences by which the Creator and Preserver of all other entities, is referred to the class of real ones, should refuse to him a place in that class, the class to which such person would find himself, in a manner, compelled to refer to that invisible and mysterious being would be, not as in the case of the human soul to

to all of this lies in the relation between prison warden, or inspector, even public spectators, and the inmates, students, patients, or whatever. For the inspector's authority relies on not being seen by the inmates: they think the inspector is present, ever-vigilant, that they are constantly being watched, but they can never see the inspector. If they did, then this would lessen the effect of his absence and unravel the whole arrangement, for the direction of the inspector's eyes, as well as his presence and absence, would be noted. Although the inspector can see and hear (through elaborate voice pipes) all that goes on, it is absolutely essential that the inspector, his movements, comings and goings, remain hidden from the inmates, even during chapel, and Bentham goes to great lengths, by means of an elaborate lantern with holes, colored and smoked glass, the production of a silhouette and a trap door beneath, to ensure that this is the case (1995, 105–9). What counts is the "*apparent omnipresence* of the inspector" combined with "the extreme facility of his *real presence*" (1995, 45). This is, then, the fiction that lies at the heart of the panopticon: perpetual surveillance. But does not the inspector become, with omniscience, omnipotence, and omnipresence added to the ability to see everywhere, more and more godlike? "What has to be staged in the panopticon for the gaze of the prisoners is reality itself, that is, God. Whereas the innocent are deterred from offending by real punishment, by the real suffering of the punished, the prisoners in the panopticon are deterred from transgressing by the *fiction of God*" (Bośovič 1995, 11). Yet it is a hidden God, *deus absconditus*, one who by definition cannot exist. This God exists as long as his subjects believe so, in the same way that the authority of the inspector exists as long as the inmates believe he is there and watching. The repeated invocations of Providence by the explorers of which I will speak in a few moments take on a distinctly new hue in this light.

For the veins and capillaries of the explorers also flowed with the new panopticism as they surveyed the land. Over against the general and quite unremarkable practice of climbing hills to look around, I would like to set the new eyes that gradually looked upon lands, "old" and "new," as things to be measured, mapped, controlled, and possessed. And it is the visual that is dominant: Ryan speaks of "exploration methodology's heavy reliance on sight" (1996, 87). But not merely the visual—it is the view from a height: "The cartographic necessity of gaining elevation and seeing great distances offers a particular point of view and demands the arrogation of a visual power over the land, opening it for inspection" (1996, 88). This opens up the vast area of

---

that of fictitious entities, but that of non-entities" (1995, 120). The convoluted syntax here partly obscures the conclusion drawn by Bośovič.

cartography and its transformation into a "precise" discipline that relied on a different set of ideological assumptions from those earlier ones that depicted the world and its various sectors according to religious or theological categories. What is interesting here is that such a change in the practice and theory of cartography coincides by and large with the rise of the bourgeoisie, the development of modern science, and the complex minute patterns of surveillance and the policing of life and the body that Foucault designates as panopticism.

I want to focus, however, on a certain set of practices that became the norm in the era of classical and imperial capitalism as the various European colonial powers set out to conquer those areas of the globe outside Europe itself. Thus, the Royal Geographical Society in England sponsored a string of expeditions in the "new" lands that attempted to traverse them from one end to the other, or to "penetrate" their interiors. All the while the various explorers were expected and compelled to keep verbal and graphic traces of their moves, experiences, and reflections in various diaries and journals. These were subsequently published, under the auspices of the society in question, with the expected advancement of the career of the explorer in question. The range of what was surveyed in these texts—land forms, flora and fauna, indigenous people, the impressions of the writer, potential places of settlement—ensured that at least the impression of comprehensiveness had been achieved. Ryan usefully traces the ideological constructs that operated in such observation: the aesthetic ideals of the picturesque (active alteration of the land according to codes of looking), panoramic (perceptual construction of the land according to similar codes), mimeticism (since this was the high period of realism), and perspectivism. Often, however, the agenda was one of pastoral profit and human settlement: Where were the best pasture lands, the best possibilities for grain and especially grazing? Where might the squatters and farmers be able to move in the new worlds for the maximum gain of the industries back "home"?

But how might all of this be designated as panopticism? To begin with, there is the view from the height, the sine qua non of the aesthetic category of the panoramic. The best possibilities for a surveying view were to be had on any rise: ridges, hills, if not the occasional mountain itself. Mountains presented either a barrier that hindered further surveying and possession of the land—as in the perpetual question in the first convict colony in Sydney about what lay beyond the "Blue Mountains"—or as a peculiar vantage point from which to view the land about. This may take a number of forms: the first view of a valley or plain upon passing through a ridge; the distant rise that is finally attained after much effort; the mountain that is desirable as a place of aesthetic advantage (the beauty of the view and the aesthetic code of the picturesque); and the mountain as the best point for surveillance itself.

Time and again the explorers mount a mountain, ascend an ascent, clamber up a climb. For instance, in a little over a hundred pages, Eyre crests Mount Deception (1845, 1:64–65), Termination Hill (87), Mount Searle (117), Mount Distance (126), Mount Hopeless (127–30), Baxter's Range (139), Mount Hill (151–52), and Mount Hall (193). When he is not on them, he sets his bearings by them (1845, 1:110). Although Eyre finds the desert views disconcerting, "the realization of my worst forebodings," rendering the expedition futile (1:118), Giles likes his eagle eye: viewing Birthday Creek (Ernabella) from a nearby mountain, he crows, "We had a perfect bird's eye view of the spot.... Having completed our survey, we descended barefooted as before" (1889, 1:170). And so it goes on from explorer to explorer: Grey climbs a ridge "and a magnificent view burst upon us" (1841, 1:161); "there burst upon my sight a most enchanting view" (1841, 2:28); the country "lay like a map at our feet" (180). Sturt names the directions in which he looks, as though the land it were a map itself, northeast, southeast, southwest, northwest (1833, 1:25–27). Leichhardt, upon Mount Stewart, "obtained a very extensive view from its summit," being able to espy "as far as the eye could see" (1947, 113). And of course Mitchell embodies all of them, surveyor-general that he was, ascending every hill with a utilitarian purpose, such as Warrawolong, north of Wiseman's Ferry in what is now the Yengo wilderness (Mitchell 1839, 1:9–10).

Further, the view from the height gives control. Explorer texts favor military terms such as "command" (see Ryan 1996, 89). Apart from repeated references in the journals about commanding positions or views, the question of control also surfaces when there is a contest (real or otherwise) with Aborigines for the high ground, as when Eyre found that the native had taken a position a little higher and more commanding than his (Eyre 1845, 1:237–38).

With this visual, and at times belligerent, control comes the idea of possession and ownership. The land is possessed, in proxy as it were, for the British-style estates and manors that are to follow. Certain vantages are more than the means of visual control and possession of the land viewed; they themselves become desirable for their commanding prospects. So, Grey writes of Western Australia, "I painted in fancy the rapid progress that this country would ere long make in commerce and civilization, and my weakness and fatigues were all forgotten" (1841, 1:163). He also reflects on the territory's commercial prospects (1:265–88) and the "Overlanders" who made the first treks to dispossess the Aborigines (2:183–204). The progress is so rapid that Eyre can note, after narrating his initial journey through the fertile land north of Adelaide in 1840, that by the time he revises his journals for publication some five years later, "all this country, and for some distance to the north, is now occupied by stations" (1845, 1:38). Of course, he had prophesied this himself: "I however felt conscious that within a few years of the moment at which I stood there, a British population, rich in civilization, and the means of transforming an unoccupied country to one teeming with inhabitants and produce, would have followed my steps" (1841, 1:359). Like all prophecy, it was all the more true having been written after the event—*vaticinium ex eventu*.

Alongside this conjunction of vision and power is the desire and requirement for meticulous detail, the minute recording of a whole range of items that were regarded as significant. Indeed, the explorers' journals often read as the early, faltering efforts of the later, apparently more sophisticated ethnographers and anthropologists who were to comb the world in search of the most authentically indigenous tribe. This is particularly true of Grey's accounts (1841, 1:11–20, 37–64, 202–5, 238–64; 2:116–80, 207–388, 391–482) and those of Sturt (1833, 1:ix–lxxx, 105–6, 151–81; 2:50–55, 249–56; 1984, 118–264; see also Leichhardt 1847, 351–61; Mitchell 1839, 1:xvii–xxi, 14–16; 2:340–415; Stuart 1865, 484–507), interspersed as they are with smatterings of linguistic material (lists of words with English "equivalents"), descriptions and inventories of specimens of flora and fauna, natural history, climate, nature of soil, landforms, commercial opportunities, advice for other explorers, and of meticulous observations on Aborigines, their appearance (including the presence of lighter-skinned people), life, customs, burial practices, law, kinship, ritual, life span, production, preparation and consumption of food, song and culture, and details of cave paintings and styles—in short, a list comparable to the web of biblical references that I noted above, particularly with regard to the natives.

Not only do these practices signal the functioning of panopticism in the activity of English explorers of Australia, but they also suggest that panopticism is crucial for the exercise of colonialism. That this is not restricted to exploration or the early stages of colonial expansion is suggested by David Spurr's *The Rhetoric of Empire*, which begins with a treatment of surveillance as one of the prime motifs by which journalists perceive and process the lands they visit and report about. The act of surveillance is made invariably from a height, although for these contemporary "explorers" that height may be as much a hotel tower, helicopter, or airplane as the mountain of former surveyors of lands that were open for "possession." The way surveillance operates may well be problematized—the reporter may question the surveying function in the process of doing it—yet the action itself remains in place.

I have taken some time with this, since it seems to me that not only is the panoptic gaze a particular production of consolidating capitalism, but it is, as I argued above, a distinctly theological notion. Its ideology, in other words, is one that is constructed in theological terms. With the explorers this happens in two ways. First, the land, traditionally presented in cartography about Australia as a blank, is textualized. It is both a *tabula rasa* on which the explorers must inscribe themselves and a text that speaks of the Author of nature. The divine signification, common enough in nineteenth-century European writing, is also applied to Australia, of which God also is the author (see Ryan 1996, 123).

Second, the depiction of surveillance, whether in writing or illustration, often includes the explorer: the explorer appears as knowledge gatherer and as surveyor, viewed by yet another eye, which is immediately that of the writer/illustrator and reader. The explorer is, in other words, there in the picture: the writer writes himself, or the drawer draws himself, into the text. But this superior eye, the one that sees the explorer seeing is not only the writer (explorer) or reader but often God. "The point of view of the eye of God is not simply a well-worn trope, but continues in the explorers' texts the association of height and surveillance" (Ryan 1996, 91–92). God is the ultimate watcher, the last in a hierarchy of vision. Not only does this justify the explorers' role, giving divine approval, but it provides reasons for survival itself:

> in the wide field of nature, we see the hand of an over-ruling Providence, evidence of care and protection from some unseen quarter, which strike the mind with overwhelming conviction, that whether in the palace or in the cottage, in the garden, or in the desert, there is an eye upon us. (Sturt 1849, 92)

The panoptic view of God is then a wider theological position—the eye of Providence—that applies in the explorer's own experience. The explorer looks upon the land, and especially the Aborigines, as though he were the divine, or perhaps Bentham's inspector (so Ryan 1996, 133). But the explorer is also one item in that greater vision that only God can command. Colonial exploration is but a particular example of this larger practice, which is then watched over by God. Of course, at the same time, God's eye is constructed in terms of the explorer's panoptic view: "The eye of God looking down on the solitary caravan, as with its slow, and snake-like motion, it presents the only living thing around, must have contemplated its appearance on such a scene with pitying admiration" (Giles 1889, 2:318).

This, finally, is an elision of explorer and God, usually through vision. So Giles writes of a "corrugated range ... spread by the great Creator's hand," which was rescued by him and his companion Tietkens "from its former and ancient oblivion" (1889, 1:282). Without being seen it may as well not exist: their act of viewing is comparable to that of creation.

It is not for nothing, then, that the favored term for God is "Providence," the one who sees before, or who sees ahead. So Sturt, in a speech reiterated by Eyre:

> Nevertheless, gentlemen, I shall envy that man who shall first plant the flag of our native country in the centre of our adopted one. There is not one deed in those days to be compared with it, and to whoever may undertake so praiseworthy and so devoted a task, I wish that success, which Heaven sometimes vouchsafes to those who are actuated by the first of motives—the public good; and the best of principles—a reliance on Providence. (Eyre 1845, 1:9)

One must not actually desire to be the first to plant the flag, since that smells of naked competition, but must be drawn above all by the equation of the public good and a reliance of Providence. Only then, as is proper under Providence, will one be duly rewarded with the other prize.

It goes without saying that Providence, or "Heaven," has the commercial good of both (South) Australia and England at heart: "Go forth, then, on your journey, with a full confidence in the goodness of Providence; and may Heaven direct your steps to throw open the fertility of the interior, not only for the benefit of the province, but of our native country" (South Australian Register, 20 June 1840, quoted by Eyre 1845, 1:20). With the heavenly being clearly with his party, hidden in the saddlebags perhaps, Eyre can leave the outcome of the expedition to such a goodly force. "The result we were willing to leave in the hands of that Almighty Being whose blessing had been implored upon our undertaking, and to whom we looked for guidance and protection in all our wanderings" (Eyre 1845, 1:28).

And so my discussion folds back to its earlier theme of the reliance on the Almighty Being, Providence, Heaven, or whatever, particularly in rescue from moments of dire distress, recklessness, and plain stupidity. Eyre again:

> Such are the mysteries and inscrutable ways of providence and so impossible is it for man's private comprehension to estimate the result even of his own simplest actions, still less to judge of the more general ordinations of Divine Wisdom. In my progress thro' life I have frequently found trivial circumstances conduce to important events, and influential occurrences take place when least expected; an experience no doubt shared in by others, but which I think ought to teach us to distrust ourselves and our own judgement and to place full reliance on the wisdom and goodness of God, who can, and in his own good time often does, make plain and clear what once seemed dark, inexplicable or unimportant. (Eyre 1984, 214)

If readers look hard enough through the lines of the text, it may be possible to discern the diminutive silhouette of Bentham himself, casting his controlling eye over his prison, school, infirmary, or whatever. For this text is soaked with the transformation of the central theological notion of Providence in terms of panopticism, with its focus on the trivial and everyday, the use of these by God to produce great events in a person's life, momentous occasions from the minutiae of life, and the shedding of light and reason on the dark and inscrutable. Yet is it not the case that the perception of God here is not only determined by such panoptic categories, but also that the theological traditions of divine surveillance, foreknowledge, and predestination, influenced the construction of panopticism, and thus of the ways the explorers saw the land?

In the end, the Providential eye that oversaw the explorers' strange wanderings also monitored the spread of Christianity—inextricably tied in with civilization and English commerce—throughout the globe. Ever evangelical, Grey writes: "Christianity and civilization are marching over the world with a rapidity not fully known or estimated by any one nation; the English are scarcely aware what has been effected by their own missionaries and commerce, and they are utterly ignorant of what has been already done, and is now doing, by the Americans, Dutch, and Portugese" (Grey 1841, 2:224).

A Queer Land?

Let me close, however, on a different note, a little more surreptitious but all the more intriguing. A recurring feature of postcolonial study is the argument that the colonial land is gendered as female, lying recumbent, awaiting penetration by the male explorer's eye and caravan. That is to say, colonial desire is in many respects also sexual desire. Freud's designation of woman as the "dark continent" only adds to such an argument, although it is also compounded by the overlapping of colonial and precolonial patriarchy, and by the complicity of Western white feminism in the exclusion of colonial women (Mohanty 1993, 196–97). Yet one of the weakest arguments in recent work on the explorers is to argue that their desire for Australia is the sexual desire of colonial male for exotic female. Indeed, Ryan's attempt to make this argument turns, symptomatically, from the explorer texts on which he focuses to colonial fiction (Ryan 1996, 196–205). Michael Cathcart (1997) has also attacked this idea, suggesting that Sturt's famous passage about a veiled central Australia draws not so much upon the notion of the veil of a harem girl as upon the veil of the holy of holies in the temple of Jerusalem, where the greatest mystery was hidden from view, until it was torn in two with the death of Christ in the Synoptic Gospels. Devout and evangelical Anglican that he was, knowing his Bible, Sturt viewed the center as the hidden, mysterious, divinely charged place, the holy of holies from which the female was excluded:

> Men of undoubted perseverance and energy in vain tried to work their way to that distant and shrouded spot. A veil hung over central Australia that could neither be pierced nor raised. Girt around by deserts, it almost appeared as if nature had intentionally closed it upon civilised man, that she might have one domain on earth's wide field over which the savage might roam in freedom. (Sturt 1849, 2:2)

Like Christ, his duty was then to break through the curtain to this mystery as well. For Cathcart, Sturt "was imagining 'the center' as a place of Christian mystery which he alone could reveal" (1997, 7).

However, if the female is largely excluded from the explorers' desire—in part due to the aridity of much of the land, in contrast to the America discussed by Kolodny (1975)—then what form does that desire take? A queer desire, it seems to me. In this pinkish light, the bands of men traveling together for months on end become homosocial bands, bonding and squabbling as they travel, thirst, starve, and explore. The land is rarely soft and receptive but rather harsh, unforgiving, testing them, in short, manly. The explorers pit their strength against a tough land; some lose, some win, but it is a contest of man against man. Yet as any reading of such masculine contests will attest, a queer desire inflects such contests. Homosocial groups and homosocial contests are also the place of homosexual desire, and the paradigmatic case of this is Giles and his Aboriginal boys.

Most of the time Giles treats Aborigines as no better than cannibals, troglodytes, cave dwellers, as he calls them. However, he does like little black boys: so he begins his expeditions buying one, after patting his head and admiring his curly hair, only to lose him later on: "I suffered another loss," he laments, "as a bright little black boy called Fry, a great favourite of mine, with splendid eyes and teeth, whom I intended to bring with me as a companion for Tommy, was also dead" (1889, 2:157). Tommy, on the other hand, was drawn by Giles from his initiation rites, making them partners in conspiracy as Giles took advantage of the adolescent's rebelliousness. Giles keeps him with him for the trip from Port Augusta to Perth: he cuts off his initiation hair growth, allows him near women, and so on, so that he can have him for himself and so that the elders will reject Tommy. When a group of sexually inquisitive native girls follow the party at the beginning of the return trip from Perth to Adelaide, Giles notes Tommy's reluctance to be with them, "though they tried very hard to make love to him," as Tommy, "being a very good-looking boy, was an object of great admiration to a good many of them" (1889, 2:270). In the end, however, Giles "was anxious to get rid of them; they were too much of a good thing" (1889, 2:272). Other boys and young friends appear. In 1882 on a trip to the Everard Range he has a black boy with him, Billy, and a "very young friend" named Vernon Edwards (1889, 2:331).

Giles cannot refrain from commenting on his ability to attract the younger boys to him. So when he meets a small group of Aboriginal males, he writes: "This old party was remarkably shy; the elder boy seemed a little frightened, and didn't relish being touched by a white man, but the youngest was quite at his ease, and came up to me with the audacity and insouciance of early youth, and pulled me about. When I patted him, he grinned like any other monkey" (1889, 2:326). And then there is the remarkable poem to youth, recited as a waking dream: "O lovely youth, with thine arrowy form, and slender hands, thy pearly teeth, and saintly smile, thy pleading eyes and radiant hair; all, all must worship thee" (1889, 2:154).

4

HOME IS ALWAYS ELSEWHERE: EXODUS, EXILE, AND THE HOWLING WILDERNESS WASTE

There is a place I was born
It is a place I've never seen
Don't even know where it is
Don't even know my name
Where is home? Where is my home?
(Midnight Oil, 1996)

A significant debate has been boiling along for some time now relating to the use of the Bible in postcolonial theory, all of which turns on the use that has been and may be made of certain deep motifs of the Hebrew Bible. The debate is curious on two counts, for it comprises a unique moment in an exploding postcolonial criticism that seems singularly uninterested in the role of the Bible in both colonialism and postcolonialism (the other exception is Bhabha's essay "Signs Taken for Wonders" [Bhabha 1994, 102–22], which is to be discussed in chapter 6), and it is a debate that has been pursued by scholars whose major discipline is not the Hebrew Bible.

While I touch on some of the broader uses of the themes of travel, displacement, and exile in a swathe of literary and cultural figures, I am interested more specifically in the explicit use of biblical motifs and the Bible itself. Apart from engaging at this level, my final reflections are interested in the various mutations, absences, and inversions that happen in the way such motifs are appropriated in Australia.[1] To speak about exodus and exile is to consider not so much how various individuals and peoples may have moved within modernism and postmodernism but, as Caren Kaplan notes with regard to

---

1. It is a disappointing to note that such crucial works as Richard White's *Inventing Australia: Images and Identity, 1688–1980* (1981) or Geoffrey Serle's *From the Deserts the Prophets Come: The Creative Spirit in Australia, 1788–1972* (1973) do not even have a passing reference to the Bible.

travel itself, how these motifs refer "to the construction of categories in criticism that engender specific ideas and practices" (Kaplan 1996, 2). Further, I am taken with the ambiguity of exodus, nomadism, and the wilderness: they can be read as signs of barbarism for settled peoples or as a utopian state of existence over against the corruption of settled life. What is interesting in all of this is not so much the particular valorizations themselves as the function of such contradictions in the ideologies of various cultures.

Exodus

> A lost and wandering Aramean was my ancestor; he went down into Egypt and lived there as an alien. (Deut 26:5)

As with so many things, Edward Said initiated the debate over exodus in 1984 (reprint 1988) with a strong critique of the use of the biblical exodus story in contemporary Israel. Basing his argument on a review of Michael Walzer's *Exodus and Revolution* (1984), Said points out that Walzer's appropriation of the biblical exodus as a religious, non-Marxist model for mildly left social democratic movements is deeply troubled. Although Said spends little time with the biblical story itself (except to point out that the Israelites were, according to the story, by no means oppressed in Egypt), and although he deals mostly with Walzer's efforts to justify Israeli oppression of the Palestinians, what interests me here is Said's point that the exodus cannot be separated from the story of invasion, occupation, and oppression in the "promised land" of Canaan, that the image of God (the Hebrew Yahweh, but this must include El, Elohim, and Baal) that comes through is one who bloodthirstily commands total annihilation of the Canaanites and others, a motif found throughout the laws in Leviticus and Numbers. This of course raises significant questions about the appropriation of exodus by South African Boers, English Puritans, African American slaves in the U.S.A., the Pilgrims leaving Europe for the "New World," the fight against apartheid in South Africa, in liberation theology (e.g., Croatto 1987), and of course in the establishment of the modern state of Israel. Indeed, to go beyond Said here, the exodus itself may be read as an ideological justification for precisely such acts of brutality, as a discourse, to echo Said's use of Foucault, that legitimates the inflicting of oppression on others because of the purported experience of oppression of the invaders. What Said skips by in his response—and he makes it clear that he is no biblical scholar—is a consideration of the biblical text itself, a matter to which I return below.

Said is in fact reacting to a tradition of nonbiblical scholarship in which it has been argued that the biblical story of the exodus is one of the originating stories, or inaugural myths, of liberation and freedom from the weight of oppression. Walzer's book (1985) attempts a rereading of the story in Exodus, Numbers, and Deuteronomy in order to delineate the original counters of the distinctly Western pattern of the revolution: oppression, liberation, social contract, political struggle, and a new society with its danger of the restoration of oppressive systems. Revolution is its well-known name, but Walzer attempts to wrest the tradition away from Marx and calls it exodus politics. Indeed, Said would have more in sympathy with Lewis Feuer's study of a decade earlier, *Ideology and the Ideologists* (1975), where the same pattern Walzer determines, with some elaboration (1975, 2), is also seized upon as the revolutionary spring, only to attack such exodus politics as pernicious, feeding into Marxism, fascism, and the bourgeois state. Using the old Marxist notion of ideology as illusion, Feuer seeks its end, along with the myth of the exodus.

The strongest point of Said's argument is its least articulated, and it is Ella Shohat's achievement to have done precisely that (Shohat 1992, 137–40): in the same way that the Holocaust ("burnt offering") of World War II acts as an ideological justification for the establishment of Israel and oppression of Palestinians, so also the exodus functions as the ideological justification for the occupation of Canaan and the expulsion of the Canaanites, Perrizites, Gibeonites, Jebusites, and so on in the biblical story.

Indeed, the tide seems to be turning against the exodus, for in a book widely read outside biblical scholarship, Regina Schwartz has provided for this readership a distillation of much current discussion in biblical studies (Schwartz 1997). Her basic argument is that monotheism is an ideology that is entertained by, and one that feeds into, those groups that would seek a land, a "home," an ethnic unity and national or at least group identity. That is, in the same way that there is one God, so also there should be one people, one land, one nation, to the exclusion of others. The outcome of this is a perpetual history of violence and slaughter as those with monotheistic faiths—Judaism, Christianity, Islam—have sought to dominate others in the name of the one God. Such a drive to unity manifests itself in the Hebrew Bible, a common scriptural source for the three religions mentioned, through such things as the continual reconstructions and pure invention of genealogical lists in order to create the fiction of a people united by kinship, and by the story of the exodus, a myth of the origin of the people through being led out of Egypt under the power of a single deity. In the end Schwartz makes the same point as Said: the exodus functions as a legitimating myth for the destruction of other peoples in Canaan: "the haunting biblical myth of the Exodus" is to be read "as a massive justification of Ancient Israel's conquests" (Schwartz 1997, 56). Two myths, of exile and conquest, have been yoked together, so that they cannot be disentangled. What she does manage to do is make it clear that biblical scholarship by and large does not treat the exodus, or Moses, as historical figures but rather as the result of a search for a myth of origin by a disparate and diverse group of people in Canaan. The weight of biblical scholarship, made available to a wider audience through Schwartz's work, seems to render the exodus more suspect than ever.[2]

The theme of the exodus has been used in many different places on the globe: the Boers saw themselves as Israelites on trek in South Africa seeking the promised land; the Puritans who sailed to North America regarded themselves as on their way to the land God promised; the slaves of the U.S.A. appropriated the story of liberation and freedom for their own struggles from oppression; the liberation theology whose seeds lie in Latin America has seen the exodus as a powerful myth of liberation; and, of course, the construction of the modern state of Israel has found the exodus story fundamental to its own emergence. The questions raised by Said, Shohat, and Schwartz apply urgently to these struggles, but what of Australia? Is exodus used here as well? I touch base with three critics in different fields who have reflected on such questions. Deborah Bird Rose, an anthropologist who has done extensive work with Aboriginal peoples, relates (personal communication) how she was somewhat perturbed and annoyed to find, upon coming to Australia from the U.S.A. that the exodus myth was not used in Australia by the non-Aboriginal population in order to understand and justify its presence here. What she finds is that the myth of exclusion from the garden of Eden is the key: "The expulsion myth situates Home as Eden, the monarch as God, and the convicts as sinful people doomed to a life of toil and sweat amidst thorns and thistles" (Rose 1996, 205). I will return to this, since Rose resonates with a particular strand of depictions and descriptions of Australia.

By contrast, historian Ann Curthoys sees some comparison to the exodus myth, particularly in the perception of many immigrants who left the old world "to find salvation, redemption, and to start anew" (Curthoys 1998, 177). Although she agrees with Rose that many coming to Australia found the colonies hell on earth, feeling as though they had been expelled from Eden, she also argues that many took to the new land, identifying with it more positively as a land of promise and hope. She wants, as Andrew Lattas suggests (1997), to blend expulsion from Eden and the possession of the land. The curious twist is that the exodus in Australia assists in creating a victim

---

2. In an interview with Homi Bhabha, Schwartz admits that monotheistic faiths are not the only ones to have carried out programs of slaughter and oppression (see Schwartz 1997).

mentality, reflected in the ANZAC legend, Phar Lap, Les Darcy, and so on. It seems to me that Curthoys has indeed identified a particular fragment of the exodus myth in Australia, but it is, as I will argue, a peculiarly truncated one, a mutation of the myth that gives it a strange cast.

John Docker, one of Australia's leading public intellectuals, feels that the myth of the exodus, specifically in its form as a story of dispossession and subjugation of one people by invaders, is a strong one in Australia (see Docker and Fischer 2001). Following through the work of Said, Shohat, Schwartz, Rose, and Curthoys, he argues that the myth of exodus is a terrible narrative that justifies expulsion and oppression. Over against the severity of monotheism, with its demands for one people, one God, one land, he wants a return, like Schwartz, to a multiplicity of gods rather than monotheism, to generosity rather than scarcity. The exodus, which inseparably links the wandering in the wilderness with the invasion of the land, is a huge mistake and is best discarded.

It seems to me that Rose, Curthoys, and Docker are correct in their own ways, although the themes with which they are concerned invert in their use in Australia. So, as I will explore a little further in the final section of this chapter, Australia was indeed seen as the land God had forgotten, as that which Adam and Eve found after their expulsion from Eden. Where the use of the exodus appears, it is distinctly muted and truncated.

So, from a characteristically marginalized location (Arno Bay on the Eyre Peninsula in South Australia) a narrative poem by one of the "pioneers" in the area, Frank Masters (first car owner, chairman of Cleve council, local preacher and choir director, and managing director of the Eyre Peninsula Co-operative, died 1947) speaks of the process of dispossession, settlement and hardship:

> It was the over-flow Westward of the mainland expansion
> That surged first to the plains of this goodly land,
> Then tackled scrub (clearing with roller and axe),
> An exodus obedient to the great Biblical command.
> "Be fruitful and multiply and replenish the earth
> And subdue it!," with its accompanied blessing.
> (Masters 1982, 195)

The blending of the story of creation, especially the quotation from Gen 1:28 spoken to the humans by God, and the exodus has already been noted, although here it is the command to subdue that jumps out rather than the exclusion from Eden. However, what slips away from the appropriation of the exodus story is liberation, release, escape, except for a faint association with the westward flow of European, particularly Anglo-Celtic, settlement.

The exodus reference here, then, becomes one that justifies—"the great Biblical command"—expropriation. And indeed the Aborigines feature here as unworthy of the land, not knowing how to develop it, squandering, to use another biblical allusion, the talent they had been given. What is curious about all of this, except for the worn, weary, and filthy faces in the photographs of the "pioneers" in the volume from which the poem comes, is that this exodus citation refers not to the first settlers, the squatters who ran sheep, but the grain farmers, growers of crops and fruits, Cains not Abels. It was they who displaced, by divine right, both Aborigine and squatter.

The inevitability of dislocation, of the replacement of one people by another, is a dominant motif in other places, read in terms of the Israelite overrun of the Canaanites in the biblical story, but also overlaid with other themes. Lancelot Threlkeld, Congregational missionary and first Bible translator and advocate for the Awabakal people of Lake Macquarie and Newcastle, NSW,[3] searches for a theological reason:

> It is a matter of fact that the Aborigines of these colonies and of the numerous islands of the Pacific Ocean are rapidly becoming extinct. The cause of their extinction is mysterious. Does it arise from the iniquity of this portion of the human race having become full?—or, that the times of these Gentiles are fulfilled?—or, is it but the natural effects of iniquity producing its consequent ruin to the workers thereof in accordance with the natural order of God's government of the universe? Whatever may be the result of these speculative theories in answer to these queries, there remains one grand question incontrovertible, "Shall not the Judge of all the Earth do right?" (Threlkeld 1892, 125)

The exodus echo here lies in the notion of the sin of the Canaanites, their destruction and removal an appropriate punishment for unknown evil. Threlkeld throws forth suggestions—divine punishment for sin, apocalyptic closure, or the natural working out of sin—only to close with the question (is it rhetorical?) about the global judge. In the end, Threlkeld's doubts must dissipate, good dissenter that he is:

---

[3]. At the time I wrote these lines on Threlkeld in 1999, he and Biraban were barely remembered. I recall digging out an old volume or two from the University of Sydney library, dated sometime in the nineteenth century. Since then, by curious turns, I have ended up living in Newcastle. What did I find? Threlkeld and Biraban are invoked everywhere! On signs as one walks beneath a crumbling cliff or along an old Aboriginal track from the coast to Lake Macquarie, in histories about the area, in claims that Threlkeld's description of Awabakal is the most complete that we now have of any Aboriginal language.

> The providence of God has permitted ancient nations, together with their languages, and numerous tribes, with their various tongues, to pass away and others to take possession of and dwell in their tents, just as we in New South Wales and the neighbouring colonies do now, in the place of the original inhabitants of the land. (Threlkeld 1892, 125)

The allusions strengthen here somewhat, without explicit mention of exodus, Israel, or Canaan, but now New South Wales becomes the locus of Canaanite replacement by the "providence of God"—the same phrase encountered time and again in the explorers' texts of the previous chapter. Yet the strongest evocation of the exodus story is with the allusion to Ps 78:55: "He cast out the heathen then also before them, and divided them an inheritance by line, and made the tribes of Israel to dwell in their tents" (KJV). Again, the story is read in terms of the possession of the land.

At other moments the Jordan is reread as the boundary between Christendom and civilization, between a perilous wilderness and ordered, capitalist Christianity. So Mitchell: "The ford of Wallanburra was now our only separation from the christian world. That once passed, we might joyfully bid adieu to pestilence and famine, the lurking savage, and evil peril of 'flood and field'" (1839, 1:139). If Mitchell comes out of the pestilential wild lands, Giles overlays his reading with a callous social Darwinism that produces the same ideological effect as Threlkeld's more theological effort. Its only mitigation is that he then includes himself within the schema:

> No creatures of the human race could view these scenes with apathy or dislike, nor could any sentient beings part with such a patrimony at any price but that of their blood. But the great Designer of the universe, in the long past periods of creation, permitted a fiat to be recorded, that the beings whom it was His pleasure in the first instance to place amidst these lovely scenes, must eventually be swept from the face of the earth by others more intellectual, more dearly beloved and gifted than they. Progressive improvement is undoubtedly the order of creation, and we perhaps in our turn may be as ruthlessly driven from the earth by another race of yet unknown beings, of an order infinitely higher, infinitely more beloved than we. (Giles 1889, 1:183–84)

Despite the way these citations allude to and evoke the moment of dispossession as that which assists in the construction of the European experience of Australia, it is a theme that takes time to uncover. No presidential speeches or endlessly reiterated claims to being a chosen people, liberated and freed in order to set out for the promised land here, just the appropriation of land and the decline of the indigenes.

However, what I have been doing is taking the exodus story itself as somewhat untroubled, as a story that speaks of release from Egypt, wandering in the wilderness, and the invasion of the land. And this is the way it has wormed its way into the cultural unconscious of Western thought and culture. It seems to me that it may in fact be worthwhile to visit the story again in the Hebrew Bible, taking up as it does the bulk of the Pentateuch, or the first five books, and appearing time and again in a myriad of ways in other places throughout the Hebrew Bible.

What appears is a profound ambivalence over the exodus and its function in the biblical text. On the one hand, it is seen as a sorry episode of reluctance to leave Egypt, of critique of Moses for having led them to death by starvation in contrast to the fleshpots of Egypt (Exod 16:3), or for giving them nothing but bread in contrast to the fish, cucumbers, melons, leeks, onions, and garlic (Num 11:4–6), of perpetual rebellion, murmuring, complaining against Moses, Aaron, but above all God, mostly with regard to food and water (Exod 15:24; 16:2, 7, 8, 9, 12; 17:3; Num 11:1; 14:2, 27, 36; 16:11, 41; 17:20/5, 25/10), of apostasy and worship of the golden calf (Exod 32), and of outright rebellion and insurrection, such as those by Korah (Num 16) or Miriam and Aaron themselves (Num 12). Echoes appear in both psalms (Ps 78:12–20) and prophets (Ezek 20:10–17). It is this pressure for perpetual rebellion that led Freud to suggest that the Israelites killed Moses and then, in a moment of guilt, elevated him as the supreme leader and God (1939). And Ernst Bloch reads this incessant rebellion against Yahweh, the demiurge, as one of the seeds of atheism within Judaism and Christianity (1995, 1266–74). Further, the paradigmatic wandering in the wilderness for forty years is itself the punishment for lack of faith, believing the tales of the spies about tall, fierce warriors in Canaan, before whom the Israelites appear as grasshoppers, rather than trusting Yahweh (Num 13–14, especially 14:34). The part of the story that covers the departure from Egypt and the wandering in the desert is then a period of sin, rebellion, and punishment that leads, despite everything, into the land of Canaan.

On the other hand, this time is pictured elsewhere as one of purity of worship, of a simple earlier time in which the people were faithful to Yahweh and did what was right. For the prophets who evoke this version of the exodus tradition it is used as a counterexample to the present practices of the Israelites, who, of course, have fallen away from what they should be doing. It becomes a time of Yahweh's great bounty and provision, even unto fatness from the land they came to occupy (Neh 9:19–25). Rebellion becomes a problem later, contrasted with the ideal wilderness. Following Yahweh, the people are provided with strong guidance and rain (Ps 68:7–8). For Jeremiah, evoking the troubled image of marriage, the wilderness is a honeymoon period, a time of devotion to Yahweh, of faithful following, of trust in the midst of pits, drought, and deep darkness, that has been sullied by rebellion and turning away in the land given to the people (Jer 2:2–7). It is, finally, that moment before the elaborate ritual of sacrifice, of burnt offerings, grain offerings, and fatted animals that the text of Hosea despises so much (Hos 2:21–25).

At the end of the story, the invasion of Canaan, the ambivalence of the biblical material has led to the two great positions on the arrival of Israel in Canaan, that is, before the publication of Norman Gottwald's *Tribes of Yahweh* in 1979. Thus, William F. Albright (1957) and those who followed him, particularly G. E. Wright (1950) and John Bright (1980), regarded the literary and archaeological evidence as sufficient for an invasion, however piecemeal, a concerted effort by a collection of tribes to take the land of Canaan. Archaeological material was argued to indicate not only new architecture (four-roomed house) and pottery (collared-rim jar) but also a string of towns destroyed in the later part of the thirteenth century B.C.E. in southern Palestine—Debir, or Tell Beit Mirsim (Josh 10:38–39), Lachish, or Tell ed-Duweir (Josh 10:31–32), Eglon, or Tell el-Hesi (Josh 10:34–35), Hazor, or Tell el-Qedah (Josh 11:10–11)—that coincide with the biblical text that speaks of a conquest. Even though these scholars agree that the situation is obviously more complex than appears, the story of conquest, campaigns in the center (Josh 7–9), south (Josh 10), and north (Josh 11), and subsequent distribution of the land (Josh 13–21) is correct in its depiction of a sudden and violent incursion. What is remarkable about the profound influence of Albright is his evocation of an evolutionary supersession that echoes the words of Giles I noted earlier, although with the theological twist of Threlkeld. Of course, the mention of Australia is more than fortuitous:

> From the impartial standpoint of a philosopher of history, it often seems necessary that a people of markedly inferior type should vanish before a people of superior potentialities, since there is a point beyond which racial mixture cannot go without disaster. When such a process takes place—as at present in Australia—there is generally little that can be done by the humanitarian—though every deed of brutality and injustice is infallibly visited upon the aggressor. (Albright 1957, 281)

As is well-known, this position, cautiously and popularly[4] presented by Bright (1980, 129–33), for one, constituted a reaction to the dominant position in biblical scholarship that had been established by Albrecht Alt (1966) and Martin Noth (1960). For them the account of a lightning campaign was

---

4. The book ran to three editions between 1959 and 1980.

to be discarded as a wishful reconstruction, for other material in the text itself suggested a long, sporadic infiltration, at times violent but more often peaceful, of nomadic pastoralists who gradually became sedentary farmers. Texts such as Judg 1, Josh 13:2–6; 15:13–19, 63; 23:7–13 indicate such a situation. To avoid the problem of merely relying on one set of texts over against another, the archaeological evidence was brought to bear. Not only did Noth in particular point to the absence of evidence of destruction of a string of cities purported to have been knocked over in the Hebrew Bible—Jericho (Josh 6), Ai (Josh 7–8), Gibeon (Josh 10:2), Hebron (Josh 10:36–37), Arad, and Hormah (Josh 12:14)—he also questioned the identification of the sites mentioned above in his characteristic skepticism about any historical evidence. What we have, then, for these scholars, is a collection of separate traditions of dubious historical value.

Both positions constitute variations on an origin of Israel external to Canaan, since it was felt that only an external force could have brought about the change. Yet, following some earlier hints by G. Mendenhall (1962), but in a vast wealth of sociological and biblical research, Norman Gottwald put forward his hypothesis of a major rebellion by the marginalized and exploited groups of Canaan against their city-state lords (Gottwald 1979; 1992). While he allows for external groups, such as a small Levite group from Egypt who provide the exodus myth, the major impetus was internal, a bloody revolution that accounts for the destruction of certain cities in the thirteenth and twelfth centuries B.C.E. Using the new technologies of iron implements, terraced farming, and lime pits to hold water in a zone where there was no regular water supply, this rough group of people, argued Gottwald, moved into the highlands of Judah to become Israel. Initially attacked for the absence of biblical evidence, critics failed to realize the use of a Marxist perception of modes of production, although with a heavy moral twist: an exploitative tributarian system (the Marxist Asiatic mode of production) is replaced with an egalitarian communitarian one (or Marxist primitive communism). In this light, Gottwald was able to read vast amounts of biblical tradition as either the ideological material of a tribal, communitarian system (e.g., the stories of the mothers and fathers of Israel) or of a tributarian one (e.g., the covenant between God and the kings).

What is distinctive about this proposal is that it posits early Israel's appearance in Canaan as an internal affair; it shares with the American tradition of Albright, despite its attacks on this tradition, the notion of a relatively sudden revolutionary moment. Not unexpectedly, and almost in order to fill out all the logical possibilities of Aristotle's table of logical opposites, or Greimas's semiotic square, the proposal came that early Israel arose as a gradual withdrawal, a settlement shift, of people into the highlands of southern Palestine, most likely as a result of economic and social disruption. Of course, what the archaeological material (including pillared buildings, silos, and collared-rim ware along with iron, cisterns, and terracing) that indicates settlements in these highlands cannot tell is the identity of those who established villages and settlements there, nor where they came from. Thus, in this position, put forward by Robert Coote and Keith Whitelam in particular (Coote and Whitelam 1987; Coote 1990; see also Ahlström 1986; 1993; Lemche 1985; Thompson 1992), Israel is by no means unique in Canaan: it is a Palestinian tribe or tribal confederation. It does not stand radically opposed to its Palestinian environment but is very much part of it, socially, culturally, materially, and religiously. Yet it can still be identified as Israel. Later Whitelam questions such an identification, pressing the point that all the archaeological evidence can tell us is that the "growth of highland settlements is the most evident result of the realignment of Palestinian society but it can hardly be described as unique or the result of the intrusion of a new ethnic group" (1996, 230).

If I add to this the work of Jamieson-Drake (1991), who argues that the archaeological material can provide us with no evidence of a kingship or a political entity any earlier than the ninth century, well after David and Solomon (see also Whitelam 1996, 160–73), or the work of Philip Davies (1992), who argues that "biblical Israel" is an identity constructed even later, after the exile to Babylon by Persian period scribes, or Keith Whitelam (1996), who regards "ancient Israel" as largely a work of fiction, then the origin of Israel and its presence in Canaan becomes even more murky. Even the texts that suggest, going back to the first model I investigated, a direct invasion begin to look more uncertain when interrogated a little more closely, as I will argue in the next chapter, with regard to the ambiguity of Gibeonite/Israelite identity in Josh 9.

Apart from the ambivalence over the liberation from Egypt and the wandering in the wilderness that the biblical text exhibits, the whole opposition of Israelite/Canaanite becomes exceedingly troubled, except as a reading back of later, constructed identities. What if the Canaanites, Perrizites, and others are also Israelites? In this light the great opposition in the Hebrew Bible between wilderness and arable land, tent and fixed dwelling, nomadism and settlement, Moses and David, may be understood as a wide-ranging ideological opposition, a contradiction that must be read in a different way, namely, as signs of other conflicts and tensions.

Finally, perhaps the most curious twist of all is that the exodus stories themselves seem not to have had currency at least until the exile to Babylon in 587 B.C.E. (some six hundred to seven hundred years after their purported happening), when they were first collated and written down, since these stories provided a model for understanding the stay, of the ruling and intellectual elites, in Babylon itself. The exodus story thereby becomes a vast political myth, justifying a later return and conflict over possession of the land. Of course, this has been its function in a host of places throughout the world ever since, but it is worth noting that the biblical material upon which such subsequent appropriations are based is anything but clear.

What is the impact of this research on the debate over the use of exodus that I traced a little earlier? To begin with, it seems as though the dominant reading of exodus outside biblical scholarship but drawn from the Hebrew Bible—as liberation from Egypt, wilderness wandering, and the conquest of the promised land—must be understood as a political myth. The function of myth is such that efforts to counter it with either moral arguments for or against, or historical arguments in search of the facts, fail to account for the force of ideology itself (understanding myth as one form of ideology, which is itself crucial for social and individual self- understanding). Nor is it sufficient to argue for a recovery of indigenous or native discourses, however justified that might be, for this merely inverts the myth with a recourse to nativism—as Said does, and as Keith Whitelam carries out in his polemical reading of the "invention of ancient Israel" (Whitelam 1996). Yet what Whitelam unwittingly does is point out not only that the biblical evidence is largely fictional but that the scholarly positions I have traced are also ideological in their own way, influenced in many ways by international politics at their time of writing.[5] To my mind, any effort at attacking this particular myth must work at a number of levels: to point out that it is a myth; that it may have a distinctly pernicious turn, as with its use in Israeli-Palestinian relations or with its truncated usage in Australia to justify dispossession; that any scholarship relating to it will also be ideological; that it will contain contradictions that point to social, political, and economic contradictions (I am thinking here of the nomadic-settled contradiction in particular). In the end the only way around such ambiguous myths is to avoid or discard them altogether; not easily done, unless circumstances help out. It may then be read as a small plus that the exodus myth in Australia is muted and sidelined.

However, if the exodus story first gained currency during the exile in Babylon, it may be appropriate turn to the theme of exile itself.

---

5. Unfortunately, the way he does this is to suggest that each model reflects political debates and tensions regarding Palestine at the time they were written. This reflection follows a one-to-one correspondence between biblical scholarship and Palestinian politics that vitiates the remainder of his argument.

Exile

> I have lived that moment of the scattering of the people that in other times and other places, in the nations of others, becomes a time of gathering. (Bhabha 1994, 139)

> "When exactly ... does the 'postcolonial' begin?" queries Ella Shohat in a discussion of the subject. Misreading this question deliberately, I will supply here an answer that is only partially facetious: "When Third World intellectuals have arrived in First World academe." (Dirlik 1997, 52)

The traveling, diasporic desire of postcolonial intellectuals gains a distinctly biblical note in the work of Jonathan and Daniel Boyarin (1995), foundation figures in what is now known as the "new Jewish studies." They have sought to reclaim the exodus through a model of exile, thereby avoiding the charge leveled at the exodus myth by Said. The crucial move here is to distinguish sharply between the Mosaic and the Davidic: the former connotes wilderness, nomadism, antitotalitarianism, and exile; the latter brings up notions of settlement, cultivation, and totalitarianism. In the exodus story there are both moments, the nomadic existence in the wilderness under Moses and the invasion of Canaan, the dispossession of the inhabitants and the eventual establishment of a monarchy of which David is the prime exemplar. In making this distinction the Boyarins wish to drive a wedge between them, to cleave them asunder with a huge meat axe, or perhaps circumcising knife. Davidic totalitarianism, not unexpectedly, is cut away and discarded, like a useless but highly charged flap of skin, while Mosaic nomadism is held up as the ideal. They valorize the first part of the divide and vilify the second (see especially Boyarin and Boyarin 1995, 328).[6]

These two strands carry a further load within contemporary Judaism, they claim, one connecting land and people, providing a claim to autochthony and indigeneity, which is to be opposed by another that "is perpetually an unsettlement of the very notion of Jewish identity" (1995, 327). Here it is that questions of travel and identity connect with each other in a reading of the Bible. In doing so, they oppose the main tenets of Zionism, foregrounding the notion of diaspora, a permanent exile as the "generation and ground of Jewish identity." However, not only does this counter Zionism, it also

---

6. Another way of dealing with Jewish identity that arrives at the diaporic for the Boyarins is historically. In broad periods, that history begins with the "tribe" in the land, then there are the troubles of the tribe (the Hellenistic period and Paul's challenge to universalize and break with body and land), and finally diaporic existence.

provides a distinctly Jewish way of being with the current value placed on nomadic ways of being among postmodern and postcolonial peoples and, especially, theorists.

But they find themselves in a bind, for this then undermines indigenous claims to the land the world over, for whom the land in some sense is invariably meaningful for identity. In response, they revert to the language of what is "real," meaning presumably what is historical, political, and economic: "The uncritical valorization of indigenousness (and particularly the confusion between political indigenousness and mystified autochthony) must come under critique, without wishing, however, to deny the rights of native Americans, Australians, and Palestinians to their Lands precisely on the basis of real, unmysterious political claims" (1995, 327). All the same, such claims must be suspicious, given that the diasporic nature of Jewish identity is in the end not to be restricted to Jews.

Further, in response to the question that most people in diaspora find themselves forced into such situations, the Boyarins argue for a "Diasporized, that is, disaggregated" (1995, 335) identity that is voluntary, not forced. "We want to propose a privileging of Diaspora, a dissociation of ethnicities and political hegemonies as the only social structure that begins to make possible a maintenance of cultural identity in a world grown thoroughly and inextricably interdependent" (1995, 335), and, one should add, a theoretical climate grown thoroughly antiessentialist. The biblical story, then, is "not one of autochthony but one of always already coming from somewhere else" (1995, 327).

In what has by now become something of a habit, Ella Shohat has suggested an underside to all of this. Before the advent of Zionism—to which the Boyarins are opposed—as a dominant ideological position after the late 1940s, the uniquely Jewish narrative was that of diaspora, exile, and return to the motherland. But this "privileged status on the margins of Europe and Euro-America" (Shohat 1992, 133) was enhanced through a singular focus on the Holocaust (capital H), so that other claims to exile or diaspora threaten such a uniqueness. The Boyarins then risk a similar exclusion of other exiles and diasporas by claiming the model for Jews: their only escape is to refuse the constructed ethnic marker.

Yet the Boyarins present a recent variant on a philosophical and literary theme that has a significant modernist pedigree. Indeed, the notion of an itinerant identity, in the wilderness, is something that has been felt to be the peculiar nature of the Jewish God, Yahweh of the Hebrew Bible, one who is noted for errancy and the desert, the realm of the wilderness—so, for instance, Hegel, Benjamin, and Jabès (see Vitiello 1998, 137–146).

Perhaps the most influential recent use of this motif is by Gilles Deleuze and Felix Guattari in their working out of a rhizomatic or nomadic thought, of nomadology. In a remarkable chapter Deleuze and Guattari (1987, 111–48) take up the ideological opposition of nomadic-settled and rewrite it in psychoanalytic terms. They seek to make a distinction "between a paranoid, signifying, despotic regime of signs and a passional or subjective, postsignifying, authoritarian regime" (1987, 121). The former, paranoid and despotic form is characteristic of ancient imperialism, whether Egyptian or Babylonian; its determining feature is an irradiating circular network, a circular system of signs in which items continually refer to one another and ultimately the central imperial face, the faciality that determines language, signification, and tribute itself (see 1987, 115). (The relation between this depiction and Marx's Asiatic mode of production needs to be explored elsewhere.) The other, passional and authoritarian, regime or "plateau" is that which the Israelites claim for themselves in moving into the desert or wilderness. This is the nomadic realm, the line of flight that follows the trajectory of the scapegoat, which is simultaneously cursed and blessed but which also unravels the circular signification of the other regime. Here we find the animal-raising nomads, whose semiotic system operates by arithmetic and numeration (hence the book of Numbers in the midst of the wilderness wandering of the Hebrew Bible), by mobile and plural distribution, by arrangements and distributions rather than central collection and tribute, whose social organization is by the war machine directed against the state, and whose methods involve secrecy, spying, and the hiding of the face of God (1987, 118).

The crucial markers for Deleuze and Guattari are the ark of the covenant and the two temples, destroyed in 587 B.C.E. and 70 C.E., the two dates that function as the title of this chapter. The temple of Jerusalem can only be understood as destroyed or awaiting destruction, as therefore fragile and mobile.

> The whole history of the Temple—the mobility and fragility of the ark, then the construction of a House by Solomon, its reconstruction under Darius, etc.—has meaning only in relation to renewed proceedings of destruction, the two supreme moments of which came with Nebuchadnezzar and Titus. A temple, mobile, fragile, or destroyed: the ark is no more than a little portable packet of signs. (1987, 122)

The exodus may then be understood as this group or packet of signs that detaches from the Egyptian (and, I would add, the Babylonian) imperial network and "sets off in a line of flight into the desert" (1987, 122), turning the scapegoat into a positive sign. But this produces a vagabond monotheism, an atheistic monotheism that operates in "an infinite succession of local operations" (1987, 383).

What Deleuze and Guatari then do with all of this is to connect the nomadic with, first of all, the notion of smooth space—desert, steppe, or ocean (1987, 380–84, 474–500)—and then with their favored model of the rhizome. Desert vegetation is rhizomatic, temporary and shifting in location, as are roots and weeds and hives and warrens, as are gaps, detours, subterranean passages, and holes, as is "variability, the polyvocality of directions" (1987, 382), as is the organization of their own work (1987, 10–12). In other words, they appropriate the nomadic, via the Hebrew Bible, for themselves.

How should such a tour de force be read? Apart from the perpetually promising interpretation of Marx, Deleuze and Guattari recast the opposition evoked by the Boyarins: what was Davidic totalitarianism becomes a paranoid, despotic regime of signs; what was Mosaic nomadism becomes a passional, postsignifying scheme. Yet they still designate the settled over against the nomadic, the empire and kingship over against the desert and diaspora. Whereas the Boyarins valorize the latter more readily as postmodern mode of identity, Deleuze and Guattari equivocate a little more, and one has to read a few transitions before seeing the connections with their own work. Indeed, with the series of oppositions and contradictions that run over and through the many plateaus they traverse, there is a distinct impression that the one is not possible without the other, however more desirable one may be than the other.

Yet there are some problems with the reading of the Hebrew Bible by Deleuze and Guattari: they take the settled-nomad opposition from the text and read it in psychoanalytic and Marxist terms, rather than questioning the function of the opposition itself. They do indicate ways that the opposition may be questioned, but these must be developed by the reader of their work. In taking up the nomad-settled distinction, they also trade in the problem with the exodus that I noted in the previous section. That is, one cannot have the nomadic without imperial settlement, diaspora without land, wilderness wandering without conquest. The duality of the exodus myth is thereby replicated. If myth is understood as an effort to deal with social and ideological contradiction, as Lévi-Strauss and Jameson suggest, among others, then to perpetuate the myth is to perpetuate the contradictions it seeks to resolve. Second, there is a dangerous use of the circular-linear opposition in characterizing their opposition: the imperial system is circular, while the line of flight of the nomadic follows a linear trajectory of number. This opposition has been used time and again to contrast Western, modern ways of understanding the world, time, and history to the agricultural, cyclical patterns found in tribal, ancient, and non-Western ways of thought. The next step in this argument is to locate the origins of a linear approach within the Hebrew Bible: God is a God of linear history, and the Hebrews are the originators of such a way of thinking. While the use made by Deleuze and Guattari shifts the valences somewhat, their use is quite similar, and equally problematic, for the Hebrew God and gods are no less linear or circular than any other society or divine being. Further, to locate the origins of Western civilization in the Hebrew Bible is to make all sorts of mythical claims about the inherent Judeo-Christian nature and origins of Western society and to place those origins in religion rather than socioeconomic areas.

Others also have made use of exile and diaspora as markers of identity. I restrict myself to two central postcolonial theorists—Edward Said and Homi Bhabha—in order to note how strongly the nomadic-settled distinction runs through their work. Said has vigorously claimed exile as a slogan for his own autobiographical position—a Christian-Arab raised in the Middle East but Western-educated—and critical practice, especially in his "Reflections in Exile" (Said 1990). In eliding the modernist secular notion of exile, especially as George Lukács located it as a generic factor of alienation (a "transcendental homelessness" [Lukács 1993]) in the modern novel, the Jewish tradition of diaspora as religious displacement, and the forced reality of exile for millions, Said comes to a conclusion not dissimilar to the Boyarins: although no one chooses exile (then they are émigrés), one can opt to make it a viable alternative to the mass institutions of modern life, an opportunity that catapults the exile beyond the humdrum observances of others.

For Said, literature is able to bridge this modern condition and the history of terrible and forced exile. Exile allows an investigation of the various layers of modern existence; it becomes a metaphor of modernity. But exile is not merely a modernist or theological category, as suggested by Said's juxtaposition of the theme in Western thought—Dante, Joyce, Conrad, Nabokov, Hemingway, Fitzgerald, Simone Weil, and Theodor Adorno—and Third World writers—Faiz Ahmad Faiz (Pakistan), Rashid Hussein and Mahmud Darwish (Palestine), and Noubar (Armenia). In the end, Said is committed to exile as an intellectual and philosophical alternative. Not a privilege or a choice, exile provides an opportunity for profound perception, for finding a "home," like Adorno in his *Minima Moralia* (1993), in writing itself. In fact, the loss of home in modernity provides the situation in which home may be found in writing: the impossibility of dwelling becomes the possibility of writing. Exile, of course, becomes the perspective of so many postcolonial authors (witness Salman Rushdie) and critics, cut off from roots and past and nation, yet vitally concerned with it. "Exile is life lived outside the habitual order. It is nomadic, decentered, contrapuntal; but no sooner does one get accustomed to it than its unsettling force erupts anew" (Said 1990, 366; see also Roy 1995). As far as Ella Shohat is concerned, Said has not merely adopted the role of exile; it is a lived reality: "Said in this sense brings to the often amorphous postmodernist sense of exile a telling material and historical edge" (Shohat 1992, 122). Yet, as is so often the case with Said, he slips between bourgeois markers (the solitary middle-class exile) and radical politics (the mass of exiled and displaced persons). Indeed, as Kaplan suggests, the "plight of historically constituted refugees might be said to *authorize* Said's discourse on exile" (1996, 120). This slippage between elegiac-romantic reflections on exile and political engagements, between singular and mass exile, between the romanticized exile and political refugee, trades on such a relation.

However, it is precisely these political engagements that show up the other side of Said's diaspora. His strong, public, and polemical interventions in favor of the Palestinian intifada, of a Palestinian state, and his continual efforts to overturn the discourse in the West that favors Israel and demonizes the Palestinians, must be seen as that perpetual longing for a "home." Said's habit of traveling heavy, with as many things as he can take with him, must not be read merely as the mark of an exile, of one who does not know whether this trip will be another flight; it should also be read as the perpetual expectation of going home, of the establishment of a Palestinian state. Thus, in Said's work the very opposition with which he critiques the exodus appears—diaspora and home, nomadic and settled, wilderness and land—although now in its own mutation.

Homi Bhabha also valorizes itinerancy, modeled as it is on Frantz Fanon, a French-educated Martiniquan who became an Algerian nationalist, the eternal return of Bhabha's work. Yet Bhabha foregrounds the indispensable link between exile and homecoming, as in the quotation used in the epigraph to this section. Scattering and gathering come together, which then become the basis for a consideration of the nation, whose cohesion and appeal relies on its perpetual dissemination. Elsewhere, through a reading of Toni Morrison and Nadine Gordimer, home and identity are disrupted by Freud's notion of the *unheimliche*, or "unhomely" (Bhabha 1992). There is, in the end, no continuity for the self in a particular location, except as unhomely. The home is unhomely, the nation disseminated, the gathering scattered.

Like the others, Bhabha evokes the nomadic-settled opposition that I have been tailing and criticizing. But there is another problem in all of this, and that hinges on the crucial difference between exile and travel, for it seems to me that there is some significant slippage in these terms with the writers I have been considering. Indeed, I would suggest that valorization of exile and diaspora in these writers must be understood in its context of modern and postmodern travel, itself the focus of a considerable body of writing, whether in terms of the history and nature of tourism itself or of the theorist as itinerant, nomad.

The widespread practice of contemporary travel and tourism would seem to have provided the socioeconomic and ideological background for the valorization of travel in contemporary theory. Despite evidence of travel by peoples such as the Vikings or migratory travel over large bodies of water by Pacific Islanders, travel as a widespread practice of a particular class, especially a newly formed middle class, takes on a new dimension in the early Renaissance,[7] although the literature itself owes much to the "marvelous voyage" of medieval and Arabic writing (Zumthor 1994[8]). The mercantile expansion undertaken as part of an entrepreneurial and then imperial capitalism was generated through the activity of increasing travel by individuals to further and further parts of the globe. This misnamed "age of discovery" saw exploration as a vital factor in both the construction of capitalism and of travel. The distinctly Eurocentric focus of exploration saw explorers moving through "uncharted" lands, or at least places where no "civilized" human being had formerly been. Explorers, then—and the Australian explorers traced in the previous chapter are prime examples of this—proceed to find places for the first time and rename them in Adamic rapture, even though time and again the local people often led them there, or at least to water so they could survive and continue. "In addition to such physical explorations, however, 'travel' also began as the imaginative reconstruction of other people and places" (Ashcroft, Griffiths, and Tiffin 1998, 96).

A crucial element of these travelers' activities was the production of journals and travel accounts, by explorers, missionaries, merchants, and so on. As the genre develops, there is less of the day-to day-monotony of the journey or of scientific reporting and more of the dangers, threats to life, reflection on the nature of life, and embellishments that became part of the growing genre of travel literature, developing the whole category of the exotic/erotic. Thus, the exploration journals of Giles have a much greater emphasis on these factors, targeted at a growing audience for travel literature, in comparison to those of Eyre, Grey, Mitchell, Stuart, or Sturt.

Contemporary tourism is then an extension of this possession by exploration, dividing itself between adventure or safari tours—whitewater rafting, trekking, wilderness tours, and so on—and the mass tourism of conventionally identified tourist sites. While the latter admits that tourism is the discovery of the already-known and makes that a virtue in itself, the former trades on the contradiction of much contemporary travel—the search by

---

7. For a useful coverage of the question of travel and tourism, see variously Urry's work (1990), as well as Behdad (1994), Belasco (1979), Kaplan (1996), MacCannell (1976), Prato and Trivero (1985), and Van den Abbeele (1992).

8. Indeed, Zumthor argues for a lively writing of travel narratives—pilgrimage, missionary, navigation logs, marvelous tales—and so on until the seventeenth century, after which there was a pause before the new generic explosion of the nineteenth century that I am interested in here.

tourists for the nontouristy sites, only to find others tourists there doing the same thing. Yet this was already a problem for earlier travelers such as Flaubert, for whom travel to the exotic East was to a place already traveled, already discovered, and therefore deflating in its belatedness (see Behdad 1994, 53–72).

It seems to me that this provides the social and economic context for the valorization of the diasporic and nomadic by postcolonial theorists, who have appropriated the idea of homelessness and diaspora and provided it with a different loading.[9] The attraction of travel, common for the backpacker, middle-class family, retired couple is also that which attracts the theorist. The lecture circuit, global conference, movement from job to job is that which draws the theorist to emulate in her or his own way the pattern of professional life more common to late capitalist travelers, or, for that matter, to the business executive than a former academic life (although colonial academics nearly always traveled back and forth from "home," as I have discussed in the introduction—it was those in metropolitan centers who remained put).

All the same, it is not merely that (postcolonial) theorists are travelers as such. Rather, it may well be argued that travel has a deeper place in modernity, being a crucial matrix for Flaubert's universe (see Gourgouris 1995) or as both the trigger of Locke's crucial breakthrough in his theory of knowledge and the linguistic information and terminology itself—voyages, possessions, sure footings, discovery—that he used as evidence for his theories (see especially Paxman 1995). Travel becomes, then, a metaphor not only for modernity but one that may be claimed theoretically (see Gwin 1996). In fact, it would seem that the postmodern theorist is the quintessential tourist, linked, as van den Abbeele shows in his brilliant review (1980) of MacCannell's book (1976): in the intellectual's disdain of the tourist, she or he exhibits the fundamental feature of the tourist and thereby is one by default; Deleuze's and Guattari's "nomadic thought" and "nomadology" (1983, 105–6; 1987, 111–48, 315–423), or Hodge and Mishra's "nomadic syntax" (1990, 152–53), or Baudrillard's travels in *America* (1988) and *Cool Memories* (1990)[10] merely bring this to the surface.

---

9. Is it not a little ironic that I write these words while living in a tent in Canberra, during a stint as Visiting Fellow at the Humanities Research Centre of the Australian National University (1 January–14 February 1999)?

10. Baudrillard himself is not averse to the odd biblical allusion. So: "Only the exiled have a land. I know some people who are only close to their country when they are 10,000 kilometers away, driven out by their own brothers" (1990, 83). The allusion here is to Joseph being sold into slavery and exiled by his brothers in Gen 37:12–36. And then, with a touch on the story of the Israelites seeking to leave Egypt for a sacrifice in the desert

Travel provides one signal of the capitalist socioeconomic context for theories of diaspora, as well as recourse to the Hebrew Bible in developing such theories. Another is the assertion that the only valid diaspora is a willed one, chosen rather than forced. Exile is by definition that which is forced upon a person or a people, those who are banished from a "home" (whatever that means) where they would rather be. Diaspora, however, whereas it may have originated and may often be perpetuated by force, bears with the association of a voluntary stay in a place in which one first arrived by force: the exile in Babylon for the Israelite political, religious, economic, and intellectual leadership is again the paradigmatic example. In the case of the Boyarins in particular, one must choose diaspora for any valid claim to a postmodern identity. It is precisely this voluntary diaspora that postcolonial critics tap into, the possibility and decision to move into a major First World academic center on the strength of a master work. Spivak, at least, refuses to make her constant travel more than it is: she travels for "reasons that have more to do with an unexamined life than with exile. I'd like to say that an exile is some one who is obliged to stay away—I am not in that sense an exile" (Spivak 1990, 68). Indeed, for Dirlik, postcolonial theory is constituted by Third World academics in First World institutions. Yet what makes all of this a distinctly capitalist enterprise, and ties in very closely with travel, is that the elevation of individual choice is central to the ideology of liberalism. The ability and inviolable right of the individual to choose as she or he wishes lies at the heart of such an ideology, masking the socioeconomic factors that enable and disable such possibilities. In the same way that one chooses to travel, so also one may elect diaspora. Indeed, the easy celebration of travel, exile, and the related terms of hybridity and multiculturalism is premature and elides socioeconomic factors: in the end transnational business likes these things too (see Mitchell 1996).

I have, then, leveled three major criticisms at postcolonial appropriations of exile: that it trades on a nomadic-settled opposition derived from the Hebrew Bible; that it presupposes the practice of travel in a capitalist context; and that it valorizes voluntary diaspora, migrancy, and itinerancy.

Antipodal Images

General depravity—prevalence of it in New South Wales, as attested by general impressions.... Main cause of non-reformation, drunkenness—uni-

---

(Exod 5:1, 3, 8, 17): "Death Valley is as big and mysterious as ever. Fire, heat, light: all the elements of sacrifice are here. You always have to bring something into the desert to sacrifice, and offer it to the desert as a victim" (1988, 66).

versality and incurableness of it in New South Wales. (Bentham 1843, 217, 230)

He found him in a desert land, in a howling wilderness waste. (Deut 32:10)

It remains to consider the fate of the exile motif in Australia, where I have already found that the exodus has undergone its own somewhat vicious mutation. The first moment in this search is a more contemporary one, namely, that of Stephen Muecke's appropriation of Deleuze and Guattari's nomadology. However, what Muecke does is connect this focus on nomadism, which I have suggested derives in part from the Hebrew Bible, with Aboriginal nomadism. The appeal in this case is with the nomadism of indigenous people, fringe dwellers, the vagrants and ferals of earlier social formations that are now charged with an alternative and positive value. And so, in the volume *Reading the Country: Introduction to Nomadology*, a collection of artwork, story, poetry, dialogue, and quotes from French theorists by Muecke, along with artist Krim Benterrak and Aboriginal Paddy Roe (1984), exile becomes nomad in content as well as form. A similar thematic underlies Muecke's exercise in ficto-criticism, *No Road: Bitumen All the Way* (1997). Here nomadic Aborigines become, through the very terminology itself, a model of thinking and acting for intellectuals and others seeking a new way of being. The same possibility is sought as the Boyarins, but from a different source. This is a curious, solitary effort that draws upon the popular ideology of Aborigines as aimless wanderers, as going on "walkabout" for no good reason, rather than the anthropological concept of nomadism, where movement takes place in set economic and social patterns and in clearly demarcated areas.[11]

---

11. The whole ideological construct of the popular perception of Aboriginal nomadism needs a separate study, which would need to include reflection on the narrative and graphic, along with the more usual legal, development of the doctrine of *terra nullius*; the effect of the Mabo and Wik decisions at a popular level; land-rights claims at the same level; the work of historians such as Bill Gamage on land use; or archaeologists such as Donald Pate on chemical analysis (for protein, calcium, nitrogen etc.) of Aboriginal bones, particularly the bone collagen, in comparison with those of contemporary animals, as well as plants, in order to ascertain dietary patterns and movement; the construction of nomadism in explorer texts (e.g., Eyre 1845 1:41; 2:218, 247; Grey 1841, 2:297) despite repeated references to fixed dwellings and sedentary food gathering practices (e.g., Grey 1841, 2:11–12; Leichhardt 1847, 109, 290, 307, 331, 527; Mitchell 1839, 1:77, 237, 240, 262, 305; Sturt 1833, 1:89; 1984, 70, 92); and the work of popular conservative historians such as Geoffrey Blainey's *Triumph of the Nomads* (1975; see also Chaseling 1957; Mountford 1976; Strehlow 1961).

In contrast to Muecke, a dominant biblical motif that was and is used of Australia is that of wilderness, desolation and waste, without water or hope. It is more the place of exile, with little consciousness of exile itself. So Grey writes of his first view: "At first streak of dawn, I leant over the vessel's side, to gaze upon those shores I had so longed to see. I had not anticipated that they would present any appearance of inviting fertility; but I was not altogether prepared to behold so arid and barren a surface, as that which now met my view" (1841, 1:67). It is worse than his worst imaginings, so much so that he is caught off guard, shocked. For Charles Sturt, the unbearable dreariness of the country weighed him down: "Nothing could exceed in dreariness the appearance of the tracks through which we journeyed" (1833, 1:73); "It is impossible for us to describe the kind of country we were now traversing, or the dreariness of the view it presented" (1833, 2:59). Similarly, although from a different social location, a letter from Georgina Molloy, one of the first settlers in western Australia, writing about her lost child some three years earlier to her friend, Helen Story in Scotland, who had just lost hers: "Its grave, though sodded with British clover, looks so singular and solitary in this wilderness, of which I can scarcely give you an idea" (quoted in Hodge and Mishra 1990, 145). The wilderness here is contrasted with the desired and missing Edenic place of Scotland, signified by the clover of the grave.

Similarly, Ernest Giles almost fifty years later, who found the arid wilderness an occasion for some literary flourishes: "It was totally uninhabited by either man or animal, not a track of a single marsupial, emu, or wild dog was to be seen, and we seemed to have penetrated a region [the Great Victoria Desert] utterly unknown to man, and as utterly forsaken by God" (1889, 2:191). Of course, the Aborigines, for Giles, were not really "men," closer to animals on the evolutionary scale, and so the presence of Aborigines and the encounters with them that he notes on every second page do not count. But what Giles manages here is a narrative clearing of the space, the creation of a literary *terra nullius* in which not even God is interested, let alone animal or human.

It is indeed the land God forgot, or forsook: "Even the great desert in which we have so long been buried must suggest to the reflecting mind either God's perfectly effected purpose, or His purposely effected neglect" (1889, 2:227). It goes without saying that Giles's is the only "reflecting mind" in this particular space.

And then there is the favored motif, the howling wilderness: "Here, too, we find in this fearful waste, this howling wilderness, this antre vast and desert idle, places scooped out of the solid rock, and the mighty foundations of the round world laid bare, that the lower organisms of God's human family may find their proper sustenance" (1889, 2:228). Finally, another presence is noted and then immediately dismissed as "lower organisms." It is not so much that God is present but merely that some of his creatures are. What interests me here, however, is the double biblical presence in this text. To begin with, Giles quotes Deut 32:10, where the "howling wilderness waste" appears, a phrase that recurs in other places (see below). But he also makes the land primeval, prehistoric, providing a glimpse of the moment of creation itself, "the mighty foundations of the world laid bare." Indeed, what happens with the wilderness motif in Australia—referring as it does not merely to the deserts but to the whole land and its society—is that it is often connected with the biblical stories of creation.

Before a final glance at such a use of the Bible, I want to trace the use of the "howling wilderness" a little further. In his useful study of the landscape in Australian poetry, Brian Elliot (1967) shows how rarely, if ever, the notion of a promised land appears in depictions of Australia. Whereas biblical images are often used especially by explorers such as Mitchell, as I noted in the previous chapter, and many of the early and not so early poets in order to give evidence of the antiquity of the land and its inhabitants—it was as though civilized Europeans had happened upon a time warp, or an anthropologist's dream—the common motif is one of the wilderness, the "howling wilderness" (see Elliott 1967, 137). The other biblical image that appears in the poets is Egypt, an ambiguous place at best in the Bible—it is both a place of oppression from which to escape and a refuge from persecution—but one that also carried a mystical loading for the early poets, a locus of esoteric knowledge and exotic traditions of knowledge. Egypt was also at the other side of the wilderness from the promised land. Alongside the ambivalent space of Egypt, Babylon too was invoked as a non-Israelite place outside the promised land. The writers and poets John Dunmore Lang, Marcus Clarke, A. L. Gordon, A. D. Hope, and Christopher Brennan all used the Egyptian reference (see Elliott 1967, 21–22, 25, 82, 96, 196, 275, 325).[12]

As for the howling wilderness, it also appears in the work of Henry Lawson, in his story "Hungerford," although with a further twist: "The coun-

---

12. Lang: "or the busy ant rearing his slender pyramid of yellowish clay, as if in mockery of the huger monuments of the Pharaohs" (Elliot 1967, 21). Gordon's gum trees as "weird columns Egyptian" with their hieroglyphic markings in *The Sick Stockrider* (Elliott 1967, 196). A. D. Hope in *Australia*: " those endless, outstretched paws / Of sphinx demolished of stone lion worn away" (Elliott 1967, 196); or in *Pyramis or the House of Ascent*: "Those terrible souls, the Pharaohs, those great Kings / Taking, their genius, their prerogative / Of blood, mind, treasure ... / I think of other pyramids, not in stone, / The great, incredible monuments of art" (Elliott 1967, 325). Brennan in *Poem 54* speaks of a valley like "the Egyptian crypt outspread" (275).

try looks as though a great ash-heap had been spread out there, and mulga scrub and firewood planted—and neglected. The country looks just as bad for a hundred miles around Hungerford, and beyond that it gets worse—a blasted, barren wilderness that doesn't even howl. If it howled it would be a relief" (Lawson 1976, 122). Lawson takes the biblical image a step further, for howling, a sign of life, is itself absent.

The literary stereotypes that were settled early and against which later writers fought were of wilderness, exile, and disappointment (see further Elliott 1967, 143–44). The howling wilderness was connected, as I noted, with motifs drawn from creation itself, particularly the curse. Australia was the best exemplar of a land subject to the primeval curse for the original sin, full of rocks and thorns and back-breaking work (see Gen 3:17–19). So, not unexpectedly, Ernest Giles: "but truly the curse must have gone forth more fearfully against them, and with a vengeance must it have been proclaimed, by the sweat of their brows must they obtain their bread" (Giles 1889, 2:228). Here he designates the Aborigines as bearers of the curse against Adam and Eve, although now much more concentrated. John Dunmore Lang was also keen on this idea, which is related to the suggestion that Australia was not so much the land that exhibits the curse after the fall but was that region that escaped the words of Gen 1, "And God saw that it was good" (1:10, 12, 18, 21, 25). So Barron Field's "Kangaroo" (1819) from *The First Fruits of Australian Poetry*, the first book of verse printed in the colony:

> Kangaroo! Kangaroo!
> Thou spirit of Australia,
> that redeems from utter failure,
> From perfect desolation,
> And warrants the creation
> Of this fifth part of the earth;
> Which would seem an afterbirth,
> Not conceived in the beginning
> (For GOD blessed his work at first
> And saw that it was good),
> But emerged at the first sinning,
> When the ground therefore was curst:-
> And hence this barren wood!
> (Field, quoted in Elliott 1967, 48)

The curse precedes the garden and the fall, anticipating the subsequent curse by missing the initial blessing.

All of this might be termed a theological or biblical antipodality, Australia being cast as the diametrical opposite of England, the land outside Eden, whether before its creation or after expulsion and curse. The response to this characterization remains within the same logic, where Australia is then presented as an Eden itself. Early hints of this may be found in the journals of Thomas Mitchell: "They prefer the land unbroken and free from the earliest curse pronounced against the first banished and first created man.... we cannot occupy land without producing a change, fully as great to the Aborigines, as that which took place on man's fall and expulsion from Eden" (Mitchell 1848, 66). Here the Aborigines live in a land comparable to Eden before the fall, and it is the English who bring about the fall, now understood as both necessary for progress, inevitable, and with dire consequences, already noticeable, for the indigenes.

A. D. Hope also seeks to invert the antipodean perception of Australia, finding value in precisely those elements that others found so much part of the "wilderness." The drabness, stupidity, cultural dependency, cheapness of Australia is precisely the wilderness from which, in his famous phrase, the prophets come:

> Yet there are some like me turn gladly back
> From the lush jungle of modern thought, to find
> The Arabian desert of the human mind,
> Hoping, if still from the deserts the prophets come,
> Such savage and scarlet as no green hills dare
> Springs in that waste, some spirit which escapes
> That learned doubt, the chatter of cultured apes
> Which is called civilization over there
> (Hope 1973, 8).[13]

Yet the clearest sign of this antipodean inversion lies in the popular assertion that Australia is the best place on earth to live, an assertion often made by those who have traveled overseas.[14] Even from earlier moments this inversion may be found, whether in the Jindyworobak movement of the 1930s and 1940s that sought a positive Australian art and spirituality through Aboriginality or the claim that artists first really "saw" Australia in the late 1800s, as with Arthur Streetson's "The Purple Noon's Transparent Might," the notion of a "worker's paradise" (see White 1981, 29–43), the "lucky country" (itself

---

13. The presence of A. D. Hope has another referent, which is that nearly all of the research and writing for this book took place in the A. D. Hope Building at the Australian National University in Canberra, where I undertook a visiting fellowship. Images of Hope greeted me as I walked in every day and when I departed every evening.

14. Indeed, more than once people responded to me in this way after public presentations of earlier forms of this chapter, feeling that I had in some way maligned the country.

an ironic phrase coined by Donald Horne), "Arcadia in Hell," and the propaganda presented to immigrants from a war-torn Europe promising a rich and fertile land with jobs for everyone. That much of this turned out not to be the case only reinforces the function of this mythic opposition. In a strange way this contrast between Eden and curse, the garden and the howling wilderness, seems to remain part of the way Australia is perceived.

5

Green Ants and Gibeonites: B. Wongar, Joshua 9, and Some Problems of Postcolonialism

Go the ant, thou sluggard; consider her ways, and be wise. (Prov 6:6)

The explorers' paths have now been left behind, as have the themes of exodus and exile, for it is time to draw a little nearer to that perpetual absence in so many colonial texts, the Aborigines. In order to do so, I focus on two problems—those of the (il)legitimacy of subject positions and identities and the question of essentialism—both of which have a perpetual, if at times submerged, presence in postcolonial theory. Since I have found that dialectical methods are often the most fruitful ones, it seems useful to set together in some sort of tension both a biblical text and a postcolonial text, distant from each other in time of composition and reading habits but also curiously similar in that the questions of speaking voices and essentialism are important for both texts.

The biblical text is Josh 9, a story about the deception of Joshua and the invading Israelites by the Gibeonites, while the postcolonial text (or rather, texts) is the written corpus of Sreten Bozic, a Serbian immigrant to Australia and writer of poetry, short stories, and a number of novels in the name of B. Wongar, an Aboriginal person, sometimes female. But before I consider these texts more closely, I need to indicate what is meant by vocal dialectics (as a frame for the question of subject positions and identity). This refers to the continual movement or slippage in the nature of the "voice" (although I need to be suspicious about that word too) of postcolonial speakers or subjects. In other words, those who speak within/to/from—that is, with some sort of prepositional relation to—postcolonial situations find that their ability to speak or write is always (over)determined by a range of conflicting factors, derivative mostly from the former colonial contexts themselves. For example, the very ability to be heard outside one's own context is paradoxically enabled (and then limited) by the language and connections bequeathed by the former colonial masters—an ambiguity embodied in the famous "What have the Romans done for us?" sequence in *The Life of Brian*.[1]

Wongar/Bozic attracts me, for he provides a means to write my own troubled situation in a postcolonial country into this text: the marginal European who writes as an Aboriginal and who raises questions about identity and essence is the site for my own libidinal investment. But Bozic/Wongar also attracts me for a different reason, for one of the problems with much postcolonial criticism is that colonial discourse is understood as taking place between colonizer and colonized, or rather, between the postcolonial (now understood as a replacement for Third World) and overdeveloped world, and never between one colonized and another, or between one postcolonial and another (see Loomba 1998, 179–80). In Australia, postcolonial criticism has—as I have tended to do in the chapters up until now—favored the British-Australian relation, the center of colonial power and its colony. The elevation of this relation, focused mostly on the nineteenth and early twentieth centuries, has neglected the fact that approximately two thirds of Australians have not arrived or descended from the United Kingdom. This means that the question of what (post)colonialism meant and means for these people has been neglected, as have their relations with Aboriginal people, particularly where that varied from the dominant paradigm of British-Aboriginal relations. Wongar/Bozic provides a glimpse a different type of relation.

A word on the plan of this chapter: it differs from the preceding in that it does not seek out the use of the Bible, neither in explorer texts nor in those who speak of and claim exile and exodus. Rather, it dialectically plays off a biblical text against a postcolonial text, a little like the first chapter. I begin with Wongar/Bozic after my reflection on essentialism and nominalism, for in a sense the troubled and ambiguous presence of Bozic/Wongar is the persona (the allusion to theater is not accidental) who will read Josh 9.

Essentialism and Nominalism

Part of the attraction of a dialectical method is that it requires one to "step back," to flick the lever, slip into another gear, and seek out the possible reasons for a particular problem. In this case the question to be asked is why

---

1. In this scene, the leader, played by John Cleese, of the revolutionary group asks at a cell meeting, "What have the Romans done for us?" One by one various members of the group list the things the Romans have done—aqueducts, hospitals, education, peaceful streets—so that Cleese is forced to include an increasing number of concessions: "Apart from…, what have the Romans done for us?" It seems to me that colonialism is similarly ambiguous.

the issues of subject positions, identities, and speaking voices are issues in the first place, to which an initial response might be to move more explicitly into the realms of philosophy and history. The whole area of the slippage of speaking voices, and its related question concerning subject positions, have peering over their shoulders the philosophical problem of essentialism, a problem visited with increasing frequency in certain areas of the discourses of postmodernism and postcolonialism. That this is paired with a resurgence of nominalism is something I want to suggest a little later on, but it is essentialism and the closely related questions of the subject and identity that I will place in detention for a while and subject to some systematic interrogation.

It is with the political emergence, or at least naming, of particular groups characterized by social, racial, sexual, and gender difference that the problem of essentialism has become most acute. What does it mean to be identified as poor, black, indigenous, gay, lesbian, or feminist? An initial avenue is then provided by an essentialist explanation: the key is to locate that which makes a person or a group of people distinct, that which marks off individual and group identity from other identities. And it turns out that what we are looking for is some essential quality, some deeper "thing" (to evoke Žižek and Lacan) or "essence" that serves as an explanation for the nature of the person or group in question. The search for essence is often intimately bound up with origin: the location of the origins of a particular group of people or of a person then becomes a major component in specifying the identity of the group or person in question. This may happen in all sorts of complex ways: for instance, at a popular level it is common to explain a particular character trait or psychological state in terms of ethnic affiliation—the Dutch are arrogant, Australians are laid back, and so on. But essentialism has also been important in the older waves of feminism over the last century, or in the self-perception of lesbians and gays, or in the postcolonial political consciousness of indigenous peoples. Thus gender, Aboriginality, ethnic identity, and sexual orientation become the determining features of identity and psychological makeup.

The political gains of essentialist group identities have been significant, yet the basic strategy of such an approach as a whole is that it wants to claim existing terms and then reinvest them with a range of different meanings; however, this merely leaves the structure of such terminology intact. It has accepted the terrain of its enemy, as it were, in order to engage in the struggle, for there is little that is formally distinct between the claim, for example, that indigenous people are essentially lazy alcoholics and the claim that they are deeply spiritual people with long and profound cultural and religious histories. The substance is distinct and has often seemed to be worth battling over, but both statements operate on the essentialist assumption of a deep

Aboriginal essence—it is what constitutes the essence that is contested, not the question of essentialism itself. If there have been political gains with such a position, then there have also been some drawbacks, the most urgent of which is the restriction of people to specifiable groups and behavior patterns. If some attributes are identified as essentially male, female, indigenous, or ethnic, then these attributes and behaviors are not open to any other group. This has dire consequences for any political action that wishes to effect social change, since the aim to which the change is directed, such as an egalitarian human nature, may simply not be possible for a vast majority.

So it would seem that the traps of essentialism may be too great in the long run, which then opens up the possibility that the "notion of an essential self—a self presumed to have its origins in a specific culture, ethnicity, or nation—is debunked by the performative and discursive configurations that participate in the production of these selves" (Sawhney 1995, 216). The problem then becomes one of recognizing difference without recourse to essentialism, something more obvious in the postmodern debates surrounding the subject and what has been termed antiessentialism. The by now commonplace observations about the subject—that it is decentered, disintegrated, dispersed, and so on (and always has been so)—bear with them the assumption that without an illusory essence, any pretence at integration and unity has now quietly slipped out the back door. It is of course Donna Haraway's "A Manifesto for Cyborgs" that powerfully claimed this discourse for Marxism and feminism, but in speaking of the subject and antiessentialism in the context of postcolonialism, I am edging closer to the remarkable essay of Gayatri Chakravorty Spivak—"Can the Subaltern Speak," as well as its partner, "Subaltern Studies: Deconstructing Historiography"—in which the question of what it means to speak of a postcolonial subject rises to the surface. Spivak, accomplished interpreter of both Marx and Derrida, affirms a resolutely antiessentialist position, arguing strongly for the sheer constructedness of what once counted as "real," for the inescapable artificiality of institutions, experiences, ways of thinking and feeling, and especially the constitution of the subject. In a characteristic Derridean move,[2] in which an opposition is reversed in order to problematize the opposition, Spivak speaks of a "subaltern subject-effect":

> A subject-effect can be briefly plotted as follows: that which seems to operate as a subject may be part of an immense discontinuous network ("text" in the general sense) of strands that may be termed politics, ideology, econom-

---

2. But she also notes its presence in Deleuze and Guattari's *Anti-Oedipus*, which is "[t]he most, perhaps too, spectacular deployment of the argument" (1988a, 200 n. 16).

ics, history, sexuality, language, and so on. (Each of these strands, if they are isolated, can also be seen as woven of many strands.) Different knottings and configurations of these strands, determined by heterogeneous determinations which are themselves dependent upon myriad circumstances, produce the effect of an operating subject. Yet the continuist and homogenist deliberative consciousness symptomatically requires a continuous and homogeneous cause for this effect and thus posits a sovereign and determining subject. This latter is, then, the effect of an effect, and its positing a matalepsis, or the substitution of an effect for a cause. (1988a, 204)[3]

In the light of such an antiessentialist construction of the subject, Spivak concludes, after a long consideration of the ambiguous abolition of sati, or widow sacrifice, in India, that the subaltern, the postcolonial subject, for Spivak the colonized Indian woman, cannot indeed speak, since this requires an essentialist approach to the subject in question; or rather, she cannot speak since that which serves to construct her subject denies her speech.[4] The subject is thus both dispersed and overdetermined, and with this argument she criticizes the Subaltern Studies Group's search for a subaltern consciousness. Yet, in a moment of endorsement, in order to attain positive political results, Spivak speaks, in her discussion of the Subaltern Studies Group, of a "strategic use of positive essentialism in a scrupulously visible political interest" (1988a, 205; see also 206–7; 1984–85, 183–84), a sort of limited identification of an essential will or consciousness that recognizes at the same time that that subject, the "subaltern," is itself an unstable category (see on this Sharpe 1993, 17; also Parry 1996). This may be read in at least two ways: a positive antiessentialist essentialism, on the one hand, a voice that takes on an identity for a few moments only to move on soon afterwards (so Fuss 1989, 31–32); or a condescension to people in colonial spaces in which they

---

3. I have quoted this at length since it has significant repercussions not only for the discussion of Bozic's work but especially for my consideration of the "subject" Israel when I turn to Josh 9.

4. This piece has sparked considerable debate. Thus, Loomba (1998, 233) sees Spivak saying that the subaltern cannot speak because of colonialism and patriarchy. Others suggested that she does not let the subaltern speak or does not allow such speech (see Spivak 1996, 287). Griffiths and Tiffin (1998, 79) argue that this is not Spivak's point; rather, the subaltern can never be isolated in some essentialist fashion from the play of discourses and institutional practices that give it its voice. Spivak indicates the unruly confusion of the paper in an intellectual crisis of her own but goes on to outline the various senses of "not speak": "speak" means not talk but speech-acts (which involves speaking and hearing); the subaltern is never pure, always shifting, elided and therefore not heard (see Spivak 1996, 287–90).

are permitted to be essentialist if it suits their purposes. For those in sophisticated metropolitan zones it is no longer appropriate (see Larsen 1990, 22). Stuart Hall (1996) has suggested a more dialectical play that is sensitive to specific locations and moments in which the notion of identity itself functions: at times an essentialist self based in a shared culture has been and is necessary for oppositional marginal groups, while at others a shifting, differential identity that is itself an incomplete historical and representational production is more useful.

The conventional and well-established opposition to essentialism is constructivism, the suggestion that identities are constructed by social, political, economic, and cultural histories: it is one's position in such a matrix that forms identity (see, e.g., Hall 1996). Yet in order to destabilize the essentialist-constructivist opposition, a number of options are possible. Diana Fuss, for instance, makes use of Locke's distinction between "real" and "nominal" essence (Fuss 1989, 4–5). The former designates what is irreducible and unchanging, that is, Aristotle's notion of essence; nominal essence then regards essence as a linguistic phenomenon, a system of classification that allows for categorization. Real essence is ontological, nominal essence linguistic. In this light, ascertaining a real essence requires empirical evidence, while a nominal essence is allocated or generated through language. Fuss goes on to suggest that this distinction is close to the essentialist-constructionist divide, except that recasting the debate in these terms opens up some problems with it. Her own larger argument is a dialectical one in which essentialism turns out to have a constructionist dimension, or even base, especially the notion that essence is irreducible, for such irreducibility is itself constructed. Conversely, constructionism cannot avoid essentialism, especially in its favoring of linguistic and social conditions as producers of identity and in the taking of unavoidable metaphysical positions regarding identity.

I want to take Fuss's point regarding nominal essence in a slightly different direction, for constructionism or antiessentialism may also be understood as a postmodern retooling of the older philosophical option of nominalism, worked out in great detail in the fourteenth century by William of Ockham and his followers but now, in what has become a standard postmodern pattern, mutated in certain critical ways. Ockham's nominalism undermined Thomism's natural theology and metaphysical psychology through a rejection of the assumption that universals were things (and thus existed independently of their names) and a focus on individual particulars that are intuited directly by the mind (universals having formerly been inferred from particulars). Universals thus "exist" only as names, or conceptual terms.[5] Ockham and his followers emphasized the probability of that which in the thirteenth century had the status of clear demonstrations, in particular the logical inference from one thing to the existence of other things (other people, God, etc.). This led both to a split between the synthesis of philosophy and theology but also to a greater emphasis on the role of faith, as well as the liberty and omnipotence of God (Luther saw himself as a disciple of Ockham). In order to ensure such divine freedom and power, Ockham sought to banish the theory of essences derived from classical Greek thought, and it is here that contact is made between fourteenth-century nominalism and my own discussion of essentialism.

Whereas the older nominalism attacked in the name of logic the metaphysics of Aquinas and Scotus, its revived postmodern form comes into its own with the complexities of deconstruction. In a somewhat lengthy consideration of the work, not of Derrida (although that is coming too), but of Paul DeMan, Fredric Jameson (1991, 217–59) has argued for the return to nominalism in DeMan's deconstruction, mediated through the latter's work on Rousseau. While Jameson traces in detail DeMan's interest in metaphor in Rousseau's work, it is the tension with the other category in the *Second Discourse* (on language) that suggests nominalism—naming, understood as a designation of the particular and the distinct, then as a generalizing activity enabled by the very act of naming distinct particulars with the same name. Thus, in the standard example, "tree" names a distinct particular while providing simultaneously a general category. Such a connection between particulars is then none other than the use of metaphor, and here the relation between metaphor and language opens up the link with nominalism. In postmodernism the reappropriation of nominalism is tied with the drive toward immanence (the philosophical equivalent of the now well documented depthlessness of postmodernism) and the refusal of transcendence (modernism's depth).

If the connection is made between postmodern immanence and deconstruction's interest in the constructedness of all that was once held as essential, then nominalism seems to be the most appropriate philosophical term for what has generally gone by either antiessentialism or constructivism. Spivak's emphases will then take on a different hue if they are understood as an elaborate working out of the implications of nominalism in postmodern and postcolonial theory. The political dimensions of nominalism are, not unexpectedly, ambiguous, although Ernesto Laclau and Chantal Mouffe (Laclau

---

5. Logically, only individual things can exist; it is a contradiction to assert that universals exist (on the Ockhamist movement, see further Copleston 1963, 49–61, 122–52).

and Mouffe 1985; Mouffe 1988; 1993) have been working hard at what an antiessentialist socialist politics might look like. If what counts is the named, or "staged," identity, then it is possible for a political operator to shift and mix various possible identifiers. This has the positive import of enabling allegiances across various micro-groups who would otherwise not look beyond their own, inevitably limited, constituencies, but the negative one of losing an older political stability (given certain data, you used to know where everyone stood).

I have dealt with the opposition between essentialism and nominalism, between authentic identity and between staged identity, in a more formal way, since it seems to me to be a crucial dimension of the material I will discuss in a moment. Yet I do not want to come down on either side of the divide, although much cultural criticism at the moment seeks out and destroys the last vestiges of essentialism wherever possible. The end result here is to slip into some sort of moral approbation or condemnation rather than ask the question that seems far more interesting to me: why this is an opposition in the first place, and what it is about this historical situation that has highlighted the issue once again.

Green Ants...

> The ants are a people not strong, yet they prepare their meat in the summer. (Prov 30:25).

The consequences of the essentialism/nominalism opposition, and its manifestation in the question of speaking voices, are not insignificant for postcolonial theory. Indeed, discussions of colonialism and postcolonialism have assumed that it is possible to postulate essential colonized and colonizing subjects. This has been crucial not only for the perceptions of the colonizing nation-states but also for the movements of decolonization, where the needs and desires of the colonized peoples became the focus of attention. This often expressed itself in terms of a rediscovery or return to preconquest origins and a rewriting of the postconquest histories. Yet it seems that nominalism may provide a rather different way of understanding the dialectic of voices that I have hinted already exists in postcolonial discourse.

These issues are still at the heart of the critical and popular reception of the work of B. (variously Banumbir, Birimbir, Boro, but also Bozic) Wongar. In Australia the initial reaction to Wongar's work was guarded, particularly since the identity of the writer was not clear (although it seems to have been so in some of the European circles with whom Bozic had an acquaintance). The suspicions final came to written expression in the *Bulletin* article by

Robert Drewe (1981). The charges of deception, literary fraud, and misrepresentation voiced in this article make the expected essentialist assumptions about integrity and authenticity, something that seemed to be less of a problem in the reception of Bozic's earlier work overseas. Yet the debate raises the issue that is my own focus here, although I will treat it in a very different way: the construction of identity in the work of B. Wongar, or the construction of the "subject-effect," to borrow Spivak's terms.

A few biographical details[6] might be in order here (a first step in ascertaining the total subject-effect). Sreten Bozic seems to have been born circa 1936, most likely in Serbia, although some stories place his birth in Australia with a return as a child to Serbia. His father had been, apparently, in Australia, but his mother is unknown. Given the turmoil of the Second World War and the remote location of the home where he was raised, his formal education was minimal. Some time after the war he wandered through a still-devastated Europe until he ended up in Paris, working in an auto factory and involved in the circle associated with *Les Temps Modernes*, especially Simone de Beauvoir. Sometime in the late 1950s (some put it in 1958), he arrived in Australia, doing the same sort of thing he did in Europe, wandering around. He seems to have spent time in Arnhem Land (northern Australia), the central deserts, including Maralinga (the zone in South Australia where the British undertook nuclear testing in the 1950s), and then on into Victoria. He taught himself English but also learned significant slabs of Aboriginal languages, particularly from Arnhem Land. While there (approximately ten years, according to Bozic), he also married an Aboriginal woman, Djumala, who later died along with the children before they could follow him to Victoria. The earliest stories began appearing in *Les Temps Modernes*, especially those now collected in *The Track to Bralgu*, but eventually the writing moved from French to English. After a banned photo exhibition in Parliament House in Canberra on the nuclear testing at Maralinga in South Australia, Bozic found it difficult to get his Aboriginal stories accepted for publication in Australia, and so B. Wongar, "messenger of the spirit world," arrived on the scene. The profound ambivalence over the publication of Aboriginal stories by a Serbian immigrant meant that initial publication took place overseas: the University of Illinois Press, University of Ohio Press, and Dodd, Mead are some of the early publishers. Only recently has the Angus and Robertson imprint of HarperCollins in Australia taken him on as a writer, reissuing earlier works and publishing the newer material.

---

6. Understanding biography as the highest level of fiction, apart from autobiography.

There are any number of ways of dealing with Wongar's work, such as the recurring motifs of the transformation from human to animal or plant, the compound or jail (claustrophobia and confinement), uranium mining and natural devastation, the spirit world and the relief of death, sexual exploitation, the complicity of police, clergy and mining interests; but also of the healer (or marngit), survival and knowledge of the land, and the frog with life-giving water in its belly. In fact, I would like to pick up this final motif, particularly since it appears to be a marginal feature of these narratives, as a sort of organizing device for the others. For what is interesting about the frog episodes is their repetition in story after story—a sort of nervous tic or compulsive act, even finding its way into autobiographical comments (see the interview with Willbanks 1992, 203–4), that signals other things going on within and beyond the text. The situation of the incident is one of extreme thirst in a desert environment: a non-Aboriginal traveler faces a severe shortage of water; an Aboriginal person arrives and digs up from some sand a frog (in semihibernation awaiting the next downpour of rain), and from its belly a mouthful of water is extracted by cutting it open. With thirst only partially quenched but death averted, the traveler is then able to proceed on the journey, now accompanied by the Aborigine but at the expense, presumably, of the frog's own wellbeing.

Although I am slightly guilty of Althusser's expressive causality, this repeated episode highlights a number of elements that are important for my own concerns here. There is, to begin with, the promise of death from dehydration, which is formally connected with the theme of claustrophobia and the inevitable death that the prison cell brings. And then there is a glimmer of healing, chthonic knowledge and survival against all the odds. In other words, the repeated frog episode provides a focus for all the negative and positive features of Wongar's narrative and poetic structures:[7] onto the ones I have just listed may be added those other elements I noted a little earlier—natural and sexual devastation, the various levels of exploitation, as well as the relief of the spirit world and the release of being able to go there. Yet ultimately what is interesting about Wongar's work are not so much these individual items themselves but the transitions between them, and in the life-giving frog water there is the basic transition from death to life—linked then with the shift from devastation to restoration, claustrophobia to release—however tenuous that may be and whatever form it might take. Even this is highly unstable: the life is granted only until the next supply of water and food. Yet it is in this way

---

7. Ross (1990, 36) emphasizes the destructive and regenerative forces as well.

that I want to focus on the profound ambiguity of Wongar's speaking position, mediated through the formal device of a tenuous transformation.[8]

The formal device of transformation manifests itself as content in the stories of the shift back and forth between animal and human form. The most common of these is the transition between dingo and human, one (at least the shift from human to dingo) that often signifies death, although the dingo then stays with the camp and is understood to be a human relative (as, for example, "Poor Fellow Dingo" [1992b, 29–37] or "Five-Dog Night" [1982, 80–85]). Otherwise, the interchange takes place with a cockatoo (1982, 18–26), or a crocodile (1982, 27–38), or an emu (1982, 94–99), and so on. In these and other stories, death seems to be merely a transition from one state into another, so that the nature of death is always ambiguous. At other times the interchangeability of animal and human weaves them all into a vast and somewhat amorphous mass. Such interchangeability is part of the structure of many of the short stories in the various collections (*The Track to Bralgu* [1992b], *Babaru* [1982], *Marngit* [1992a], and *The Last Pack of Dingoes* [1993]), although some of the motifs appear in the longer works as well.

However, while the question of speaking positions is signaled in the sorts of transitions I have been discussing, the question itself is also directly broached in what may perhaps best be characterized as a comprehensive reworking of an older point-of-view approach. Although such an approach appears in the short stories—often written in the first person—it becomes more sustained in the novels themselves. The best example comes from the fifth novel, *Raki* (1994; an earlier version is reported to have been confiscated by the Victorian police [see Pullan 1989–90]). The novel shifts back and forth between a war-torn Serbia and Aboriginal Australia. In Serbia the story is told from the perspective of a boy during World War II (the autobiographical echoes should not be neglected here), although patterns of suffering from the long oppression by the Ottoman Empire and the war in the Balkans of the 1990s also make their presence felt. In Australia it seems to be the same person, but now in prison with other Aborigines, who produce art works for the prison director. A mother figure appears, apparently his Serbian mother but mistaken for an Aboriginal mother by the director, who forces her to plant konopla, or hemp plants, traditionally used in Serbia for clothing over the winter. Indeed much of the focus in the Serbian location is ensuring an adequate konopla crop. In the end it is taken by the Germans in the form of rope to bind up prisoners, in the same way that a rope is the way prison

---

8. I am indebted to Livio Dobrez (1990) for the idea of metamorphosis or transformation in Wongar's work.

inmates in Australia escape from their cells, after the tribal healer, or marngit, has called.

What comes through in *Raki*, as also in the other works to a lesser extent, is the sheer inability to nail down what sort of position this novel speaks from. This is not merely the case with the inability to specify particular characters whose identities keep shifting but also in the nature of the writing itself. It is not pure, or essential, Aboriginal writing—something that the earlier short stories attempt more directly—nor is it conventionally metropolitan or European writing. The oppressors in Serbia—Turks, Germans, neighbors—line up alongside those in Australia, especially prison officers, police and benevolent anthropologists and Aboriginal workers. If there is an essentialist dimension to this, then that comes from the story being told from the perspective of poor Serbian peasants and Aboriginal people, continually seeking out survival tactics yet at the same time, with a sort of wise naiveté, showing goodwill to even the most callous of people. Yet, just when this seems to be a good way to read this material, we realize that its language is English, the language of colonialism and not that of either Bozic himself, Serbian peasants, or Aboriginal people. It is, in fact, a learned language, one that comes with colonial associations for the very stories Wongar writes and yet one that is required in order to be heard.

The speaking voice is less scrambled and more monolithic in the earlier novels (*The Trackers* [1975], *Walg* [1986a], *Karan* [1986b], *Gabo Djara* [1988]), yet even here the ambiguities continue to appear: in *Walg* (womb), the first novel of the nuclear trilogy, Wongar takes on the persona of a woman, Djumala, who escapes the breeding compound and flees to her tribal ground in order to have her child, all the while pursued by various police and authorities.[9] Some of the short stories are written in a similar way—as a mother about to give birth, a mother transformed into an animal and trying to care for her young, and so on (see "Yudu, the Children" [1982, 69–79]; "The Ant-Woman" [1992a, 29–37]; "Walpadja, the Storm-Maker" [1992a, 39–49]; "Miralaidj" [1993, 11–12]; "The Tortoise" [1993, 81–82]; "Baru, the Crocodile" [1993, 89–103]). *Karan* reverts to the more conventional male, this time an Aboriginal male, Anawari Mallee, who is in all respects "white." After some tribal initiation markings mysteriously are incised on his chest overnight, he sets out to find their meaning, first on the computers at the Tribal Research and Assimilation Centre where he worked, then on a journey to his tribal land.

---

9. For Connor and Matthews (1989, 715) the complex interaction of frame and text in *Walg* troubles any notion of a fixed identity. Gunew (1993, 8–9) develops this issue further.

Relentlessly pursued he finally turns into a tree as the ruined land floods. A similar theme is found in *The Trackers*, although this time an Asian immigrant, Dao Ba Khang, begins to regain his lost color and then ends up, while persistently pursued, identifying with some Aboriginal people who are themselves being destroyed. Finally, in *Gabo Djara*, the animal dimension of many of the stories returns: here it is the mythological "Dreaming" figure of the green ant that finds itself in numerous points of contact with power (parliament, queen of England, mining tycoons, a general, the pope, etc.) in a white world only to destroy it in what appears to be a nuclear explosion. In these cases, as well as in *Raki* and in the varying perspectives of the short stories, the ambiguities of the vocal dialectics are pushed to the extreme: European and Aboriginal narratives, Serbia (or the Netherlands) and Australia, colonizer and colonized, white European and black Aboriginal, white male and Aboriginal female, human and animal. These essentially mutually exclusive categories find themselves operating together in Wongar's work. All of this is then epitomized in the duplicity of self-designation—B. Wongar and Sreten Bozic. In Spivak's terms, B. Wongar is as much a "subject-effect" as Sreten Bozic.[10]

Yet Wongar is but one exemplar of a wider phenomenon in Australian literature and art, namely, the taking on of an Aboriginal personality in order to produce various cultural products. Most recently (1996), the "authenticity" of Mudrooroo Narogin Nyoongah (Colin Johnson until 1988), a professor of Aboriginal studies, has been called into question in print, although rumor has been circulating for some time. The issue has not unexpectedly been clouded by the importance of origins—was he taken as a child from the Nyoongah people and sent to the U.S.A., or is he African American?—and the implications for an authentic identity. In the end, Mudrooroo has responded publicly, admitting the absence of any Aboriginal "blood" in his veins but arguing that "race" is a Victorian classification, that he had been "textualized" as an Aborigine in his earlier writing (see 1979; 1983; 1987; 1991; 1992; 1993). Yet what is interesting is not so much the appearance yet again of tired old terms but the response to the accusations by some Aboriginal writers, who claim him by and large for themselves. As Ruby Langford "Ginibi" writes, "[s]o if his

---

10. In an allusion to Spivak's "Can the Subaltern Speak?" Sneja Gunew concludes her paper with "'Wongar' may neither speak nor write" (1993, 12; Spivak begins her last paragraph with "The subaltern cannot speak" [1988b, 308]). For Gunew this happens when the "god author" becomes the dominant issue: "one is refusing textuality in terms either of interpretation or of the processes whereby meanings become constructed. In this case it both refuses the overt political meanings of this text and refuses to acknowledge the ways in which these meanings are consistently denied" (Gunew 1993, 12).

own family disowns him, I'll claim him as one of mine! ... Besides, look at B. Wongar—he's not an Aboriginal but his stories about us Aboriginals are sold all over the world! So don't be too quick to judge Mudrooroo" (1996, 12). The diametrical comparison between Mudrooroo and Wongar takes another twist in all of this, since Mudrooroo has been one of the more aggressive transformers of European and American literary forms in the light of Aboriginal literature, whereas Wongar has sought to sublate Aboriginal literature itself. Both Wongar, in adopting Aboriginal literature, and Mudrooroo, as one who takes on European forms, now find the focus on their slippery identities.

Yet the list includes more than Wongar and Mudrooroo: in a mini-explosion of a nativism that resembles the Jindyworobaks of the 1930s and 1940s, Sarah Durak, of a "pioneer" settler and pastoralist family in the semiarid regions of Australia, takes on an Aboriginal persona for her painting, arguing that she "is" the person in whose name she paints. Further, the large Aboriginal mural at the Mary MacKillop shrine in North Sydney was painted by Sakshi Anmatyerre, who turns out to be Farley Warren Patrick French, born in Calcutta, India, in 1950 and "naturalized" as an Australian citizen in 1975. And in 1995, a novel, *My Own Sweet Time*, by Wanda Koolmatrie appeared. Subsequently, it won the Dobbie Award for a first novel by a woman, only to be revealed that it was written by Leon Carmen, a white male of forty-five when it was published. Even Archie Weller, a well-known Aboriginal writer, has had his identity called into question. What is curious about all of this is that it seems to be a reverse mimicry, particularly in the way Bhabha has discussed the practice. What Bhabha has in mind here is the old colonial item of double vision, the colonial man, especially native, who adopts the persona of the enlightened English gentleman, who appears more English than the English but can never quite make it (See Boehmer 1995, 115–16). For Bhabha, the result of all of this is mimicry of empire, a complex process of imitation while pulling the rug from beneath that which is imitated. In other words, it plays with the power relation of colonizer and colonized: "[Mimicry] is a complex strategy of reform, regulation and discipline, which 'appropriates' the Other as it visualizes power. Mimicry is also the sign of the inappropriate, however, a difference or recalcitrance which coheres the dominant strategic function of colonial power, intensifies surveillance, and poses an immanent threat to both 'normalized' knowledges and disciplinary powers" (1994, 86). However, with Wongar and the others, mimicry reverses, taking up the old motif of "going native" with a twist that questions the binaries of civilized-native, colonizer-colonized.

In order to set up a wider theoretical context in which Wongar's work might be placed, I want to draw some comparisons (with their own postcolonial logic in the [re]turn to England) between Wongar's work and a similar case in England that has been dubbed the "Vicar and Virago Affair." In this case some stories written under the name of Rahila Khan, a feminist from the Indian subcontinent, about young South Asian girls and adolescent white boys in Thatcher's Britain, were accepted by the British Broadcasting Corporation (BBC) and Virago, the Woman's Press. When pressured to make some public appearances the author turned out to be a middle-class Anglican white male vicar, Toby Forward. An autobiographical article in *The London Review of Books* basically saw the end of the story, with Forward discredited and the press embarrassed. The similarities and differences between Forward and Wongar probably balance out, although it is worth indicating the vast difference of the established vicar and the marginalized Wongar. However, my interest is the way the Vicar and Virago affair has generated what may well be the two possible critical responses to the situation of both writers. These are articulated in papers by Dympna Callaghan and Sabina Sawhney in the collection *Who Can Speak? Authority and Critical Identity* (Roof and Wiegman 1995).

For Callaghan, Forward's effort replicates in new forms an old pattern whereby white heterosexual males colonize and dominate the cultural expressions and identities of women, non-European and especially colonized peoples, gays and lesbians. Perhaps the strongest argument in this position is that the white heterosexual male assumes that all others are marked in some fashion by gender, sexual orientation, socioeconomic status, ethnic affiliation, education, religion, and so on, except for the white male himself, who is *tabula rasa*, as it were, or at least not affected by any of these factors. He thus assumes that he is able to take on the identities of others in a situation of commodified ethnic identity—particularly since whiteness has lost its racial specificity and is equated with blankness—in what can only be regarded as more sophisticated forms of control. The catch in all of this is that "endeavors to compensate for the exclusion of racial 'minorities' from the means of literary production can become the very means for continuing this exclusion" (Callaghan 1995, 197). Ultimately, identities for Callaghan are produced in terms of race, gender, and sexuality, but she wants to keep the political resonance of the category of identity. For Sawhney, on the other hand, this smacks a little too much of the sort of essentialism I have discussed earlier, despite the weight of Callaghan's arguments for oppositional politics. Her examples include not only the case of Toby Forward but also a joke by Spivak that makes a play on her Indian origins as a basis for the spurious cultural practice of interruption in excited discussion. The very difficulty Spivak's listeners have in discerning a "spurious" cultural practice or Forward's readers have in distinguishing the work of an English vicar from that of a somewhat naïve Indian girl signals the deeply constructed nature of the various factors that go to make up any identity, "the extent to which any cultural identity is part of a performance, a staging of the self" (Sawhney 1995, 216). This of course spills over into Callaghan's position, although perhaps not with the consequences that she anticipates: the nominalism (to revert to my earlier terminology) implicit in Sawhney's argument applies as much to the pale breeder male as to the others whom he emulates. Yet Wongar/Bozic has an advantage over Forward in that the chronic uncertainty of his identity makes its way into the form and substance of his writing. His biological existence is by no means an unexamined and comfortable one, being as uncertain and transitional (for me as for Bozic/Wongar) as the other identities found in the various stories and novels. He produces in the end a very unstable subject-effect.

I have so far been favoring an antiessentialist or nominalist/constructionist position in my discussion of Wongar/Bozic, and that position seems to make it easier to understand the various contradictions and mutually exclusive dimensions of Wongar/Bozic's life and work. Each of these mutually exclusive positions may then be reread as constructed identities, comparable to those identities continually assembled by Wongar in narrative and poetic form. The problem is that once we understand the constructed nature of terms such as "European," "Aboriginal," "white," "black," "woman," "man," "English," "Serbian," as well as "first-generation Australian," "heterosexual," and "homosexual," then we are left with nothing more than a postmodern appropriation of nominalism: they mean nothing more than their names. For this reason I want to reiterate one question from the previous section and add another to it: Why is it that nominalism and essentialism seem to be the only two options available for us at this postcolonial moment? And what is it about our socioeconomic situation that makes an antiessentialist, constructionist, or nominalist position more attractive? I will return to these questions at the end of the chapter.

... And Gibeonites

> Here is our bread; it was still warm when we took it from our houses as food for the journey, on the day we set out to come to you, but now, see, it is dry and moldy. (Josh 9:12)

The strange thing is that the issues I have raised are not restricted to postmodern or postcolonial texts such as those of Wongar/Bozic, since it seems now that we can read ancient texts, such as those in the Hebrew Bible, in the same way. It is as though the Hebrew Bible (and many other ancient texts, for that matter) contains postcolonial texts *avant la lettre*, that its authors have had access to the same theoretical material we have, that they have read Derrida,

Foucault, Spivak, Bhabha, Said, Laclau and Mouffe, and Haraway, and that they express ideas we thought were only newly discovered. This is the sort of impression I get when reading Josh 9 in the Hebrew Bible, particularly when it is juxtaposed with the work of Wongar/Bozic; or, to put it more starkly, it is the way I, whose subject-effect is now in part determined by and whose blockage in reading has been written into this text through Bozic/Wongar, read this biblical text. Joshua 9 is an appropriate text: not only has the material in Joshua been used time and again to justify invasion and colonial expansion (see ch. 3), but the idea of a ruse by the indigenous peoples makes it attractive for a consideration of issues in postcolonialism as well.[11]

As with my discussion of the work of Wongar/Bozic, my main focus is on the way identities are constructed in the text, or, to use Spivak's terminology, the way various strands or lines come together to generate the subject-effect. In some respects Josh 9 explicitly foregrounds the issue of identity (like the work of Wongar/Bozic), and I will consider this a little later, but my concern for the moment is that which builds up the identity of Israel and that of the Gibeonites. I have selected two motifs—deception and repetition (one concerned with content and one with form)—and a way of organizing those motifs.

Yet before I reflect on these different areas, I need to give some consideration to more conventional historical criticism, which normally distinguishes between three layers of activity, although there have been various suggestions as to multiple layers of the text. Identification of these layers normally follows the designations of leadership or negotiators with whom the Gibeonites deal: the oldest layer is determined by the dominance of "men of Israel" (9:4–6, 7, 11–14, 16), followed by Joshua (9:3, 8–10, 15a, 22–27), and completed with the "princes of the congregation" (9:15b, 17–21). The first forms the basis and the others serve as supplements to this foundation. More details may be found in the work of Noth (1953), Gray (1967), and Sutherland (1992), although what interests me more in their work is not so much the historical-critical suggestions themselves as the signals such suggestions give out about their modernist presuppositions and realist relics.[12] There is, however,

---

11. The texts of Joshua have been forbidding territory for many critics, preferring as they do the storytelling excellence of Judges and Samuel within this smaller horizon of biblical narrative. Apart from those with an interest in military exploits and the techniques of destruction and occupation, it is in many respects the very content that causes problems for those who find stories of divinely ordained destruction problematic. That this is very much an ethical problem has been explored by Stone (1991).

12. By this I mean the modernist assumption of a depth model: the text then becomes a deceptive surface (in its projection of a unified story about Joshua et al.) that needs to be

another dimension to historical-critical study that owes a significant debt to conventional reading habits and the bulk of literary-critical activities both within and outside biblical studies. I am thinking here of the focus on character and plot that dominates so much literary reflection, a domination that should be questioned because of the very natural feel that such readings have. This is one of the main reasons why I have opted for the alternative categories or strands noted above.

There are two elements in the construction of the deception—space and the domestic: untruth attaches to the claim to have traveled from "a very far country" (9:9; see 9:6) and to the claim that the provisions and clothes have worn out on the journey (9:12–13). The request for a treaty (9:6, 12) and the reiteration of Yahweh's deeds (9:9–10) are not deceptive as far as the story is concerned.

As for space, my interest is specifically in the function of journeying or travel:[13] the Israelites are presented in the words of the Gibeonites as having been in Egypt (9:9), while the Gibeonites themselves pretend to have traveled a long distance (9:6, 9, 22), having in fact traveled for only three days (or rather, this is how long it takes the Israelites to travel to Gibeon from Gilgal [9:17]). Joshua's reproach in 9:22 is cast in terms of space and distance: "Why did you deceive us, saying, 'We are very far from you,' while in fact you are living among us?" Space then becomes an element in the deception of the Gibeonites themselves; the purpose of the worn-out sacks and wineskins, the patched sandals, worn-out clothes, and moldy supplies is to give the impression of having traveled over a great distance. Indeed, these items become the proof called upon in the negotiations for a treaty in 9:9–13. The converse

---

overcome or bypassed in order to see the "real" picture "beneath" it. In this case the "real" situation is a complex and fragmentary textual history that competes with the unifying effect of the surface (this problem of the fragmentary and total is a modernist problem in itself, cranked up to another level in postmodernism). The realist assumption is that the history of the text, once uncovered, approximates fairly closely with "what really happened"—an ideological frame of mind that persists in many areas of scholarship and popular culture. See further my *Novel Histories* (2006, 21–46, 98–103, 169–200).

13. Other spatial features are as follows: the kings of 9:1 come from the hill country beyond the Jordan and from the coastal plains as far as Lebanon; Gibeon is but one place in this expanse, ominously associated with the now-defunct Jericho and Ai in 9:3; Joshua and company are in Gilgal in 9:6; the stretch from Egypt to Heshbon and Bashan appears in the recital of Israel's journey in 9:9–10; Gibeon is joined by Chepirah, Beeroth, and Kiriath-Jearim in 9:17, and it is at Gibeon that the final dialogue takes place. These spatial items are also the concern of historical critics seeking—with a deep desire to make some tangible connection with the real—to identify places and construct maps with the assistance of archaeological data.

of this is not so much the lack of real distance between the Israelites' present location and Gibeon but rather the suggestion that news of the deeds of Yahweh on behalf of Israel have traversed this fabricated distance to the "very far country" of Gibeon. That this is a confession of the type found in other stories of the conquest (see, e.g., Rahab's confession in Josh 2:9–11) is not of immediate interest here, although I will return to this later. What is significant is the way such a narrative statement of Yahweh's deeds becomes part of the deceptive strategy of the Gibeonites. The ambiguity of finding a perfectly acceptable (at least in terms of the ideological structures of Joshua, if not the Deuteronomistic History as a whole) confessional statement used to enhance the deception—Yahweh's deeds are so stunning that even we have heard of them in our far-flung corner—is one of the more appealing dimensions of this story.

So the confessional statement joins space as integral to the beguiling of the Israelites. But there is also what might be termed the domestic, or the homework economy, normally regarded as a peripheral device to the main storyline. Yet if Freud has left any legacy at all, then part of it would have to be the significance of the insignificant, the function of the peripheral symptom in the structure of dreams, literature, or any dimension of culture. By "domestic" I refer to the interest in the provisions for the constructed journey of the Gibeonites: the bread, wine, wineskins, sandals and cloaks that are each qualified by adjectives describing their status in the cycle of economic production and reproduction. At first mention (9:4–5) they are "worn out," "torn," "tied up," "patched," "dry" and "moldy" or "crumbly," only to become "fresh" or "hot" and "new" in the mouths of the Gibeonites as they relate their story (9:12–13), and then once again dry, burst, worn, and old. In terms of the chapter as a whole (although that in itself is a troubled division), the newness of the provisions and clothing is only in the words of the Gibeonites and thus part of their deception, yet the cycle itself, when removed from its context, indicates the basic pattern of economic reproduction—the needed replenishment and replacement of food and clothing. Now, while it is true that there is something reasonably permanent about this cycle, it is also worth reflecting on the way different socioeconomic systems, or modes of production, have formed in order to deal with the production of essential and unessential items, as well as provide the social circumstances for the dominance of certain groups or classes over others. Yet what is interesting in Josh 9 is only partly covered by reflecting on the roles of the various negotiating persons in Israel (men of Israel, Joshua, or the princes of the congregation; see Sutherland 1992), or on the marks and traces of the Asiatic mode of production (see Boer 1996:187–91). The other dimension to this is the heavily gendered nature of the supply and deterioration of the provisions: the focus is squarely on the homes where the supplies are hot, fresh, and new—that is, recently produced—and then on the distance from home that sees them become worn out, dry, and torn. That it is the men who make the journey and who are then in the presence of the worn-out material acts as a strong symptom that the women are involved in the process of domestic (re)production, in the homework economy. But this is a highly conventional pattern: the men travel and work outside the home; the women remain in the *domus* and work there, or in its near environs.

Thus there are all the marks of a domestic dimension of mode of production here, but all of this forms part of the deception by the Gibeonites. In other words, while the *domus* is apparently present, or at least implied, in the freshness of the Gibeonites' provisions at the beginning of their journey, that journey itself has been fabricated as far as the narrative is concerned. This means that the narrative excludes women at another level, that of the narrative action. The provisions have always been worn out, torn, and dry, twice removed from their initial domestic production, yet they form the major evidence in the Gibeonite ruse, their current status attesting, in the mouths of the Gibeonites, to the distance they have traveled from when they were first produced. It is curious, then, that a more conventional historical criticism should discount the story of the provisions—its possible historical reference and therefore usefulness is almost always discounted—in inverse proportion to their importance. The story would collapse without them.

I want to ask eventually what sort of contradiction might be lurking in the need for a story of deception about taking the land (itself constructed out of spatial and domestic codes), but I also want to pursue on a more formal level any other significant (as in that which signifies) features, and this is where repetition comes into play. The most obvious place to begin is the double ending of the story. An initial reading indicates nothing untoward: the first ending in 9:18–21 flows reasonably well into the second one (9:22–27), although there is a difference between the "leaders of the congregation" in the first and "Joshua" in the second that I have noted earlier. Even so, the narrative moves quite nicely from a deliberation between the leaders and the congregation first, then a subsequent summons of the Gibeonites by Joshua, who questions them and delivers the verdict. The feel of unity jars, however, when the reader's eyes reach the final verse of the second story: "But on that day Joshua made them hewers of wood and drawers of water for the congregation and for the altar of Yahweh, to continue to this day, in the place that he should choose" (9:27). Yet this seems to have been decided already. Compare 9:21: "The leaders said to them, 'Let them live.' So they became hewers of wood and drawers of water for all the congregation, as the leaders had decided concerning them."

Apart from the issue of who is responsible for decision making in this story, a reconsideration of the two endings shows a significant difference of emphasis. In the first, the "leaders of the congregation" are concerned to hold firm to the treaty "sworn to them by Yahweh, the God of Israel" (9:18, repeated in 9:19). Its sanctity is affirmed three times in succession (9:18, 19, 20), with the consequences of its breach being Yahweh's wrath (9:20). The decision to make the Gibeonites "hewers of wood and drawers of water" is thus a resolution of the dilemma generated by the unbreakable treaty or oath and the pressure from the congregation that "murmured against the leaders" (9:18). The content of the treaty is never disclosed, except for the crucial piece of information that it guaranteed them their lives (9:15)—this seems to be all that is needed for the narrative to move along to the next stage, any further details only confusing the issue—which then becomes the crux of the dilemma in the first ending.

In the second ending the shift is marked by those with the privilege of reported speech in the narrative: only the leaders do any speaking in the first ending of 9:18-21, although it seems to be in response to the congregation as such (see 9:19), while in 9:22-27 it becomes a conversation between Joshua and the Gibeonites. Joshua immediately takes the high moral ground, accusing the Gibeonites of deception and decisively stating that they are cursed (9:22-23). The Gibeonites backpedal, claiming self-defense, yet putting themselves at Joshua's mercy (9:25), who now becomes their savior, keeping them from death at the hands of the Israelites. In this second ending, notable for the inclusion of the house of God and the altar of Yahweh as places for hewing and drawing, the treaty is much more distant, never mentioned, and only alluded to in the initial question, "Why did you deceive us?" Thus, apart from the massed tide of vengeful but mute Israelites and the final punishment, the two endings are quite distinct in emphasis, dialogue partners, and tone. At the same time they finish on virtually the same note.

Rather than pursue the implications of such a repeated ending that is both different and yet the same in terms of sources and their redaction, I want to make use of a Freudian idea, namely, the "compulsion to repeat" as a mark of something else going on, or of something that has happened in the past. For Freud the traumatic neurosis comes about through the ego's effort to protect itself from the full consequences of the trauma. It does so by repeating the traumatic situation in dreams and thereby continually drawing the person back into the situation as though it had not been adequately dealt with (see Freud 1973, 314-15, 428-29). All of this begs to make the transition to literary and cultural criticism, where the search becomes one for the textual trauma that generates the repetition in a text rather than a dream. I am going to suggest that such a "trauma" may be the issue of Israel's own formation, and here deception has a crucial function.

Two further repetitions in content rather than form enhance the suggestion of a trauma regarding origins. Both are indicated by a sort of narrative tic, nervous repetitions with some small variations between them. The first of these is the treaty or oath itself, concerning which the verb "to swear" appears three times in succession (9:18–20). The nervousness of the text over such a treaty, or rather the insistence on its inviolability, may fruitfully be connected with the role of the "confession" that I noted a little earlier: to provide a means whereby entry into Israel is enabled. But then the dialectical twist here is that treaty and confession have something other to say about the formation of Israel itself. A similar point applies to the other textual tic, in this case the triple appearance of the phrase "hewers of wood and drawers of water" (9:21, 23, 27), which, while it indicates a clear colonial subjugation of an invaded people, may also reflect a displaced awareness of the origins of those who called themselves "Israel."

Apart from space and the domestic, there is a third category for this text, that of ideology. My call upon the ideological as a final phase of analysis for Josh 9 is intended to indicate the import of deception and repetition in the text. In doing so I am going to make use of two ideas from Marxist literary interpretation. The first is that ideology is inevitably conflictual. This has its material conditions in class conflict for which ideology then functions as class discourse, articulating the hopes and fears of particular social groups. The second is that texts, narratives, and ideological formations may be described as imaginary resolutions of social and economic contradictions. At the same time, the traces of such contradictions leave their marks in the texts in question, and this takes place in the very act of attempting a resolution. The paradox here is that the text would not exist if it were not for the attempted resolution, yet by undertaking such a task it necessarily shows the signs of the very thing it attempts to overcome.

I want to argue, then, that the text of Josh 9, in particular the two items of deception and repetition, signals both ideological conflict and functions as an imaginary resolution of a social contradiction. This ideological conflict and social contradiction are tied, it seems to me, to the question of Israelite origins. The imaginary resolution operating in Josh 9 is then the story as it is: the Gibeonites are indigenous people, or at least the "first nations" of Canaan, ensuring their own survival through a ruse. Joshua and company are therefore deceived by the natives into preserving their lives, despite the colonial command of God. At this level the text may become a postcolonial celebration of the duping of dull colonial forces. Yet I have already suggested that deception and repetition are symptoms of other things happening with this text. Deception may here be understood in a curiously self-referential fashion: the story of the invasion of the land and the deception by the Gibeonites is itself a deception over Israel's own origins. Similarly, the trauma both denied and continually repeated is, I would suggest, the same issue of origins and a troubled identity. It is then possible to offer a second reading of Josh 9, in which a social contradiction rises to the surface. In this case the Israelites may be no more than Gibeonites (and thus a part of the history of Palestine; see Whitelam 1996 and the preceding chapter), or the Gibeonites may be understood as Israelites; or, their story indicates a secondary narrative concerning the process by which "Israel" itself is gradually constituted in the text. The way the Gibeonites become part of "Israel" is one example of the way various groups constitute the textual construction of "Israel" in the first place, as do Rahab and her family in Josh 2. This suggestion has echoes in the model that sees Israelite origins as an amorphous mix of different peoples who retreated into the highlands of Judea, perhaps with the occasional revolutionary conflict. But the resonance may also be heard with arguments such as those of Philip Davies (1992) in which "biblical Israel" (over against the "Israel of history" and "ancient Israel") is a construct of Persian-period scribes. If I follow this line, then what appears in Josh 9 with my reading are some of the contradictions inherent in such a construct, marked by both deception and repetition. These contradictions would themselves be the traces of class conflicts, although whether such class conflicts (constructed inevitably in line with certain theories) are more characteristic of the alternative origins of my first echo or of Davies's proposal requires further work.

The very effort to construct a dominant story of origins brings the discussion back to antiessentialism or nominalism, since the various items I have traced enact a dialectic of voices, pointing to a profound uncertainty about Israelite identity, to the possibility that "Israel" is a discursively constructed entity, or an "invention," as Whitelam argues. Deception therefore has, not unexpectedly, a double role to play: it indicates the duplicity of Israel's own perception of the taking of the land, and it acts as a trace of the social contradiction that the story attempts to resolve. The repetition of the endings is then a second symptom of this double story, now from the perspective of a hidden trauma. Thus, deception and repetition indicate that Israel's overt textual presentation of its origins is part of the construction of its own identity: "Israel" exists only when it is named. In this light the other items also fall into place: it is not so much the Gibeonites who are "hewers of wood and drawers of water," but the Israelites, or rather the Gibeonites as Israelites as Gibeonites; the treaty is important not so much for the Gibeonites but for the various elements that make up Israel.

It would seem that this text is also about the question of speaking positions. Whom do the Gibeonites represent: conquered native people who avoid death by a trick or Israelites uncertain about their own identity? As with the material of Bozic/Wongar, this ceases to be a problem if "Israel" itself is understood as a construct, as a name produced by this text for a very diverse and constantly shifting entity. We are, of course, back with the problem of essentialism and nominalism, and it seems to me that Josh 9 reads better as a nominalist text than an essentialist one. Sawhney's comments apply as much to Israel and the Gibeonites as to contemporary subjects such as Wongar/Bozic: "[i]mpersonation in any manifestation of cultural articulation demonstrates the manner in which such articulation is constructed, thus subverting the notion of a homogeneous or transparent identity.... Constituted as we are, through a multiplicity of subject positions—some of which may be contradictory—any attempt to fix identity relies on a denial of these contradictions and self-differences" (1995, 216).

Conclusion

I have set up this reflection on postcolonialism, Wongar/Bozic, and Josh 9 in terms of speaking voices, subject positions, and identity, all of which is generated out of the opposition between essentialism and nominalism. I have argued that Wongar/Bozic's work insistently foregrounds the question of identity and, with the particular subject effect that I have named Bozic/Wongar peering over my shoulder or even using my eyes, that Josh 9 indicates the presence of a similar question through deception and repetition. What comes through in my readings is the profound ambivalence of the question of identity in both postcolonial and biblical texts, as well as in the postcolonial interpreter. It is of course the ways of thinking associated with postcolonialism that have raised these sorts of issues for both contemporary interpretation and that of the Hebrew Bible.

However, in conclusion I want to pick up another dialectical step and return to a problem I have mentioned on a couple of occasions in this chapter, namely, why the problem of essentialism and constructionism/nominalism should have arisen in its old-yet-new postmodern/postcolonial form. I have by and large been favoring an antiessentialist or nominalist line, since it seems at this historical conjuncture to provide better interpretive options, yet by shifting the designation from constructionism to nominalism, I have also undermined the claims of constructionism to its social base for the construction of subjectivity. Such a move becomes clearer if we ask why it is that constructionism, with its heritage from Derrida, Lacan, and Foucault (see Fuss 1989, 6–18), seems so popular now, at this particular postmodern juncture. An answer might begin with the acknowledgement that the problem itself is an intellectual one, thereby finding its place in what is termed in Marxist thought the superstructure, which is intrinsically related to the base.

The search is then on for something in the base or infrastructure to which such a tension or problem is a response. And in many respects the favoring of nominalism signals what appears to be a final break between signifier and signified, the link between them being that upon which essentialism relies. In a world of free-floating signifiers, only nominalism is possible. But this is part of the complex interweaving of economic, social, and intellectual elements that are dominated by the commodity form. Is not nominalism then a necessary transferal or translation of commodification into the realm of thought, in particular in literary and cultural analysis? It is perhaps for this reason that we find nominalism so much more obvious and desirable, saturated as we are with the rampant commodification of late capitalism. Yet assuming a desire (the desire called Marx) finally to overcome such a situation (capitalism and its associated cultural forms), the question becomes one of the means to take a step beyond both essentialism and antiessentialism or nominalism, to move past or sublate the opposition itself, without reverting to essentialism or resorting to a futile conservative reaction.

6
Dreaming the Logos:
On Bible Translation and Language

Yet gods do change names from culture to culture, from religion to religion, and from period to period of that religion. Ancient and modern gods are forever translating themselves elsewhere, taking themselves to new sects and nations. Self-translation is a mark of divine, universal power. (Barnstone 1993, 144)

And so I come, at last, to translation, itself a metaphor evoked, not without some difficulty, by critics such as Bhabha to characterize the postcolonial, in-between, spaces of the global scene, as negotiated language, porous borders, or cultural ambivalence (1994, 173–75, 227–28; see Wilson and Dissanayake 1996, 2). The mention of Bhabha is not fortuitous, for the reconstruction of the postcolonial critic in this book through the various stages of reflection, surveying gaze, travel, and identity comes to its close with the task of translation itself. For in being able to translate the words of the indigenes into the language of the colonizer, and in being able to trans-late, the critic is able to trans-fer (the words come from the same Latin root, *trans-ferro*) to the world of the colonizer. However, what interests me in this chapter is not so much the translation from indigenous languages into that of colonizer but the reverse process, the translation from the colonizer's texts—in this case the Bible—into the indigenous languages.

The question is: What happens when the text is translated into an Aboriginal language? It is not merely the transferal of the text into the language of the colonized, enabling the word to be spread a little further, for there are a range of problems that immediately come to the fore, including those raised by translation theory, the practice of translation into Aboriginal languages in Australia, the construction of such languages by linguists and translators, appropriation and agency by Aboriginal people themselves, and the tensions and curious inversions between orality and literacy. I close out with reflections on the "Word" itself, translated, appropriated, and then sliding away.

In Theory

> But no amount of tough talk can get around the fact that translation is the most intimate act of reading. Unless the translator has earned the right to become the intimate reader, she cannot surrender to the text, cannot respond to the special call of the text.... To surrender in translation is more erotic than ethical. (Spivak 1993, 183)

One of the more notable things about the development of and present state of linguistic theory is the status of linguistic specialists who began as Bible translators or whose main interest is Bible translation. The figures of Kenneth Pike and Eugene Nida have a luminescence about them, a glow that speaks of lifelong commitments to the Summer Institute of Linguistics (SIL) and Wycliffe Bible Translators. Avowed evangelicals and significant linguists in their own right, they followed and then worked with the lesser linguist but better organizer, William Cameron Townsend, whose idea SIL seems to have been in the first place. Pike (1964; 1982) developed his theory of tagmemics, whose claim was to provide an overarching view of human language (his favorite image was of a mountaineering patriarch, Moses perhaps, or the occasional explorer, climbing a height that allowed him to command a view over the whole landscape of human language). "Broadly conceived, tagmemics is discourse about linguistic patterns" (Longacre 1985, 137). The ultimate desire, the utopian wish, is to provide in each language a system of labeled patterns that parallel the system of intuitively felt patterns used by speakers and hearers, who are assumed to be pattern-bearing beings. In order to do so, tagmemics follows the increasing complexity from morpheme to stem to word to phrase to clause to sentence to paragraph to discourse itself; hence the subsequent designation of "discourse linguistics" (see Longacre 1989). Tagmemics thus seeks to provide a theoretical understanding of the structure of language from its smallest to its largest components, although the new move was to break through the upper limit of the sentence. Paragraph and the whole textual unit, or discourse, became the focus, and, as with much linguistics, a cluster of forbidding terms were brought in to strengthen the infrastructure of the new area—syntagmeme (combined tagmemes forming structured wholes), exponence (primary, recursive, back-looping, and level skipping), and a preference for wave theory in order to understand language. Among others, Richard Longacre has provided some of the more sustained examples of this in biblical studies, especially with his reading of the Joseph story (Longacre 1989).

Whereas Pike, Longacre, and others have had some influence in Bible translation projects and in the production of indigenous grammars (for instance the Pitjantjatjara grammar [1970] of Glass and Hackett, translators for the United Aborigines Mission at Leonora in the Warburton Ranges of Western Australia), by far the most dominant theoretical underpinning of translation comes from the prolific work of Eugene Nida.

There are two items of interest in Nida's written corpus, the first of which is a significant divide between his strictly technical works on linguistic theory—there are books on morphology (1949), descriptive syntax (1951), English syntax (1966), componential analysis (1975a), semantic structures (1975b), and lexical semantics (Louw, Nida, and Smith 1989)—and those that allow a distinctly evangelical voice to come to the fore, replete with anecdotes from the field, as the motivation for his linguistic work (Nida 1952),[1] as well as his commitment to and theological justification for Bible translation. This comes through in the various handbooks on anthropology for Christian missions (1954), learning foreign languages (1957), or a translator's commentary (1947). If these two areas seem like distinct fields that might just as well be occupied by two authors, or perhaps a single author living a double life, as evangelical translator and linguistics expert, then this is belied by the volumes that seek to develop a "science of translating" the Bible into indigenous languages, the focus of a youthful thirty-three-year-old Nida (1947a) that then carries through the next five decades (see Nida 1964; Nida and Taber 1969; Louw and Nida 1989).

It is with this weight of technical ability that Nida has been able to influence and express a hegemonic principle of Bible translation in both the Summer Institute of Linguistics and the Bible Society. I am speaking of course of the notion of dynamic equivalence—"Translation consists in reproducing in the receptor language the closest natural equivalent of the source-language message, first in terms of meaning and secondly in terms of style" (Nida and Taber 1969, 12; see also Nida 1964, 166; Kilham 1991, unit 3, page 1)—the idea, in other words, that what counts is accuracy to the meaning of a text in translation. Nida and Taber cast it in the following terms:

> The older focus in translating was the form of the message, and translators took particular delight in being able to reproduce stylistic specialities, e.g., rhythms, rhymes, plays on words, chiasmus, parallelism, and unusual grammatical structures. The new focus, however, has shifted from the form of the message to the response of the receptor. Therefore, what one must deter-

---

1. "The Bible is the message of life because it reveals the Living Christ who gave His life that we might live. This is the book which must be translated, published, distributed, and read in all the languages of earth" (Nida 1952, 177). It is interesting to note that in this global work, Australia does not appear.

> mine is the response of the receptor to the translated message. This response must then be compared with the way in which the original receptors presumably reacted to the message when it was given its original setting.... Correctness must be determined by the extent to which the average reader for which a translation is intended will be likely to understand it correctly. (Nida and Taber 1969, 1)

The main consequence of such a shift is to focus on the content of the message: the form must therefore be changed if that is necessary to convey the content correctly to the receptor. "Anything that can be said in one language can be said in another" (Nida and Taber 1969, 4). If form is crucial, then the possibility of translation is greatly diminished. The focus on content, which is now equated with meaning, plays down the great other of dynamic equivalence, namely, "formal correspondence" (see Nida 1964, 165–77: Nida and Taber 1969, 22–24), all of which is predicated on the priority of the audience or receptor.

Although there is some continuity between the three handbooks for Bible translators (Nida 1947; 1964; Nida and Taber 1969), there is also some theoretical development. In *Bible Translating* (1947), Nida postulates "closest equivalence" (12, 130–48) as a mean between literal translation and the translation of ideas. In the more theoretical *Toward a Science of Translating*, Nida notes that translation operates around two poles or contradictions: between literal and free translation, and between concentration on form or content (1964, 22–26). Whereas he prefers a space somewhere in between the first opposition, with the second he firmly leans upon content. By the third volume the emphasis falls on the latter opposition, with an elaboration of the argument that the "meaning" of the text is to be located in its content (although this is reflected on at length in 1964, 30–119), but that it is conveyed dynamically. As is characteristic of Nida's work, he follows up these basic moves with a swarm of linguistic detail.

"Dynamic equivalence" is also termed "meaning-based translation," for the purpose of translation is not a wooden literalness but the conveyance of the truth of the text, which in practice allows a significant degree of variation from the literal text in order to gain the meaning. In explicating the notion of dynamic equivalence or meaning-based translation, what is noticeable within the translation organizations is the hegemony of this position (so Beekman and Callow 1974; Kilham 1991; Larson 1984). In the words of Beekman and Callow, this type of idiomatic translation is one where

> the translator seeks to convey to the receptor language readers the meaning of the original by using the natural grammatical and lexical forms of the receptor language. His focus is on the meaning, and he is aware that the

grammatical constructions and lexical choices and combinations used in the original are no more suitable for the communication of that message in the receptor language than are, say, the orthographic symbols of the original. The receptor language message must be conveyed using the linguistic form of the receptor language. (Beekman and Callow 1974, 24)

This echoes the underlying theoretical position of Pike and Longacre, namely, that what counts in tagmemics and discourse analysis are the "natural" patterns of communication used by hearer and speaker. For meaning-based translation, a metaphor that is often invoked is that of a vessel and its content: the language is then the vessel in which the gospel message is contained—the message remains the same, its truth timeless, while the vessel or container may be changed:

> We can think of a story or a message as being like one cup of water. Different languages are like different containers. I could pour the cup of water into a glass, into a billy can, or into a bottle, but the water would not change; it would still be the same no matter what I poured it into. (Kilham 1991, unit 1, page 2)

I am interested in both the opposition that Nida's approach has generated—dynamic equivalence and formal correspondence—and the internal pressures that it generates. However, before passing onto my own response, it is worth noting that Nida has been attacked by people such as Barnstone, who finds the location of meaning in content, without consideration of "the sound, style, tone and form" of the sentences, "an assumption which no contemporary literary or linguistic theory of language would tolerate" (1993, 62–63). Collapsing a focus on content with the "literal," Barnstone condemns such "accurate" translations as simply bad. Meschonnic (1970–73, vol. 2), who has been a significant figure in opening out Bible translation to a wider literary readership, attacks Nida's approach as a distortion of the translator's task, and Sherry Simon denounces his "neo-colonialist evangelical versions" (Simon 1996, 132).

Yet Nida's approach cannot be dismissed so easily on ideological and theological grounds. I want to take as my starting point an alternative he is not overly keen on: the interlinear translation so favored as the ideal form of translation, the closest approximation to the ideal language, of Walter Benjamin:

> Just as, in the original, language and revelation are one without any tension, so the translation must be one with the original in the form of the interlinear version, in which literalness and freedom are united. For to some degree all great texts contain their potential translation between the lines; this is

true to the highest degree of sacred writings. The interlinear version of the Scriptures is the prototype or ideal of all translation. (Benjamin 1992, 82)

In a curious twist, Benjamin has taken literal translation to its logical conclusion, for in the interlinear translation one word matches another, producing sentences that mirror the syntax of the "original" with specific words that are selected from a range of possibilities. The result is an almost unreadable translation, which thereby qualifies as free, language released from the bounds of its own syntax in subservience to the original. In its total disregard for meaning, the interlinear translation is able to achieve Benjamin's utopian purity.[2] I do not think anything quite as contrary to Nida's program can be found (see Barnstone 1993, 254).

Yet Benjamin would seem to be returning to precisely that tradition of translation lambasted by Nida and other, the long tradition, held firmly in many evangelical circles, that the more literal translation is to be favored, for only such a translation comes closest to the sacred word. Yet this reverence for the written word itself pushes back, it seems, to the preservation of the Masoretic Text of the Hebrew Bible—although this is not to say that the Masoretes were evangelicals—where even obvious grammatical and syntactical errors are maintained and the correction noted via the vowels or in footnote commentary. Such reverence for the text presses hard for a literal translation, where translation is indeed allowed, for in many instances translation was and is regarded as a betrayal of the divine word. Over against this, the particular innovation of Nida and those who have followed him on the issue of dynamic equivalence is to break with this focus on the written word and to seek truth in the meaning, for which the written text is but a receptacle, the original language no better or worse than any other (see Nida and Taber 1969, 6–8).

But does reverence for the text translate into its inviolability? It might be argued that it is precisely sacred texts that become the focus of scribal and translational alteration for the very reason of their sacrality. Texts of power, sacred texts, attract the swarms of commentators keen to bolster their own positions with those same texts. And so it is with translation theory and practice. Thus, while Nida's target may seem to be the favoring of so-called literal translations in his own evangelical circles, the opponent, "formal correspon-

---

2. Much has been made of Walter Benjamin's dependence on Jewish kabbalah. Despite the large number of scholars who have followed Gershom Scholem (1981) in claiming that Benjamin's ideas are deeply Jewish and kabbalistic, the argument is deeply flawed. It is based on an anachronism (see McCole 1993, 65–66). The recovery of Jewish mysticism, especially the kabbalah, was carried out by Scholem himself after his close contact with Benjamin. Most of it was simply not available to Benjamin. See further Boer 2007, 60–62.

dence," is more directly the attention to form favored by Benjamin. In other words, Benjamin's interlinear translation is not to be equated with evangelical literalness, and it seems to me that Nida is keen to attack the former, while carrying the latter to a position that enables far surer contact with the original message. For Nida, then, the translator does not surrender the new text to the original, allowing its very contours to be shaped by the original and thereby creating something new that reshapes the target language—as the King James Version did, or as Luther did with his Bible, or as Buber and Rosenzweig with their translation (see Reichart 1996).

In the end, however, there is a more radically conservative dimension to "dynamic equivalence" that also strikes upon a strange contradiction. To begin with, although reverence for the written text itself, at least in the original, has been sidelined, the message of which that text speaks remains the same in its essence. It matters not where it is spoken or read, for it is eternally the same; there is, in other words, a specific meaning, that of God. Further, the meaning sought for is that of the original audience and spoken situation. Such a move is curious, in that it makes use of a finding by the now doddery form criticism, namely, that the biblical texts more often than not originated in oral settings. Yet—and here the contradiction begins to show—since the original situation of the biblical text is an oral one, and since the original hearers would have made assumptions no longer obvious in the written text (two rather large assumptions), it is therefore acceptable to add material that helps restore the assumptions of the original hearers. The single meaning of the text seems to have clouded over, obscured somewhat, and now the translator must assist in finding the meaning, becoming God's assistant, as it were, in order to clear the fog, disperse the smoke, and bring out the real meaning. It goes without saying that these sorts of additions may only be carried out when they assist with locating the original meaning, never putting forward the translator's own theological assumptions about what a text should say. A contradiction: there is but one meaning, but the interpreter or translator must assist with its birth.

As far as the practice of translation into Aboriginal languages (not only in Australia but throughout the world, given SIL's and the Bible Society's global presence and influence) is concerned, the theoretical elaboration I have outlined above follows and feeds into a three-pronged approach that is concerned not merely with translation but with literacy of the target population and the study of linguistics itself (see Cowan 1979 for a useful coverage of SIL and Wycliffe). The earnest search is for vernacular translations that will be understood. Thus, vernacular English is taken as the starting point, most commonly the Good News Bible published by the Bible Society, and vernacular Aboriginal languages become the target languages. The justification for this lays in the argument that Koine Greek, the language used in the New Testament, was also a vernacular, the language of the common people (see Kilham 1991, unit 24, page 3). For Australian Aboriginal languages, the vernacular takes on a distinct tinge, since it denotes not a colloquial spoken language over against a more formal spoken language that itself is based upon and influences a written language that in turn is always more structured than the spoken. Rather, vernacular Aboriginal languages are in most cases the languages of everyday communication either without a written language to which they refer, or acting as parent to a more recent written language constructed out of the oral. In the latter case, the vernacular refers to this colloquial written Aboriginal style into which the text is translated (see A. Eckert 1982).

It is notable that translation usually takes place from English, partly because of the ability to secure a vernacular translation in English, but also because the missionaries mainly spoke English[3] and present-day translators share this language with their Aboriginal co-translators. However, this means that the translation process begins with a translated text, from Hebrew, Aramaic, and Greek, rather than the original languages of the Bible. These originals are of course referred to in the translation process via commentators, yet, given the theoretical notion of meaning-based translation, if the meaning has been conveyed accurately into the English, then that is as good a basis to begin with as the original biblical languages. Occasionally an early missionary did in fact make use of the original languages, such as Lancelot Threlkeld at Lake Awaba or Bob Love at Ernabella (see below).

The process is painstaking, to say the least, and reflects considerable dedication to an often thankless task.[4] Aboriginal co-translators work as a team on any one piece of text, producing an initial draft from a modern English version—a step that itself involves reading the English several times, seeking authorial intention, initial audience response and understanding, focusing on the main events and outline, situating the story in its literary context, using all possible resources for difficult terms, and telling the story from memory in the target language (see Kilham 1991, appendix B). This draft is then edited, checked, and reviewed before it is put before an "unconditioned native speaker" who, ideally, has not seen the translation before. This person is then asked to read the translation and answer a series of comprehension questions

---

3. There are local variations on this, such as the German-speaking missionaries in South Australia and in the center of Australia. In fact, one of the earliest efforts was undertaken by Strehlow at the Hermansburg mission among the Aranda.

4. Yet it had produced a steady stream of dedicated translators with significant results. In 1990 Christine Kilham's survey identified eight complete New Testaments, with a ninth and tenth (the Pitjantjatjara translation) by the year 2000 (Kilham 1990b, 84–85).

to see if the translation conveys its meaning accurately. If possible, several unconditioned native speakers are called upon, reading the story and then retelling it. A final consultant will check over the translation. This person normally has no knowledge of the receptor language, relying upon a translation back into English in order to see whether the meaning has indeed been conveyed properly. The principle here is that if the translation has worked well, it may be translated back into an English that conveys the meaning, irrespective as to whether the English is the same as that from which the translation process began.[5] The obligatory copyediting, proofs, and printing complete the process, apart from the perpetual need for revision (see the detailed guidelines in Barnwell 1980; Kilham 1991, appendices 2–4).

Apart from the increasing sophistication of the process, particularly in terms of the theoretical base and training of translators, a significant shift has been from the involvement of Aboriginal people as translation assistants to co-translators. Further, in many cases the Aboriginal people are the translators and the people from Wycliffe or the Bible Society function as nonindigenous assistants or consultants. Thus, Paul Eckert notes that he and Ann were asked by the Pitjantjatjara people to take up the translation program in 1978, some twenty years after it had ceased with the work of Nancy Sheppard in the translation of 1 John in the late 1950s. The SIL has a program underway in which it trains Aboriginal translators for the work: Christine Kilham's *Translation Time* is a textbook for such a program (1991; also 1990b, 86–98), yet the ambiguity of these changes is not conveyed by my relatively calm prose.

Ambiguous Appropriation and Aboriginal Agency

> This translation of the Gospel of Luke into the language of the Aborigines was made by me with the assistance of the intelligent Aboriginal, McGill [Biraban].... Thrice I wrote it, and he and I went through it sentence by sentence, and word for word, while I explained to him carefully the meaning as we proceeded. McGill spoke the English language fluently. (Threlkeld 1892, 126)

The move to Aboriginal translators or at least co-translators is a more concrete manifestation not only of the rise of (global) Aboriginal political identity and activism, generated within the context of late capitalism, but also a postmodern and cultural studies new orthodoxy that stresses the subversive

---

5. Note that back translation is used in legal translations as well in order to check the initial translation (Cooke 1995).

agency of cultural consumers: viewers, shoppers, students, in short, anyone who is an object of late capitalist consumption (see Morris 1990). So also, Simon Ryan reads the explorers' journals as sites of cultural contact, of contestation between explorers and indigenous resistance (witness the difficulties of communication, usually in search of water, or of the repeated hostility explorers faced). Inevitably, as Ryan notes, the indigenes "look back" (see especially Ryan 1996, 153–95).

Thus we find, along with the invitation to the Eckerts to take up the translation project among the Pitjantjatjara, that the appropriation of Christianity and its sacred text takes on distinctive forms of appropriation beyond the intentions of missionaries and translators. For instance, in his study of Christian mission and translation of the Bible into Tagalog in the Philippines, Vicente Rafael (1993) notes that conversion, confession, and Christian doctrine were understood quite differently by the locals. The process is very much a dialectic: Spanish attempts to translate Christian doctrine into the vernacular altered that vernacular and the consciousness of its speakers; simultaneously, Tagalog efforts to take over Christian colonial discourse into their own language tended to change the very meaning of that discourse. In the process the fabric of social meaning and life was altered: Rafael traces the way Tagalog notions of "debt of gratitude," "shame," master, slave, fear, and desire (by the novel ideas of heaven and hell) mutated with the missionary and colonial intervention in Tagalog society, at the same time that the Christian message itself changed, its doctrines and images sliding away from their context and thus being open to recontextualization. In order to come to terms with the strangeness of the Spanish, the Tagalogs simultaneously demarcated themselves off from the Spanish while appropriating things Spanish as a way to do so. What come through in Rafael's study are the curious, side-winding modes by which two social, intellectual, and religious systems, whose sheer difference strikes one on every page, mediated their interaction.

In India, Homi Bhabha returns again and again to the overdetermination of Christian language in the Hindu tradition: thus, the notion of being reborn into Christ already bears with it the notion of the Brahman as the "twice-born" from the Ṛg-Veda, or it is understood in terms of karma and reincarnation. Quoting the missionary Alexander Duff, Bhabha writes: "every native term which the Christian missionary can employ to communicate the Divine truth is already appropriated as the chosen symbol of some counterpart deadly error" (Bhabha 1994, 101, quoting Duff 1839, 323–24).

The key essay here is "Signs Taken for Wonders" (Bhabha 1994, 102–22), where Bhabha uses the native Indian subject's appropriation of the Bible and Christian doctrine as a key instance of hybridization and mimicry: the catechist Anund Messeh in 1817 describes how his fellow believers ask about the contradiction between monotheism and the doctrine of the Trinity, about the universal claim that the Bible is God's gift and yet that it is a European book, and about the contradiction between its status as God's word given by an angel at Hurdwar fair (a learned Pundit) and yet it teaches the religion of the European sahibs. Further, they wear white as the Bible says to show their sins are forgiven, yet will be baptized next year, not this year, will be baptized but not partake of the Eucharist because the English eat meat, will partake of the Eucharist only when all countries receive the Word, and so on. It is these attachments to the literal truth of the Bible that disable its role as an authoritative English text, that breaks the God-Englishman nexus through a bewildering appropriation. The display of hybridity that Bhabha traces among the people under a grove of trees outside Delhi is termed "the *ruse* of recognition," a recognition of authority that mimics and mocks at the same time (1994, 115). Bhabha's favored quotation is that of the missionary who writes from Bengal in May 1817 complaining that people buy up a Bible not so much to read but as a curiosity, as waste or wrapping paper, to barter at the market. For Bhabha this is a sign of the "dismemberment" of the "holiest of books."

> Still everyone would gladly receive a Bible. And why?—that he may lay it up as a curiosity for a few pice; or use it for waste paper. Such it is well known has been the common fate of these copies of the Bible.... Some have been bartered in the markets, others have been thrown in snuff shops and used as wrapping paper.... If these remarks are at all warranted then an indiscriminate distribution of the scriptures, to everyone who may say he wants a Bible, can be little less than a waste of time, a waste of money and a waste of expectations. For while the public are hearing of so many Bibles distributed, they expect to hear soon of a corresponding number of conversions. (Bhabha 1994, 92 and 122)

For Bhabha these types of appropriations, especially those concerning the Bible, are signals of colonial hybridity, of the messy mesh between colonizer and colonized. It is precisely in this discussion that Bhabha develops his well-debated and criticized notion of hybridity, the shifting forces of colonial power, the "necessary deformation and displacement of all sites of discrimination and domination" (1994, 112), the rite of power and its perpetual twisting and return by the colonized. In the end, colonial power, for Bhabha, produces hybridization. However, I am not sure that Bhabha's characteristically sliding arguments[6] work here, for in a contradictory moment of historical specificity

---

6. It is appropriate to use the same advice for reading Bhabha's work that Flaubert used in his *Dictionnaire des idées reçues* for travel—"should be done fast" (see Gourgouris

for which Bhabha does not have the greatest of reputations he suggests that the undermining response of the people under the trees outside Delhi to the missionary's questions is also the product of the particular circumstances of providing books to those—Dalits and tribal people—who would only know of books and Scriptures in the hands of caste Hindus. The translations of the Bible (in at least eight languages and dialects) served as a peculiar empowerment that questioned the structures of power in which the Bible as an English book was enmeshed. "It is the force of these colonialist practices that produce that discursive tension between Anund Messeh, whose address *assumes* its authority, and the natives who question the English presence, revealing the hybridity of authority and inserting their insurgent interrogations in the interstices" (Bhabha 1994, 117).[7] For the colonial powers, they cannot be true converts, for their belief is impure, phantasmic, and insincere.

At one level, it seems to me that Bhabha has picked up a genuine spoor here, for as my closing example of the use of *tjukurpa* and *tjukurnga* to translate the New Testament "word" (*logos*) and "parable" (*parabole*) indicates, translation is always hybrid, uncontrollable, or, conversely, impossible (when it is understood in terms of direct transferability of meaning from one language to another). On a similar level, Peter Nyaningu, Uniting Church minister of Ernabella whom I met in 1988, operated his "parish" in ways vastly different from European-derived models of the church where parish boundaries, regular worship, membership rolls, finances, and so on are crucial. For Peter, tribal elder and minister, the missionary patterns of regular worship were dispensed with in favor of occasional services when the time was right, in line with another rhythm. Parish rolls were not an issue, nor indeed were finances and buildings. If anything, the whole tribe constituted his "parish."

In the end, however, it seems to me that Rafael on the Tagalog, Bhabha on India, as well as many of the translators of the Bible into Aboriginal languages, have missed something, and that is the essential syncretism, if I may put it in such a contradictory fashion, of Christianity. It is not that Christianity has a core whose Scripture's meanings may be transmitted, or whose doctrines and texts may be subverted in the colonial relation (Bhabha), or

---

1995, 343)—for to read slowly is to make the mistake of seeking a long-gone logical fixity. There is no point lingering over the phrases and sentences, trying to trace the steps of his argument, for the effect is the same, fast or slow: a perpetual sliding from image to image, metaphor to metaphor, citation to citation. Indeed, any analysis of Bhabha per se must begin with style, with the act of sentence production.

7. Bhabha also finds enmeshed in the Indian missionary's words the Burdwan Plan, which tried to use "natives" to destroy native religion and culture (1994, 117).

whose original meaning is lost in the missionary field (Rafael). Rather, as Rafael hints, Christianity is precisely such a sliding, nonfixable, slippery, and evasive religion, perpetually metamorphosing into new forms that are distinct from its other and earlier forms. And the translation of its texts is central for such a *glissage*.[8]

Alien Word

> Thus *dead, written, alien language* is the true description of the language with which linguistic thought has been concerned. (Vološinov 1986, 73)

These notions of agency and hybridity are in the end not very helpful, although they do at least unsettle the Saidian legacy of a hegemonic colonial discourse against which local indigenous people can do little but acquiesce passively. A clue that I want to pick up and pursue for a few moments begins with V. N. Vološinov's notion of the "alien word." Vološinov's study famously begins with the basic contradiction in linguistics between individualist subjectivism and abstract objectivism (the search for contradiction indicating Vološinov's distinctly Marxist method). Over against the romanticism of the former—language, as a living, pulsing being, can only be known, intimately felt, at a distinctly personal level—abstract objectivism bases its study on the "dead" languages of the past. It develops its notions of syntax and grammar from the languages of ancient Greece, Rome, and India, producing thereby an objective, detached analysis of the performance of language. Indeed, it is precisely the rules of language derived from Latin, Greek, and Sanskrit that then become the benchmark by which the living are analyzed and ordered. (One might trace fruitfully the opposition between deductive and inductive methods of teaching languages, especially "dead" ones, to this contradiction marked out by Vološinov.)

And this is precisely the function of the alien word for Vološinov: that which is brought in, usually by those of the ruling (intellectual) class, to order the vernacular language in question. Its colonizing force shapes the subjected language to that of the alien language, altering it in the process. While Vološinov is thinking specifically of the spread of Latin grammar and syntax in the ordering of English or French, or Greek for the alphabet and structure of Cyrillic and Russian, his argument applies to other situations in an analogous way. It is the analogy with Aboriginal languages in Australia

---

8. In the process, translation and Christianity become the unwitting tools of the overthrow of colonial rule. So, argues Rafael, Christianity provided the "natives with a language for conceptualizing the limits of colonial and class domination" (Rafael 1993, 7).

that interests me here—English in relation to the modes of communication used in Australia—but in order to get there I need to pick up some suggestions of Rafael.

The frustration of the Spanish linguist-missionaries in face of the indeterminacy of the traditional Tagalog script (*baybayin*) is the initial marker of what Rafael traces (1993, 26–38): in its place they sought to establish a script where the vowels and consonants were a little more fixed (significantly, after reading Vološinov, the Latin script). Further, the missionaries, in their desire to translate the Bible into Tagalog, began by designating the various local ways of communication into ethnolinguistic groups for ease of identification. Then they proceeded to order the languages so demarcated in terms of grammar, syntax, a lexicon—once again, in Latin terms. Rafael's point here is not that the missionaries were merely codifying for written purposes an already-existing language or languages but rather that they created something new in the process. Thus, grammar did not exist for the locals before the missionaries produced it, nor did syntax, nor a lexicon.

> It is as if Tagalog were alienated from the Tagalogs by the missionary-translator, who, after endowing it with a grammar and a lexicon in his *arte* [book of grammar and translation], gave it back to them in the form of prayers, sermons, and confessionals. The vernacular is thus refashioned into an object to be classified and dissected, a gift to be circulated, and an instrument for the insertion of its speakers into a spiraling network of obligations with the Father. (Rafael 1993, 38)

In order to push Rafael's argument one step further, let me return to Australian Aboriginal languages. It seems to me that a similar argument could be made about such languages, namely, that before their demarcation the various Aboriginal languages and dialects (and this was a contested issue for some time; see the comments on language by George Grey, who felt that the modes of communication in Australia could be designated as one language with minor variations [1841, 2:362–88]) did not exist with their distinct ethnolinguistic denomination, as Aranda, Wik-Munkan, Pitjantjatjara, and so on. Such "languages" are much more fluid than these borders suggest, flowing into one another in a way that belies many of the designations. Along with the language groups, the developments of alphabets, grammars, syntaxes, and lexicons functioned and continue to function as a grid that is imposed over a particular form of communication that is foreign to the origins of the grid. And, once again echoing Vološinov, the alphabets are Latin and the syntax and grammar derived from European linguistics. Further, is it not the case that the very notion of a language as an ethnic and national marker, as a signifier of ethnic, social, and political boundaries, is inextricably tied up with the nation-state? Thus, to use the same name for a designated tribal group—the separation and naming of tribes is therefore also suspect—as well as a language or dialect is to assume the connections between ethnicity, language, and political boundaries that European settlers, explorers, and missionaries brought with them. Even if there is a far greater sensitivity to the particular forms of language in reshaping the syntax and grammar of native "languages" in contemporary linguistics, the very need to produce such linguistic shape to modes of verbal communication is still there. In short, my point is that until the arrival of mainly British people who investigated Aboriginal communication, Aboriginal languages did not exist in the sense in which those of non-Aboriginal, especially European, heritage seem to think.

Thus, it would seem that the continuing difficulty of fixing precise languages and dialects is not so much the lack of precision in the terminology being used—the problem will be solved only if our tools were better!—but the resistance of Aboriginal communication to the methods. For instance, Diana Eades argues that grammars are artificial products, not reflecting the way people speak to each other (what grammar does?). Eades notes the dereifying effects of Aboriginal language practice, in opposition to the reifying nature of grammars themselves: "In South-East Queensland, for instance, it is impossible to know exactly how to distinguish one language from another. Different families speak closely related languages for which they use the same language name. But their languages, while very similar, do have significant differences in vocabulary and grammar. Such factors as multilingualism, social varieties of language and many small family differences in vocabulary cannot be satisfactorily handled within a framework restricted to grammatical competence" (Eades 1982, 63). Further, due to fluctuation in shared vocabulary, the absence of cognates, the existence of special or "avoidance" languages,[9] and the contrast between divergence of vocabulary and grammatical similarities, studies such as those by Yallop (1982, 32–38) are highly cautious about attempting classification—although of course he proceeds to do so.

A specific example of all of this is the terminological confusion surrounding Pitjantjatjara, the language to which I turn a little later. To begin with, the term designates a "dialect" spoken around Ernabella in South Australia. Yet it is also used to describe a group of "dialects" that use *pitja* as the stem of the verb "to come," namely, Nyangatjatjara, Nyanganyatjara, Ngaanyatjara, and Pitjantjatjara. The individual "dialect" of Pitjantjatjara, or the cluster of "dia-

---

9. For use with kin who need to be avoided and addressed differently, such as a man's wife's mother, mother's brothers, and sometimes wife's father and sisters (see Yallop 1982, 161–63).

lects" designated by the same name, form part of the Western Desert Group of dialects—or is that languages? For Pitjantjatjara is also called a language, with affinities sufficiently close to Yankunytjatjara to be included with it in the standard dictionary (Goddard 1987). It turns out that the designation "Pitjantjatjara" is itself somewhat arbitrary—the focus on the stem *pitja*—for if the word "man" were used as a basis for differentiation, then the Western Desert area would be divided into three groups: those who use *wati* (Ooldea, Warburton Ranges, and Ernabella); *puntu* (Mount Margaret-Kalgoorlie to the south and west); and *matu* (east of Jigalong). Then again, if "this" were to be used, the division would be fourfold: *nyangatja* (Ooldea to Ernabella); *nyanganya* (Cundalee to Mount Margaret); *ngaanya* (Warburton Ranges to Jigalong); and *ngaatja* (east of Warburton Ranges to Rawlinson Ranges). In fact, is it precisely this mode of distinction that produces the "dialects" Ngaanyatjara and Nyanganyatjara. On this basis, one would expect that the Nyangatjatjara (the "dialect" in which *nyangatya* is used for "this") that I mentioned earlier in this paragraph is the "dialect" spoken around Ernabella. But no, that is Pitjantjatjara, the name of the cluster. Perhaps it is possible to revert to a simpler differentiation: those who use directional prefixes with *pitja-*, as in *ma-pitja-*, motion away or "go," or *ngalya-pitja-*, motion toward, "come"; and those who use such prefixes with *ya-*, as in *maa-ya-*, motion away or "go," or *ngalya-ya-*, for motion toward, "come." On this basis we get two groups: Pitjantjatjara (south and west, including Ooldea, Kalgoorlie, and Mount Margaret to the east of the Warburtons); and Yankunytjatjara (east and north, from Oodnadatta to Jigalong and Fitzroy Crossing). And then Yankunytjatjara may also be Ankuntjatjara, since sometimes the stem *a-* is used instead of *ya-*, which on its own designates motion away, whereas *pitja-* means to "come." In the face of such confusion and overlapping, Bowe, from whom I draw here, notes without too much exasperation that the "notion 'dialect' is particularly problematic in connection with Australian languages because neighbouring groups maintain periodic contact as part of the social/sacred traditions.... There is not a clear clustering of variants that can easily be identified as a 'dialect,' distinct from a neighbouring 'dialect'" (Bowe 1990, 158; see also Douglas 1964, 2–3).

It is in many respects one of the advantages of looking into the study of Aboriginal languages from outside to see the way the existence of Aboriginal languages is a given before European arrival and that study of the original languages—estimates ranging from 150 to 650 (Yallop 1982, 27)—and their survivors is an attempt to describe accurately what is there. No matter how illuminating and interesting such materials are (e.g., Blake 1991; Dixon 1993; Yallop 1982), including the central role the "discovery" of absolutive/ergative systems in Australian Aboriginal languages (over against nominative/accusative systems [Dixon 1993, 79–81]), the colonial function of such study has not been investigated in any way.

That all of this—the construction of Aboriginal "languages"—is then tied to the task of translating the Bible into Aboriginal languages may be seen in the extraordinary effort of the Congregational missionary Lancelot Threlkeld (1892) and his translation of the Gospel of Luke, prefaced by a grammar of Awabakal, an enthnolinguistic designator for the mode of communication used around Lake Macquarie in the Hunter district of New South Wales. Apart from his use of a native assistant Biraban, named as McGill by Threlkeld, to whom he told the true "meaning" of the text, Threlkeld's work is remarkable on a few counts: as a Dissenter, he went against the dominant trend, which was to write off Aboriginal languages as worthy of learning, let alone translation; he produced by 1831 the only full Gospel translated in the nineteenth century (he also completed Mark, part of Matthew, and some prayers from the *Book of Common Prayer* before the mission was closed in 1841); by 1826 he had published some notes on the Awabakal language, although he used traditional Indo-European categories in the "grammar" (that is, Latin categories). The translation of Luke, published in 1892 as a curiosity (at the time of the emergence of both anthropology and linguistics), was full of a whole raft of neologisms into "Awabakal," despite the work of Biraban.

Threlkeld's preface, which deserves a detailed reading on its own, drips with melancholy, full of the imminent end of the Aborigines, a lack of understanding of their mortality rate, the abandonment of the mission by the London Missionary Society, but above all the futility of his effort.

> Circumstances, which no human power could control, brought the mission to a final termination on December 31, 1841, when the mission ceased, not from any want of support from the Government, nor from any inclination on my own part to retire from the work, but solely from the sad fact that the Aborigines themselves had then become almost extinct, for I had actually outlived a very large majority of the blacks, more especially of those with whom I had been associated for seventeen years. (Threlkeld 1892, 126)

Threlkeld writes this in 1857, although it is not published until 1892. He leaves us with him perusing his 1826 grammar notes, which he happens upon accidentally at a book-stall, reflecting on the fate of his work, a specimen of a dead language, inscribed with his failed effort. In keeping with this tone, Threlkeld's was the last effort until the Dieri translation of Carl Strehlow and Ruether in 1897, a people also decimated by disease (for a brief history, see Harris 1990, 829–46; 1995).

The great irony of Threlkeld's bravura act of grammatical analysis and translation—now the most complete one that we have from the nineteenth century—is that it went against the widespread belief that Australian Aborigines had no grammar or syntax to speak of, that their language was so primitive that it was not much better than the communication of animals, or at least subhuman species. Threlkeld's act, then, for all its imposition of an alien word, takes a full dialectical twist here, becoming, in the very process of witnessing and writing about the passing of the tribe with whom he worked, a mark of respect for the sophistication of Aboriginal communication.

Some Dialectics, or, Tjukurpa

> *dis*semination cannot be under our control. Yet in translation, where meaning hops into the spacy emptiness between two named historical languages, we get perilously close. (Spivak 1993, 180)

> Translation is so far removed from being the sterile equation of two dead languages that of all literary forms it is the one charged with the special mission of watching over the maturing process of the original language and the birth pangs of its own. (Benjamin 1992, 74)

Following Threlkeld, there are some other dialectical turns that come from the construction of Aboriginal languages, particularly as that is tied to the missionary and translation process. As in many other places, Aboriginal communication was and remains primarily an oral exercise. Writing and its culture of literacy are thereby colonial impositions. The process of translation is, then, to follow Rafael, a process of taking what is spoken and making a new product that is written: it now has an alphabet, grammar, lexicon, and is then handed back as a new work.

Yet it is both an imposition and not, for Aboriginal appropriations have their own unexpected patterns. On the one hand, some translation projects have been closed down due to lack of community support for literacy projects; for instance, the translation project into Murrinhpatha among the Wadeye community at Port Keats on the northwest coast of New South Wales was closed because the prominent culture of the community is oral.[10] Alternatively, there have been efforts to use cassettes or to develop translations to be read aloud (Kilham 1990a, 72). On the other hand, the existence of a written Bible in a community also has the effect of generating the desire to read. And in some communities the hymnbook plays an even greater role in producing such a desire, mixed in as it is with the traditional importance of song cycles

---

10. Personal communication from Tom Webb, 4 November 1998, at the Wycliffe Centre, Carlingford.

and the related valuation of Christian singing.[11] But in another turn, in larger and more remote communities, such as those that comprise the Pitjantjatjara in central Australia, the locals have appropriated the literacy generated by missionary-translators and developed their own vernacular literacy. Indeed, the literacy program, notes Paul Eckert, was so successful that by the 1970s Pitjantjatjara literacy was taken for granted. The development of an Aboriginal literacy means that a "written style of Pitjantjatjara has developed over the years that is distinct from oral style—it is not merely the transcription of oral material—and literate Pitjantjatjara people are generally well aware of the differences" (P. Eckert 1998; see also A. Eckert 1982; Kilham 1990a; 1991, unit 25, pages 24–25).[12] In a similar vein, Christine Kilham argues that translators have three options: the translation may be intended for reading and is modeled on oral speech; it is an oral style but intended for audio-visual presentation; or a written style is developed into which the translation moves but to which it also contributes. The third is preferred. Yet in another step, the oddness of all of this comes through with the stress in missionary preaching on the oral and personal gospel, that in the words of the missionary the "Word of God" may be heard. This oral focus in the midst of a substantial written tradition regarding the Bible becomes even stranger when a written culture needs to be created among Aboriginal people for translation so that the Word of God, as an oral and personal event, may be experienced. In order to reach an oral culture, the oral word must now pass through the valley of writing in order to be oral again.

Further, the intersection of various Aboriginal "languages" and European ones, especially English, has led to the well-known linguistic syncretism of Kriol. Estimated to be spoken by some thirty thousand people, making it the largest single linguistic group (which appears to be growing), Kriol has more often been denounced for its profoundly colonial markers, the destruction of Aboriginal languages, and its bowdlerized English. Yet it also exhibits the processes by which new languages are formed—analogous to the creation of new religions—having its own Bible translation project (see Harris 1988; 1993).

Another dialectical turn follows the legacy of Threlkeld, for translators in many respects now find themselves functioning as defenders of Aboriginal culture (in both literary and written terms) over against the overwhelming pressure to operate in English. It is not so much the intellectual double-flip or

---

11. Personal communication from Ken Hanson of the Finke River Mission.

12. Paul Eckert notes, however, that in the mid 1980s a small but influential group of Pitjantjatjara and non-Pitjantjatjara managed to have the literacy program thrown out of the schools in place of all English. The presence of a literary Pitjantjatjara may be under threat if this is not turned around.

suggesting that a translated Bible is indigenous (Cowan 1979, 13), although that assumption is regularly encountered. Rather, it seems that the very translation of the Bible has fostered and encouraged indigenous rights, for the transformations wrought by the presence of European languages—that is, in terms of signification, the transfer of meaning, and the encoding of interests—meant that new ways of conceiving social and political associations took place. In its own way, this has led to the connection between self and society, particularly in terms of the nation state, that has encouraged the development of a distinctly Aboriginal national consciousness. This, one of the marked legacies of missionary literacy and translation projects, is also one of its most curious appropriations. The language of the colonizer is then returned in the unexpected political form of decolonization.[13]

Yet the final cluster of dialectics appears, like a small cloud no larger than a fist on the horizon, with a single word. Here I move from the vastly general discussion of translation theory and practice and its contradictions to the particular, although my discussion has been slowly funneled in this way, with its increased interest in Pitjantjatjara and the translation project among this tribal/linguistic group. With this solitary word, I will speak also of the various points that have appeared in the more theoretical slabs above.

The word in question is the "Word" itself, the *logos* of the New Testament Gospels. In the southern summer of 1987–88 I was in an Aboriginal community in the central desert, Ernabella, once a Presbyterian mission but now a community on Aboriginal land. Apparently, I was informed somewhat deviously, the central New Testament term *logos* had been translated into the Pitjantjatjara language with the equivalent term for "Dreaming."[14] And indeed this is the case: from the first translation of the Gospel of Mark, published in 1949 by Bob Love and Ronald Trudinger, who seem to have fought bitterly over most of their time together in the 1940s, the Greek *logos* was translated as *tjukurpa*. This practice has been maintained ever since.

---

13. These issues have come to a head in other places as well, as in the difference of opinion between Chinua Achebe and Ngugi wa Thiong'o: the former argued that African writers should use English because English is now an inescapable part of African life, but it can be Africanized and loaded with different cultural and political associations (Achebe 1993); Thiong'o, however, sees culture and language inextricably tied together, English therefore designating colonialism and native languages resistance and African culture (Thiong'o 1993).

14. For non-Australian readers "Dreaming" designates a form of religious mapping, an ideological construction whereby the universe is rendered understandable in religious terms; it is the collection of myths, stories, and practices by which the land is perceived and through which a person makes sense of the world.

Like many crucial terms it is thankfully untranslatable, this Benjaminian mark being reinforced by the range of possible meanings for the word. Its possible meanings are: (1) story; (2) Dreaming or Law (with a capital; there is an emerging Aboriginal desire for this sense of the word not to be given an English equivalent any longer); (3) message; (4) news; (5) individual word; (6) what someone says, thing said; and (7) birthmark, wart, which is regarded as showing something that is distinct and personal (see Goddard 1987, 145).

A similar practice followed for the translation of the Gospel of John, carried out by Ronald Trudinger in the 1950s and published in 1960, particularly with the crucial theological use of *Logos* as a designator of Christ. In this case a personal form of *tjukurpa* was used, *Tjukurnga*, capitalized and indicating a person or a person's name (here Christ). This is a significant, and signifying, move. There seems to be an assumption of some thematic and ideational connection between the Greek term *logos*—word, creative principle, idea, thought, language, Bible, Christ, and so on—and *tjukurpa*. Further, even though Love's and Trudinger's efforts with the Gospels of Mark and Luke took place before the influence of SIL and Bible Society linguistics and translation policies under the influence of Nida, the decision to use *tjukurpa/Tjukurnga* anticipates the policy that it is better to seek equivalents in the Aboriginal language in question, even to drop a term or figure entirely and express its meaning in another way, than to retain the words from English and transform the Aboriginal language by introducing new vocabulary items (as Threlkeld had opted to do).

Strangely, the word for God itself has been introduced as a neologism into Pitjantjatjara, while the *logos* becomes *Tjukurnga*. In other cases, specific native terms are used: in Aranda "God" is *Altjira*, the "Dreaming One," whereas in Mutawanga "God" is *Mama* (father) or, more specifically, *Mama ngarnawarrajanu*, "father from above." For Pitjantjatjara, while the word "God" has made its way as a neologism—although by now it is an old neologism—it is *tjukurpa* who is the new arrival, jostling for space with God, as it were. But this dilemma goes back before SIL and the Bible Society: whether to use native terms for central Christian concepts (*tjukurpa*) or to introduce neologisms (God). And old is the practice: as with the Catholic missionaries to Latin America and the Philippines (see Rafael 1993, 29–30) and as with Threlkeld's translation of Luke into Awabakal, certain terms such as "God" are untranslatable—it being assumed that the English, or perhaps Castilian Spanish or whatever, word has a closer fit between word and referent than any indigenous word. Indeed, one cannot help noticing that in Threlkeld's translation of Luke reams of non-Awabakal words are introduced, taken not from English so much as from Greek. These are marked on each page so as to stand out even more, and perhaps not to be confused with properly Awabakal words. The effect here, apart from the construction of grammar itself, is to create a new register of terms into the target language, a series of leaps or moments of aporia before the text continues. Rafael also traces the "untranslatability" of key terms in a native target language (1993, 110–35), indicating how terms referring to God and Jesus, or to practices such as extreme unction or the use of the name of Jesus to avert temptation, invariably altered when indigenous equivalents were used, or generated gaps in linguistic intelligibility when Castilian or Latin terms were mingled with Tagalog.

But let me focus for a few moments on a specific text. In order to get a sense of the translation process, and the way new theories have influenced the practice, I compare, via back translation, the original Pitjantjatjara translation of John 1:1 by Trudinger with the revision by Paul Eckert's team:

> 1960: Kuwaripatjara mulapa Tjukurnga nyinangi, munu Tjukurnga Godala nyinangi, munu Godanya nyinangi. (British and Foreign Bible Society 1960, 69; 1969, 283)
> Right at the beginning was Tjukurnga, and Tjukurnga was in God, and he was God.
>
> 1997: Kuwaripatjara mulapa[15] uwankara wiyangka Godanya nyinangi, ka palula tjungu kutjupa nyinangi ini Tjukurnga. Panya paluru Godanya alatjitu. (Bible Society in Australia 1997, 691)
> Right at the beginning, when there was nothing, God existed, but together with him there was another one named Tjukurnga. He was really God, that one.

A few items are worth noting here. Most obviously, Trudinger's translation is much more "literal," or tends to follow what Nida designates as formal correspondence. By contrast, the Eckert team revision favors a much looser use of the form in order to produce a text that runs in closer to dynamic equivalence. Apart from the criticism of Ken Hanson of the Finke River Mission—that many translators pay lip service to dynamic equivalence—it seems to me that the opposition, in proper ideological fashion, serves as much to open up new possibilities as close down others.

Let me make my point with *tjukurpa*, whose semantic field ranges from Dreaming to wart. For the translators, it is not so much that the term is a neologism in Pitjantjatjara but that it is used to convey a new meaning cluster, determined, it is hoped, by Christian usage and its scriptural context, that both overlaps with its former cluster but also claims a new space that excludes

---

15. The same clause is used for Gen 1:1.

DREAMING THE LOGOS

certain old meanings and introduces new ones. I am not so sure that refilling the terms with Christian and biblical content is achieved so easily. My uncertainty operates at two levels. To begin with, there is the profound otherness of the two languages and their ways of thinking. Thus, in relation to the complexity of legal translation, Cooke writes: "Difficulty in translating patterns of thinking across cultures becomes pronounced when one is attempting to get a member of the other culture to accept one's own culture's brand of logic, supposition and argument" (1995, 41[16]).

On the other hand, it seems that with *tjukurpa* it is not so much the untranslatability of Christian and Aboriginal ideas but the potential for a word such as this to release the controls and spin out in all sorts of unexpected direction. For what takes off here is precisely the "Word." Not only does *tjukurpa* designate the Word,[17] the *logos*, the meaningful expression or creative principle—or indeed story, saying, message, news, birthmark, Law ...—but it is also used at times for parable (Mark 4:13; Bible Society in Australia 1997, 486; Mark 4:10 in the Pitjantjatjara Bible Translation Project 1998, 15),[18] for the translation of "word" elsewhere (Mark 4:14), and for gospel itself.[19] Thus, Mark 1:1 has *Tjukurpa Palya*, good *Tjukurpa* (with a capital!) for "gospel" or *tou euanggeliou*. The Gospel of Mark itself is named *tjukurpa palya Markaku*,[20] the good news of Mark, that of John *tjukurpa palya Johntu walkatjunkunytja*, and so on. The same thing happens with the translations into Ngaanyatjara with parable, gospel, and word, where *tjukurpa/tjukurrpa* is also used (Bible Society 1973; 1976). Once let loose, it is as though *tjukurpa*

---

16. Cooke is critical of what he feels is the minimalist approach of the SIL in Australia.

17. With a remarkable resonance with Nida: "WORD: A term equivalent to English 'word' may be almost impossible to find in an Aboriginal language. Normally, Aboriginal peoples have not studied their own language sufficiently to have discovered any linguistic unit which they call a 'word.' It should be noted, moreover, that the Greek *logos*, translated 'Word' in John 1, does not necessarily mean 'a single word,' but rather 'a meaningful expression.' The nearest native equivalent to the *logos* of John 1:1 will probably be some word which covers an area of meaning included in the English words *phrase, sentence, speech, conversation, statement,* and *expression*" (Nida 1947, 217).

18. Although the Love/Trudinger translation of Mark 4:10 has *tjukurpa* for parable (British and Foreign Bible Society 1960, 11), it is replaced by in the 1969 and 1997 translations (1969, 120; 1997, 486) but reappears in the 1998 revision (Pitjantjatjara Bible Translation Project 1998, 15).

19. Nida again: "GOSPEL: A descriptive term for 'gospel' may be constructed in almost all languages. The gospel may be called 'the good news' or 'the good message'" (Nida 1947, 218).

20. In the 1998 revision this has become *Tjukurpa Markalu Walkatjunkunytja* (Pitjantjatjara Bible Translation Project 1998).

cannot stop, for the whole mini-Bible, comprising most of the New Testament and sections of the Hebrew Bible, is itself *Tjukurpa Palya: Irititja munu Kuwaritja*, the good *Tjukurpa*: old and new. And the capital *Tjukurpa* that was restricted to Dreaming and Law above now appears in these places as well. Although not the gods per se,[21] there is a significant transfer/translation taking place here between key religious terms that is found taking place within the Bible itself (and here I agree with Barnstone 1993, 135–52, 174–83). Indeed, there is what Barnstone, following Benjamin, calls a "maturing process" for the original here, as the Word, parable, and gospel undergo a change in the afterlife of translation.

> Although a translation cannot aspire to a likeness to the original, it can cause the original to be transformed; even the words in the original can be renewed, and their once fixed meaning begin to grow and mature, as translation endows the original with afterlife: "For in its afterlife—which could not be called that if it were not a transformation and a renewal of something living—the original undergoes a change. Even words with fixed meanings can undergo a maturing process." (Barnstone 1993, 244, quoting Benjamin 1992, 73–74)

It would seem that, despite the best intentions to give a word such as *tjukurpa* a new, distinctly Christian resonance, it is not possible to restrict a word like this when it is able to evoke the range of meaning that it does. But this is the beauty of language and especially of translation: such a riotous flowering—reminiscent of the impossibility to contain the myriad variations of Aboriginal communication that I noted earlier—of sense and meaning is what a "living" word should do. The Babelian babble of voices, of many translations, is of course in its very plethora of words a glimpse of the universal language (so Barnstone 1993, 137) that Benjamin saw only in the interlinear translation of the Bible. There is just a glimpse here of the utopian ideal language.

Before I become too ecstatic, I would like to invoke the old formalist challenge that seems to be called for with this explosion of *tjukurpa*: What if the content were the mere means by which the language sought to spread its wings and take to flight, its various techniques and skills put out for show by means of the content—here the Christian gospel—of the text? The biblical messages are then mere vehicles for the construction of new, specifically writ-

---

21. Jan Assmann (1996) suggests that under normal circumstances religion is the promoter of cultural translatability, shifting the gods into one another, until one religion claims absolute truth: then there is no translatability of the gods.

ten, forms of Aboriginal languages. And there are some notable examples of this, such as Luther's creation of a new type of German with his translation,[22] or of the profound effect on English of the King James, or of the translation of Buber and Rosenzweig, which sought not to bridge the gap between the languages but to keep open the distances, to point to them, so that the myth of a transfer of content is avoided. The task (like Benjamin) is to reshape the language, make it sound strange, in order to make the alien sound audible.

The purpose of biblical translation is not the transfer of meaning into a new form, not even the attention to form as such, but the creation of a new language. And it is the content of the Bible that enables this.

---

22. "It must be borne in mind that the German into which Luther translated was to a large extent his own creation … a new language out of the clumsy usage in the high German chancelleries by amalgamating it intertextually with the language actually spoken in everyday life, in the marketplace, in the nursery, by peasants and citizens, and forging it into a new literary medium" (Reichart 1996, 168–69).

Conclusion: (E)Strange Dialectics

In the preceding chapters I have sought the ways the Bible, strange canonical document that it is, skews the issues of postcolonialism with which I have dealt: globalization, exploration, panopticism and the gaze, home, exodus and exile, identity, essentialism and Aboriginality, and translation. This is by no means an exhaustive list, and so my readings may be regarded as local forays, in zeroing on strategic points to argue for a consideration of the Bible at precisely these points. That I have felt it necessary to do so is due not so much to a professional interest in the Bible as from my awareness of the severe neglect of the Bible by postcolonial critics. Conversely, for many biblical critics, and indeed many of those who have an investment (political, social, ecclesial, and so on) in the Bible itself, this presence of the Bible in the colonial endeavor and the complicity with colonial governments of those who purveyed the colonial Bible is one of those bad secrets, best not acknowledged.

My study has been less a reading of biblical texts (I have done so with Dan 4 and Josh 9) than of the Bible in colonial and postcolonial situations: globalization, explorers, postcolonial critics on exodus and exile, and translation. It is, therefore, mainly a reading of the use and influence, past and potential, of the Bible in postcolonial theory and practice. Yet there are moments too when postcolonial theory sheds its diffuse light on the biblical text, enabling a different reading of the marks on the page, of the world tree in Dan 4, or of exodus and exile, of Josh 9 and the identity of Israel, and translation itself.

It is not that I want to be apologetic about the Bible (it has more than enough apologists) but that it is curious to encounter the various blind spots, blank areas, censored zones of a critical practice. So, I have been tracking, across the wastes of postcolonial theory, a pattern of absence and presence of the Bible itself. At times it emerges from beneath the sands, a relic of its former presence, and one or two stop by for a moment. Espying their occasional but rare visitation, I have engaged with these characters, whether explorers in Australia (Mitchell, Eyre, Stuart, and so on), poets and writers, Bible translators, or critics, a Bhabha, Said, the Boyarins, Deleuze and Guattari. At other moments I have introduced the Bible and postcolonial theory (globalization, essentialism, and identity) to each other, passing about some water in the shade of the heat of the day, standing back to see what might result: an argument, a friendship, an affair maybe. In the end, I hope they are both richer for the experience, however long or fleeting it may be.

Yet two tasks remain, both arising from the individual explorations of the preceding chapters: a necessarily broad reflection on the role of the Bible in the colonial and then postcolonial eras; and a recasting of the notion of opposition in postcolonial theory in light of the Bible's own curious career in postcolonialism itself. The very effort to speak more broadly of practices that one would expect to vary according to the particular configurations of local places and spaces has a little too much of the search for a total picture about it that is out of favor in postcolonial discussions (and many others). It is by now well enough established that such opposition to totalizing arguments is misdirected, falsely connecting totalizing with totalitarianism, and thereby missing some of the crucial dimensions of a chronic capitalist globalization.

BOOMERANG: THE STRANGE DIALECTIC OF THE BIBLE

Thus, in regard to the Bible, a consistent mistake in the consideration of its role in the European colonialism that was constitutive of global capitalism is to see the missions as always complicit with the political and economic forms of colonialism. The missionaries, for whom the Bible was part of the reason for being there in the first place, often did indeed support the colonial endeavor, closely associating themselves with the colonial government officials and seeing themselves as part of a wider process of civilization. This was particularly the case with those from established churches, such as the Catholic or Anglican churches, for whom the primary task of priest or minister was to serve the colonial faithful, those who found themselves at the frontier of the empire, for whatever reason. Given the inviolable assumption that religion, and especially the Bible, was indispensable for morality itself, the presence of a religious professional was absolutely necessary if the fabric of civilized society was to remain intact. Whether such postings on the imperial fringe should be classified as missionary is a moot point, but it is more likely that a colonial appointment in an established church would be taken as a demotion, a removal and banishment comparable to many other colonial appointments.

Another group with less official status—the ministers and pastors of Dissenting churches (Methodist, Baptist, Free Presbyterians, and so on)—also made their way to the colonies, often to serve small and far-flung communities of the faithful. In this case they brought with them the various Dissenting ideologies and practices that framed their own existence back in the metropolitan center. More often, however, it was the practice in these churches

CONCLUSION: (E)STRANGE DIALECTICS

to use lay preachers, people from their own ranks who might be able speak coherently about certain topics, biblical or otherwise. This of course made Dissenting churches more flexible and adaptable to the sparse colonial populations and greater distances often to be found. As far as support for the colonial powers and the immediate government are concerned, these groups were more ambivalent about such support, not always so concerned about the particular form of civilization others felt called upon to support. The Dissenters were quicker to condemn the vices of the rough frontier—alcohol, prostitution, economic and social exploitation—and uphold a tougher moral code, although still with the Bible as a key to morality.

In Australia, the Catholics were held as equivalent to Dissenters, especially since the majority of the early convicts were Irish Catholics. The Church of England, by contrast, assumed without question its established role: the first church in Australia is St. John's in Parramatta, claiming from the beginning a string of "firsts": first worship, first communion, first church building, and so on. Dissenters tended to move out of the small urban zones to take up lots in remoter bushland. For instance, John Dunmore Lang, a Presbyterian, worked for many years in the Hunter Valley north of Sydney with the Scottish settlers in the area, while the Methodists spread into the hinterland of the valley and its surrounding hills and mountains.

Of course, the particular situation in Australia has its own peculiarities: one might take the Catholic presence in the Philippines, the Dutch Reformed Church in Indonesia or South Africa, the various efforts by many groups in India and trace the various contours of the local scene. I would suggest, however, that one major use of the Bible was in the provision of religious structures and institutions for the immigrants from the colonial center.

Although there was a perpetual interaction with indigenous people, and even though the religious professional might at times see himself (as they were invariably male) an agent for civilizing the Aborigines, it is important to distinguish between the greater number of those professionals ministering to fellow colonial invaders and the smaller number who sought to bring the Bible to the indigenous inhabitants. Where large numbers of such indigenes remained—as in India, Africa, Pacific Islands—there were considerably greater efforts to convert them to Christianity, with widely varying success. In the Pacific Islands such efforts were quite successful, whereas the missions in India foundered time and again, some missionaries themselves converting to Hinduism. With the rapid retreat and high numbers of early deaths through warfare and disease, the Australian Aborigines were the subject of less missionary activity, and the apparent lack of success led many early missionaries to give away the effort. A significant feature of the missionary efforts in Australia is that they were undertaken by churches more on the fringe of early colonial society (although the newly federated government did in 1901 establish four churches, the Anglican, Presbyterian, Methodist, and Catholic churches). For example, the Catholics established missions in the Kimberley Mountains of Western Australia, the Lutherans and Presbyterians in Central Australia, and, as we saw, the Congregationalists with Threlkeld in New South Wales. For the Protestants at least there was a strong evangelical zeal that was closer to the spirit of many Dissenting churches, a zeal that saw the Bible as central for salvation itself. So they shared a more critical attitude toward the colonial governments and their practices that was characteristic of the Dissenting groups, seeing the establishment of the missions as a means to protect the Aborigines from economic, sexual, and social exploitation at the hands of less-scrupulous settlers. That many of the mission superintendents were no better goes without saying, but it is worth observing that in so many ways—unseen to those who sought what they perceived as only the best for Aboriginal people—these missionaries with oppositional ideologies reinforced all the more the colonial cultures from which they came.

What interests me in all of this is the role of the Bible, for apart from various spasmodic translation efforts of the Bible into indigenous languages (efforts that continue in a similarly piecemeal fashion today), the Bible was a central document for the missionaries, translated or not. Apart from the usual expectations of the Bible—the text from which the key myths of Christianity were drawn and from which they gained their life, the text that provided a basis for a certain moral way of life, the text that formed the foundation of preaching to the variegated congregations of the missionaries—it was also a tool used for the production of a written literacy where none had formerly existed. Thus, the Bible became both the justification for a new form of literacy—the provision of a new and very artificial set of skills in order to read the Bible—and the very means of that literacy—the biblical stories became the literacy lessons themselves.

All of the previous discussion remains at the level of missionary intention, however befuddled and vague that might have been. This is not to say that such processes where the end and means merge into one another are not without interest; rather, what is more intriguing are what the indigenes did with the Bible when they got hold of it, way beyond any possible intention of the missionaries. This realm is precisely that of Ernst Bloch's intense focus, atheistic Marxist that he was, on the strange ubiquity of the Bible, its ability to be appropriated by the most diverse groups of people in vastly different times and places (see Bloch 1972, 21–25). So, in the case of Australia, which has been the focus of this particular study, what did the Aborigines do with the Bible once they had taken it?

CONCLUSION: (E)STRANGE DIALECTICS

I cannot proceed without stressing how foreign the Bible at first is to any group like the Australian Aborigines: it contains stories about certain somewhat legendary, mythical, and possibly real people in a small location in the Middle East quite some years ago, appropriated by a medieval and then imperial Europe, which then takes it on its various journeys of colonial conquest throughout the world. Unexpectedly in terms of both time and place—the Indian Brahman class was uninterested, whereas the Dalits were more so, as also were the Australian Aborigines after a time and in their own way—the Bible has been adopted by a vast range of people. It is the terms of such an adoption that has always been beyond the expectation of its purveyors.

Particularly for those for whom the Bible led to a whole new set of technical skills and its associated cultural dimension, that is, literacy, the Bible became a central feature of altered forms of communication, authority, and social interaction. Even when, as in many Aboriginal communities in Australia that are still primarily oral cultures and in which the written word plays a vastly different role from dominantly written cultures, the appearance of the Bible as a written document has brought a whole new realm of culture hitherto unknown. For literacy, as in the case of Ernabella in central Australia, which I discussed in the previous chapter, entails the production of a new, written language that differs not just in medium (oral or written) but in its very nature from oral language. It is as though the Derridean ban on *hors texte* begins to threaten the patterns of (oral) language that had existed until the arrival of the Bible.[1] Literacy, of course, has a whole range of institutions from which it can hardly be separated: education, a book industry (however small), lexica, grammars, and the creation of the "writer." In some form or another, these institutions also arrived, along with the dominant institutions of government and church, along with the Bible.

There is a specific feature of literacy that will kick my discussion onto another level, namely, the adoption of literacy as a strategy by all socialist revolutionary movements and governments. Cuba, Nicaragua, Eritrea, South Africa are perhaps the better known examples where literacy is a revolutionary strategy, despite, or perhaps because of, its indelible Enlightenment credentials (for at one time the Enlightenment was a distinctly revolutionary movement). This is not to say that literacy is inherently revolutionary, or even socialist, for its use has time and again been reactionary, and often where the Bible has played a key role in literacy itself.

---

1. One might want to argue, in another place, that Derrida's argument, no matter how much he seems to set it up in terms of Greek philosophy, takes the Bible as its primary referent.

Even in these situations it is somewhat dangerous—in the eyes at least of ecclesial and state power—to let the Bible out of the hegemonic cage, however much the desire may be to use the Bible as a key for that cage. For in it may be found stories of exodus, of freedom from oppression, or, as Ernst Bloch puts it, the "leap from the Kingdom of Necessity to that of Freedom" (Bloch 1972, 69) that he identifies as the root of Marx's own passion, of prophetic condemnations of oppression and exploitation, of the promise of a new thing, a new dispensation in which there will be no more oppression and evil, parables of a radically different order and the urgent expectation of the early church for the parousia, the *eschaton*. Of course, these stories, as I have argued earlier, are profoundly ambiguous and have often led to the justification of oppression itself.

But there is another cluster of ideas that seems to have played an equally important role in the consciousness of those who adopted a very foreign Bible as their own. There runs a thread through the Jewish and Christian Bibles that speaks of the chosen people, of a people called by God from all other peoples to be a chosen, divinely sanctioned group of people, whether ancient "Israel" or the early Christians in all their splintered and conflicting forms. In the appropriation of the theme to a Christianity that was European rather than Jewish, the chosen people become those who believe and, more often than not, belong to the church, which then becomes the location of the chosen, especially in Catholic and Orthodox forms. For indigenous people to indicate belief and join such a church also means taking on the idea of being part of God's chosen people.

Further, in the historical form that such an understanding of the chosen people took—that is, in Europe—there was an inevitable connection with the rise of the nation-state. Indeed, it might be argued that, since the nation-state did not arise out of the blue, the Bible itself played a part in the development of the nation-state itself, that certain ideas, appropriated as they were in a particular way within capitalism and within the form the state took in this socioeconomic formation, were drawn from the Bible. Of course, then the various nation-states of Europe were read back into what was perceived as the nation-state of "Israel," which in a curious dialectical move became the Ur-state, the model upon which it was felt all subsequent states depended, ordained as they were by God.

It is this conjunction that was both part of the language of collective human existence used by the missionaries and was so different from indigenous forms of understanding human interaction and social life. In other words, the emergence of the Bible among indigenous people, and especially their appropriation of that text in their own ways (as I tracked in some way in my discussion of translation), was foundational in the formation of a language and a consciousness of being in some way a distinct people, a "nation" with a distinct identity, culture, linguistic grouping, and ethnicity. Thus, the indigenous people of Canada call themselves the "first nations," and the Australian Aborigines increasingly see themselves as "Koori," with an identity much older than and distinct from the invaders and settlers of other nations. And all the appurtenances of a nation-state begin to appear: new forms of government, a flag or two, a distinct culture, new institutions—although all of these are adapted in the distinct forms of local history and social formation. For instance, the idea of a judiciary, unthinkable in that sense before a European presence, becomes an adaptation and mutation of older practices of oral law and the peculiar European practices that have become an inescapable part of the scene. What I want to stress, however, is that no matter what shape such an institution takes, its existence as an institution is a new thing.

The point of all of this is that these various ideas and the institutions and practices to which they relate are different dimensions of what it means to be a distinct people, a nation in its own right. And it is this that was fundamental in the growth of independence movements, of anticolonial struggles and the desire for new nation-states now independent of their colonial maters. To be sure, this took a myriad of forms—a first wave for those where the European settlers became numerically dominant (the United States, Canada, Australia, New Zealand), a second wave that crested in the middle decades of the twentieth century in a host of countries (India, Cuba, the Pacific Islands, and so on), and then a third wave of indigenous peoples left out of the picture and now struggling for a sense of independence. Not only is this third wave remarkable for its global range (representatives of different indigenous peoples confer and share strategies as though they were distinct political entities from distinct nation-states), but the very terms of indigenous politics cannot but help speak of preserving "culture" or "society," of fostering "language," of land "rights," of need for "independence." It is a coincidence, it seems to me, that the religious affiliation of these peoples is, for better or worse, Christian. Thus, in the case of the Australian Aborigines, to speak of Aboriginal religions is to speak first of Christianity, however different it may now be in indigenous hands. And among Aborigines the Bible remains a central document that has entered into their consciousness. For more often than not, they too identify with Israel, with God's chosen people, especially since the devotion to Christianity is of a distinctly conservative type.

So, in a pattern that can only be understood in a dialectical fashion, the Bible twists and turns from being a text central to the culture of the colonial invader to that which provides, in part at least, the ideological means for independence from that colonial power, appropriated, turned, reread in a way that goes well beyond any colonial intention. Whether this is to be assessed as a positive or negative move is something I have consciously left out of consideration, partly for political reasons, since I do not wish to attack something that is crucial for Australian Aboriginal politics. Yet, as with my critique of the use of the exodus theme in an earlier chapter, the debilitating effects of such a strategy, inevitable though it might be in many respects, must not be forgotten, for the Bible is not always, to allude to Bloch again, good news for the poor and downtrodden nor bad news for the rich and powerful.

Shaking the World

If I have sought to track, in a somewhat cursory fashion, a blind spot of postcolonial criticism in the preceding section, then in what follows I veer into the wind, as it were, to take on a central motif of postcolonial criticism. It is virtually unexamined that opposition is a key to the very definition of postcolonialism, for its very existence as a discourse, to use a term that I like less and less, is that it constitutes and enables a stand over against the forces of global capitalism, and colonialism in particular.

Yet much of the criticism written under the banner of postcolonialism is quite wearying, reiterating time and again this search for some oppositional form or other in particular local sites. Even when there is an awareness of the global saturation of capital, of the ways reification and commodification have structured our social and psychological selves, the discussion turns repeatedly to a regressive search for specific oppositional groups and practices. I would suggest that this theoretical move derives from the political practice of the anticolonial wars, which invariably began with the location of an alternative space from which the insurrections might be launched. The most obvious example is that of the *foco* theory and practice in the Cuban revolution, but it also includes Gandhi's passive resistance. By and large, however, the anticolonial effort took the form of guerilla warfare, from Ireland to Angola, which brought about in various ways the postcolonial state, however much it replicated the colonial forms and institutions of government, even down to the patterns of corruption, after ousting the colonial power itself.

This oppositional space drew on alternative ideological forms as well, often of a Marxist variety, since the wars were being fought against colonial powers that were at the center of imperial or global capitalism. It was then quite unremarkable that the wars of anticolonialism should be drawn into the global Cold War, with opposition to the new postcolonial states drawing its ideology and material resources from capitalist powers, most notably the United States; Nicaragua and Vietnam are the two best-known examples. And so, as Bart Moore-Gilbert traces so well, the initial long wave of postcolonial criticism was determined and informed by Marxism, its significant figures then recuperated in later episodes of postcolonial criticism: Frantz Fanon, Che Guevara, Paolo Frere, and so on. Moore-Gilbert, as I noted earlier, distinguishes between postcolonial *criticism* and postcolonial *theory* in order to highlight the difference between this earlier, more Marxist phase and the later phase that is informed more directly by poststructuralism and postmodernism and, as Dirlik reminds us, is carried out by stellar critics in top First World universities (Said, Spivak, and Bhabha being the most notable).

But it is the inseparable bond between Marxist theory and practice of the earlier phase that has made opposition, specifically from spaces not yet colonized (whether geographical, ideological, cultural, psychological, or political) a crucial element that has remained with postcolonial theory, to adopt Moore-Gilbert's nomenclature. However, as Fredric Jameson reminds us, this is a particularly modernist form of Marxist oppositional practice and theory, predicated upon the incomplete dominance of capitalism in the global scene. Indeed, Jameson's argument that the development of modernism is heavily indebted to the cultural impact of colonialism itself upon the metropolitan centers, that it is inconceivable, in other words, without colonialism, stresses my point from another angle. That is to say, if colonialism was a crucial feature of both global or monopoly capitalism and its respective culture, modernism, then opposition to colonialism—in economic, political, and cultural modes—of necessity had to take a distinctive modernist shape. And that shape was marked with holes, enclaves, regions of the minimal presence, if not complete absence, of capitalist economic and social relations. So it was possible, and often highly successful, to launch anticolonial moves from precisely such spaces.

The time has, of course, changed, and despite the continuing of many modernist cultural and intellectual practices, it is now a minor partner to postmodernism and all that that entails. Bart Moore-Gilbert's distinction between postcolonial criticism and theory can now be seen as a difference between modernist and postmodernist types of postcolonialism (however cumbersome a postmodern postcolonialism might look). One of the features of postmodernism is the rapid disappearance of these enclaves and spaces of resistance, the rampant plundering by the agents of capitalism of those last hideouts, whether of the psyche, or of culture, or of nature. In fact, these spaces become the research arms, if you like, of capitalism's relentless search for self-renewal, the swallowing up of everything that is distinct and different into the commercial machine. For instance, Australian Aboriginal art is taken up into the global art market, indigenous religion becomes "spirituality" and is drawn into the conglomeration of New Age spirituality, nature is preserved only in spaces set aside by human being ("parks") that become sites for eco-tourism, the very opposition to multinational and transnational business is merely the conflict of one form of capitalism (small business, local culture) to another.

For those keen on the possibility of activism in this late capitalist global order, this is a somewhat bleak picture. In speaking of capitalism, I use the threefold distinction between classical capitalism (the first, exploratory establishment of capitalism, the age of exploration of the new bourgeoisie), monopoly or imperial capitalism (colonialism), and late capitalism (the era of multi- and transnational companies, of the digital revolution, and so on). In this third and most relentlessly global form, trade unions, eco-activists, indigenous movements, debt warriors, and economic militants must seek new ways of operating, since those of the past are increasingly unsuccessful. And it is only regressive to lay claim to older forms of political and social organization in order to oppose the new dispensation, or to make use of other forms of capitalism to oppose those that are felt to be debilitating. (I am thinking, for instance, of the valorization of the nation-state as an inviolable zone over against transnationals, or of the drives to purchase only certain types of consumer goods).

This situation creates all sorts of difficulties for the bulk of postcolonial criticism and theory in its search for those zones of opposition, for they turn out to be in various ways already saturated with capitalist social and economic relations. For instance, even in Aboriginal communities where money, commodities, art sales, tourism, the sale of labor power, and so on are appropriated in ways different from those in other places, the very presence of these and other features of capitalism has already altered the nature of these communities. Is the only answer capitulation, acquiescence, with a sigh of resignation, into the world system?

The beginnings of answer may be found in two places: the Bible and Marx. The pattern I traced a little earlier in this conclusion of the Bible's own curious path from colonial text, to an adopted, owned, and reread text by those colonized, to the profound effects on religious, cultural, and political sensibilities, to being a key text many, many postcolonial places. So much so that there are more Christians in these formerly colonial spaces than in the lands from which the colonial marauders and missionaries began. This should be qualified slightly, since I am thinking here of those that undertook the second wave of anticolonial activity in the twentieth century.[2] Here

---

2. A valid objection is that some colonial places were and are Muslim (the Middle East and North Africa) or Hindu (India) or Buddhist (China). While I feel that the situation is somewhat different in China, the Muslim countries have of course the Hebrew Bible or Old Testament as Scripture as well, apart from the perpetual Christian undercurrent in

a thoroughly foreign tool, a colonial text, becomes a key factor in the anticolonial drive and postcolonial status of these countries.

It is a somewhat homeopathic option, to be sure, but one that I would like to reinforce with Marx's own argument, one that is often forgotten even by Marxists. Given Marxism's desire to move beyond capitalism and thereby sublate itself, we need to return to Marx's insight that only when capitalism is global, when no enclaves are left, does it become possible to generate an opposition from within the contradictions of capitalism. Ironically, it is with the "fall" of communism in Eastern Europe that such a possibility is again on the agenda, for not only is capitalism more radically global than ever before, but its contradictions are more glaringly obvious on the other side of the Cold War. To evoke an example contemporary to the writing of this conclusion, the "five days that shook the world," the massive protests that derailed the World Trade Organization's meeting in Seattle in November 1999, took place through a widely organized alliance of many groups—unions, students, ecoactivists, antipoverty fighters, anarchists, socialists and so on—in the most overdeveloped capitalist place in the world.

For it seems to me that such contradictions presage what might be termed postcapitalism. In the same way that the "post" of postmodernism and postcolonialism functions as a burning-off, to evoke an Australian Aboriginal practice to encourage new growth, a clearing out of the space and debris of the past (Appiah 1996, 61), so that the new may be thought and practiced, so also postcapitalism might, in this context, begin to be thought. What is needed, then, is to search for glimmers and shards of new ways of being that are global, that seek to leap forward from the "enabling violation" (Spivak 1996, 19; 1988, 90; 1990, 147), of global capitalism and begin to imagine what a changed human nature might look like.

---

these places, and India had both an anticolonial leader who read the Bible deeply (Gandhi) and a long Muslim era ended by the British Raj.

Bibliography

Achebe, C. 1993. The African Writer and the English Language. Pages 428–34 in Williams and Chrisman 1993a.
Adam, I., and H. Tiffin. 1991. Introduction. Pages i–viii in *Past the Last Post: Theorizing Post-colonialism and Post-modernism*. Edited by I. Adam and H. Tiffin. London: Harvester Wheatsheaf.
Adorno, T. W. 1993. *Minima Moralia: Reflections from Damaged Life*. Translated by E. F. N. Jephcott. London: Verso.
Afshar, F. 1994 Globalization: The Persisting Rural-Urban Question and the Response of Planning Education. *Journal of Planning Education & Research* 13:271–83.
Ahlström, G. W. 1986. *Who Were the Israelites?* Winona Lake, Ind.: Eisenbrauns.
———. 1993. *The History of Ancient Palestine from the Palaeolithic Period to Alexander's Conquest*. Sheffield: JSOT Press.
Ahmad, A. 1992. *In Theory: Classes, Nations, Literatures*. London: Verso.
Albright, W. F. 1957. *From the Stone Age to Christianity: Monotheism and the Historical Process*. New York: Doubleday.
Alt, A. 1966. The Settlement of Israel in Palestine. Pages 133–69 in idem, *Essays on Old Testament History and Religion*. Oxford: Blackwell.
Amin, S. 1990. *Delinking: Towards a Polycentric World*. Translated by M. Wolfers. London, N.J.: Zed Books.
Appadurai, A. 1993. Disjuncture and Difference in the Global Cultural Economy. Pages 324–39 in Williams and Chrisman 1993a.
Appiah, K. A. 1996. Is the Post- in Postmodernism the Post- in Postcolonialism? Pages 55–71 in Mongia 1996.
Ashcroft, B., G. Griffiths, and H. Tiffin, eds. 1989. *The Empire Writes Back: Theory and Practice in Post-colonial Literature*. London: Routledge.
———. 1998. *Key Concepts in Post-colonial Studies*. London: Routledge.
Assmann, J. 1996. Translating Gods: Religion as a Factor of Cultural. Untranslatability. Pages 25–36 in *The Translatability of Cultures: Figurations of the Space Between*. Edited by S. Budick and W. Iser. Stanford, Calif.: Stanford University Press.
Bakhtin, Mikhail. 1981. *The Dialogic Imagination: Four Essays*. Translated by C. Emerson and M. Holquist. Austin: University of Texas Press.

Barnstone, W. 1993. *The Poetics of Translation: History, Theory, Practice*. New Haven: Yale University Press.

Barnwell, K. 1980. *Introduction to Semantics and Translation, with Special Reference To Bible Translation*. 2nd ed. Horsleys Green: Summer Institute of Linguistics.

Baudrillard, J. 1988. *America*. Translated by C. Turner. London: Verso.

———. 1990. *Cool Memories*. Translated by C. Turner. London: Verso.

Beekman, J., and J. Callow. 1974. *Translating the Word of God*. Grand Rapids: Zondervan.

Behdad, A. 1994. *Belated Travelers: Orientalism in the Age of Colonial Dissolution*. Durham, N.C.: Duke University Press.

Belasco, W. J. 1979. *Americans on the Road: From Autocamp to Motel, 1910–1945*. Cambridge, Mass.: MIT Press.

Bell, S., and B. Head, eds. 1994. *State, Economy and Public Policy in Australia*. Melbourne: Oxford University Press.

Bello, W. 1994. *Dark Victory: The United States, Structural Adjustment, and Global Poverty*. London: Pluto Press in Association with the Institute for Food and Development Policy and Transnational Institute.

Benjamin, W. 1992. The Task of the Translator. Pages 70–82 in idem, *Illuminations*. London: Fontana.

Benterrak, K., S. Muecke, and P. Roe. 1984. *Reading the Country; Introduction to Nomadology*. Fremantle, Western Australia: Fremantle Arts Centre Press.

Bentham, J. 1843. *Panopticon Versus New South Wales: Or, the Panopticon Penitentiary System, and the Penal Colonization System, Compared. In a Letter Addressed to the Right Honourable Lord Pelham*. Pages 173–248 in vol. 4 of *The Works of Jeremy Bentham*. Edited by J. Bowring. Endinburgh: William Tate.

———. 1995. *The Panopticon Writings*. Edited by M. Bośovič. London: Verso.

Berquist, Jon L. 1995. *Judaism in Persia's Shadow: A Social and Historical Approach*. Minneapolis: Ausburg. Repr., Wipf & Stock, 2003.

Beyer, P. 1994. *Religion and Globalization*. London: Sage.

Bhabha, H. K. 1992. The World and the Home. *Social Text* 10/2–3:141–53.

———. 1994. *The Location of Culture*. London: Routledge.

Bible Society. 1973. *Tjukurpa Tjiitjanyatjara*. Translated by D. Hackett and A. Glass. Canberra: The Bible Society.

———. 1976. *Tjukurrpa Tjiitjanya Ngaarnmankutja*. Canberra: The Bible Society.

Bible Society in Australia. 1997. *Tjukurpa Palya: Irititja Munu Kuwaritja*. Translated by translation team with P. Eckert and A. Eckert. Canberra: The Bible Society in Australia.

Blainey, G. 1975. *Triumph of the Nomads: A History of Ancient Australia*. Melbourne: Macmillan.

———. 1983. *The Tyranny of Distance: How Distance Shapes Australia's History*. Revised edition. Melbourne: Sun Books.

Blake, B. J. 1991. *Australian Aboriginal Languages: A General Introduction*. 2nd edition. St. Lucia, Queensland: University of Queensland Press.
Bloch, Ernst. 1972. *Atheism in Christianity: The Religion of the Exodus and of the Kingdom*. Translated by J. T. Swann. New York: Herder & Herder.
———. 1995. *The Principle of Hope*. Translated by N. Plaice, S. Plaice, and P. Knight. Cambridge, Mass.: MIT Press.
Boehmer, E. 1995. *Colonial and Postcolonial Literature*. Oxford: Oxford University Press.
Boer, R. 1996a. *Jameson and Jeroboam*. Semeia Studies 30. Atlanta: Scholars Press.
———. 1996b. Green Ants and Gibeonites: B. Wongar, Joshua 9 and Some Problems of Postcolonialism. *Semeia* 75:129–52.
———. 1999. *Knockin' on Heaven's Door*. London: Routledge.
———, ed. 2001a. *A Vanishing Mediator? The Absence/Presence of the Bible in Postcolonialism*. Semeia 88. Atlanta: Society of Biblical Literature.
———. 2001b. Introduction: Vanishing Mediators? Pages 1–12 in Boer 2001a.
———. 2003. *Marxist Criticism of the Bible: A Critical Introduction to Marxist Literary Criticism and the Bible*. London: Continuum.
———. 2005. Marx, Postcolonialism and the Bible. Pages 166–83 in *Postcolonial Biblical Criticism: Interdisciplinary Intersections*. Edited by Stephen Moore and Fernando Segovia. London: T&T Clark International.
———. 2006. *Novel Histories: The Fiction of Biblical Criticism*. Repr., Atlanta: Society of Biblical Literature, 2006. (Orig. 1997)
———. 2007. *Criticism of Heaven: On Marxism and Theology*. Historical Materialism Books Series 18. Leiden: Brill.
Bośovič, M. 1995. Introduction: An Utterly Dark Spot. Pages 1–27 of J. Bentham, *The Panopticon Writings*. Edited by M. Bośovič; London: Verso.
Boyer, Robert. 1990. *The Regulation School: A Critical Introduction*. Translated by Craig Charney. New York: Columbia University Press.
Bowe, H. J. 1990. *Categories, Constituents and Constituent Order in Pitjantjatjara, an Aboriginal Language of Australia*. London: Routledge.
Boyarin, D., and J. Boyarin. 1995. Diaspora: Generation and the Ground of Jewish Identity. Pages 305–37 in *Identities*. Edited by K. A. Appiah and H. L. Gates Jr. Chicago: University of Chicago Press.
Brett, Mark. 2000. *Genesis: Procreation and the Politics of Identity*. London: Routledge.
Brewster, A. 1995. *Literary Formations: Post-colonialism, Nationalism, Globalism*. Melbourne: Melbourne University Press.
Bright, J. 1980. *A History of Israel*. 3rd edition. London: SCM.
British and Foreign Bible Society in Australia. 1960. *Tjukurpa Palya Markaku Munu Tjukurpa Palya Johnku*. Translated by J. R. B. Love and J. Trudinger. n.p.: The British and Foreign Bible Society in Australia.
———. 1969. *Tjukurpa Palya Jesunya*. Canberra: The British and Foreign Bible Society.

Brown, D. 1991. An Institutional Look at Postmodernism *Journal of Economic Issues* 25:1089–1104.
Buckley, K., and T. Wheelwright. 1988. *No Paradise for Workers: Capitalism and the Common People in Australia 1788–1914.* Melbourne: Oxford University Press.
Callaghan, D. 1995. The Vicar and Virago: Feminism and the Problem of Identity. Pages 195–207 in Roof and Wiegman 1995.
Cathcart, M. 1997. Eyes of the Beholders. *The Australian's Review of Books* 2 March:6–7.
Cerny, P. G. 1994. The Dynamics of Financial Globalization—Technology, Market Structure, and Policy Response. *Policy Sciences* 27/4:319–42.
Chakrabarty, D. 1996. Postcoloniality and the Artifice of History: Who Speaks for Indian Pasts? Pages 223–47 in Mongia 1996.
Chaseling, W.S. 1957. *Yulengor: Nomads of Arnhem Land.* London: Epworth.
Collins, J. J. 1993. *Daniel: A Commentary on the Book of Daniel.* Minneapolis: Augsburg Fortress.
Confoy, M., D. A. Lee, and J. Nowotny, eds. 1995. *Freedom and Entrapment: Women Thinking Theology.* North Blackburn, Victoria: Dove.
Connor, M., and D. Matthews. 1989. In the Tracks of the Reader, in the Tracks of B. Wongar. *Meanjin* 48:713–21.
Cooke, M. 1995. Understood by All Concerned? Anglo/Aboriginal Legal Translation. Pages 37–63 in *Translation and the Law.* Edited by M. Morris. American Translators Association Scholarly Monograph Series 8. Amsterdam: Benjamins.
Coombes, A. E. 1994. The Recalcitrant Object: Culture Contact and the Question of Hybridity. Pages 89–114 in *Colonial Discourse/Postcolonial Theory.* Edited by F. Barker, P. Hulme, and M. Iversen. Manchester: Manchester University Press.
Coote, R. B. 1990. *Early Israel: A New Horizon.* Minneapolis: Fortress.
Coote, R. B., and K. W. Whitelam. 1987. *The Emergence of Early Israel in Historical Perspective.* Sheffield: Almond.
Copleston, F. 1963. *Ockham to Suárez.* Vol. 3 of idem, *A History of Philosophy.* London: Burns & Oates.
Cowan, G. M. 1979. *The Word That Kindles.* Huntingdon Beach, Calif: Wycliffe.
Cowhey, P. F., and J. D. Aronson. 1993. *Managing the World Economy: The Consequences of Corporate Alliances.* New York: Council on Foreign Relations Press.
Coxon, P. W. 1986. The Great Tree of Daniel 4. Pages 124–41 in *A Word in Season: Essays in Honour of William McKane.* Edited by J. D. Martin and P. R. Davies. Journal for the Study of the Old Testament Supplement Series 42. Sheffield: JSOT Press.
Croatto, J. S. 1987. *Biblical Hermeneutics.* Maryknoll, N.Y.: Orbis.
Curthoys, A. 1998. National Narratives, War Commemoration, and Racial Exclusion in a Settler Society: The Australian Case. Pages 173–90 in *Becom-*

ing Australian. Edited by R. Nile and R. Peterson. Brisbane: University of Queensland Press.

Dandeker, C. 1994. New Times for the Military: Some Sociological Remarks on the Changing Role and Structure of the Armed Forces of the Advanced Societies. *British Journal of Sociology* 45:637–54.

Darby, P. 1998. *The Fiction of Imperialism: Reading Between International Relations and Postcolonialism*. London: Cassell.

Davies, M. R., J. Greenwood, and L. Robins. 1995. Public Administration Education and Training: Globalization or Fragmentation. *International Review of Administrative Sciences* 61:73–78.

Davies, P. 1992. *In Search of "Ancient Israel."* Journal for the Study of the Old Testament Supplement Series 148. Sheffield: JSOT Press.

Deleuze, G., and F. Guattari. 1983. *Anti-Oedipus: Capitalism and Schizophrenia*. Translated by R. Hurley, M. Seem, and H. R. Lane, with a preface by M. Foucault, and an introduction by Mark Seem. Minneapolis: University of Minnesota Press.

———. 1987. *A Thousand Plateaus: Capitalism and Schizophrenia*. Translated by B. Massumi. Minneapolis: University of Minnesota Press.

Derrida, Jacques. 1980. *Of Grammatology*. Translated by Gayatri Chakravorty Spivak. Baltimore: John Hopkins University Press.

———. 1994. *Specters of Marx: The State of the Debt, the Work of Mourning, and the New International*. Translated by Peggy Kamuf, with an introduction by Bernd Magnus and Stephen Cullenberg. New York: Routledge.

Devi, M. 1995. *Imaginary Maps*. Translated by G. C. Spivak; New York: Routledge.

Dicken, P. 1992. *Global Shift: The Internationalization of Economic Activity*. 2nd edition. New York: Guildford.

Dirlik, A. 1996. The Global in the Local. Pages 21–45 in Wilson and Dissanayake 1996a.

———. 1997. *The Postcolonial Aura: Third World Criticism in the Age of Global Capitalism*. Boulder, Colo.: Westview.

Dixon, R. M. W. 1993. Australian Aboriginal Languages. Pages 71–82 in *The Languages of Australia*. Edited by G. Schulz. Papers from the Australian Academy of Humanities Symposium, Occasional Paper 14. Canberra: Australian Academy of the Humanities.

Dobrez, L. 1990. Wongar's Metamorphoses: *The Track to Bralgu*. Pages 161–72 in *Aspects of Australian Fiction: Essays Presented to John Colmer*. Edited by A. Brissenden. Nedlands, Western Australia: University of Western Australia Press.

Docker, J. 1995. The Neocolonial Assumption in University Teaching of English. Pages 443–46 in *The Post-colonial Studies Reader*. Edited by B. Ashcroft, G. Griffiths, and H. Tiffin. London: Routledge & Kegan Paul.

Docker, J., and G. Fischer. 2001. *Adventures of Identity: European Multicultural Experiences and Perspectives*. Tübingen: Stauffenburg.

Donaldson, Laura E., ed. 1996. *Postcolonialism and Scriptural Reading. Semeia* 75. Atlanta: Society of Biblical Literature.
Douglas, Mary. 1993. *In the Wilderness: The Doctrine of Defilement in the Book of Numbers*. Sheffield: JSOT Press.
Douglas, W. H. 1964. *An Introduction to the Western Desert Language: A Pedagogical Description of the Western Desert Language, Based on the Dialect Spoken at Warburton Ranges, Western Australia*. 2nd edition. Sydney: University of Sydney Press.
Drewe, R. 1981. Solved: The Great B. Wongar Mystery. *The Bulletin Literary Supplement* 21 April:2–7.
Dube, Musa. 2000. *Postcolonial Feminist Interpretation of the Bible*. St. Louis: Chalice.
Duff, A. 1839. *India and India Missions*. London: Hunter.
Dussell, E. 1998. Beyond Eurocentrism: The World-System and the Limits of Modernity. Pages 3–31 in Jameson and Miyoshi 1998.
Eades, D. 1982. You Gotta Know How to Talk…: Information Seeking in South-East Queensland Aboriginal Society. *Australian Journal of Linguistics* 2:61–82.
Eckert, A. 1982. Analysis of Written Style: An Imperative for Readable Translations. *Occasional Papers—Applied Linguistics Association of Australia* 5:18–25.
Eckert, P. 1998. Translation Questionnaire. Interview by R. Boer
Elliott, B. 1967. *The Landscape of Australian Poetry*. Melbourne: Cheshire.
Eyre, E. J. 1845. *Journals of Expeditions of Discovery into Central Australia and Overland from Adelaide to King George's Sound in the Years 1840–1; Sent by the Colonists of South Australia, with the Sanction and Support of the Government: Including an Account of the Manners and Customs of the Aborigines and the State of Their Relations with Europeans*. London: Boone.
———. 1984. *Autobiographical Narrative of Residence and Exploration in Australia 1832–1839*. Edited by J. Waterhouse. London: Caliban.
Featherstone, M. 1996. Localism, Globalism and Cultural Identity. Pages 46–77 in Wilson and Dissanayake 1996a.
Feuer, L. S. 1975. *Ideology and the Ideologists*. Oxford: Blackwell.
Fitzgerald, R. 1997. *The People's Champion, Fred Paterson: Australia's Only Communist Party Member of Parliament*. St. Lucia: Queensland University Press.
Foucault, M. 1979. *Discipline and Punish: The Birth of the Prison*. Translated by A. Sheridan. New York: Vintage.
Frampton, K. 1983. Towards a Critical Regionalism: Six Points for an Architecture of Resistance. Pages 16–30 *The Anti-aesthetic: Essays on Postmodern Culture*. Edited by in H. Foster. Port Townsend, Wa.: Bay Press.
Freud, S. 1939. *Moses and Monotheism*. Translated by K. Jones. New York: Random House.

———. 1973. *Introductory Lectures on Psychoanalysis*. Translated by J. Strachey. Edited by J. Strachey and A. Richards. The Pelican Freud Library, volume 1. Harmondsworth: Penguin.

Fuery, P. 1993. Prisoners and Spiders Surrounded by Signs: Postmodernism and the Postcolonial Gaze in Contemporary Australian Culture. Pages 190–207 in *Recasting the World: Writing after Colonialism*. Edited by J. White. Baltimore: Johns Hopkins University Press.

Fuss, D. 1989. *Essentially Speaking: Feminism, Nature and Difference*. New York: Routledge.

Gandhi, L. 1998. *Postcolonial Theory: A Critical Introduction*. St. Leonards, New South Wales: Allen & Unwin.

George, R. M. 1996. *The Politics of Home: Postcolonial Relocations and Twentieth-Century Fictions*. Cambridge: Cambridge University Press.

Giddens, A. 1990. *The Consequences of Modernity*. Cambridge: Polity.

Giles, E. 1889. *Australia Twice Traversed: The Romance of Exploration, Being a Narrative Compiled from the Journals of Five Exploring Expeditions into and through Central South Australia and Western Australia from 1872 to 1876*. London: Low, Marston, Searle & Rivington.

Gill, S., and D. Law. 1988. *The Global Political Economy: Perspectives, Problems, and Policies*. Baltimore: Johns Hopkins University Press.

Ginibi, R. L. 1996. The Right to Be a Koori Writer. Letter to the Editor. *The Australian*. 7 August:12.

Glass, A., and D. Hackett. 1970. *Pitjantjatjara Grammar: A Tagmemeic View of the Ngaanyatjarra (Warburton Ranges) Dialect*. Australian Aboriginal Studies 34. Canberra: Australian Institute of Aboriginal Studies.

Gmelch G., and S. B. Gmelch. 1987. Commercial Nomadism: Occupation and Mobility Among Travellers in England and Wales. Pages 133–53 *The Other Nomads: Peripatetic Minorities in Cross-cultural Perspective*. Edited by A. Rao. Kölner Ethnologische Mitteilungen. Köln: Böhlau.

Goddard, C. 1987. *A Basic Pitjantjatjara/Yankunytjatjara to English Dictionary*. Alice Springs, Northern Territory: Institute for Aboriginal Development.

Goldingay, J. E. 1989. *Daniel*. WBC 30. Dallas: Word.

Gottwald, N. K. 1979. *The Tribes of Yahweh: A Sociology of the Religion of Liberated Israel 1250–1050 B.C.E.* Maryknoll, New York: Orbis. Repr., Sheffield Academic Press, 1999.

———. 1985. *The Hebrew Bible: A Socio-literary Introduction*. Philadelphia: Fortress.

———. 1992. Sociology of Ancient Israel. Pages 79–89 in vol. 6 of *Anchor Bible Dictionary*. Edited by D. N. Freedman. 6 vols. New York: Doubleday.

———. 1993. *The Hebrew Bible in Its Social World and in Ours*. Semeia Studies 25. Atlanta: Scholars Press.

Gourgouris, S. 1995. Research, Essay, Failure. Flaubert's Itinerary. *New Literary History* 26:343–57.

Gramsci, Antonio. 1971. *Selections from the Prison Notebooks*. Edited by Quentin Hoare and G. Nowell Smith. London: Lawrence & Wishart.
Gray, J. 1967. *Joshua, Judges, and Ruth*. London: Nelson.
Grey, G. 1841. *Journals of Two Expeditions of Discovery in North-West and Western Australia, during the Years 1837, 38, and 39, under the Authority of Her Majesty's Government Describing Many Newly Discovered, Important, and Fertile Districts, with Observations on the Moral and Physical Condition of the Aboriginal Inhabitants*. 2 vols. London: Boone.
Guha, R., and G. C. Spivak., eds. 1988. *Selected Subaltern Studies*. New York: Oxford University Press.
Gunew, S. 1993. Culture, Gender and the Author-Function: Wongar's *Walg*. Pages 3–14 in *Australian Cultural Studies: A Reader*. Edited by J. Frow and M. Morris. Sydney: Allen & Unwin.
Gwin, M. 1996. Space Travel: The Connective Politics of Feminist Reading. *Signs* 21:870–905.
Hall, S. 1996. Cultural Identity and Diaspora. Pages 110–21 in Mongia 1996.
———. 1997. The Local and the Global: Globalization and Ethnicity. Pages 173–88 in *Cultural Politics*. Edited by A. McClintock, A. Mufti, and E. Shohat. Minneapolis: University of Minnesota Press.
Haraway, D. 1998. A Cyborg Manifesto: Science, Technology, and Socialist-Feminism in the Late Twentieth Century. Pages 696–727 in *Contemporary Literary Criticism: Literary and Cultural Studies*. Edited by R. Con-Davis and R. Schleifer. New York: Longman.
Hardt, Michael, and Antonio Negri. 2000. *Empire*. Cambridge: Harvard University Press.
Harris, J. 1988. North Australian Kriol-Historical Perspectives and New Directions. *Australian Review of Applied Linguistics* 11/1:1–8.
———. 1990. *One Blood: Two Hundred Years of Aboriginal Encounter with Christianity*. Sutherland, New South Wales: Albatross.
———. 1993. Losing and Gaining a Language: The Story of Kriol in the Northern Territory. Pages 145–54 in *Language and Culture in Aboriginal Australia*. Edited by M. Walsh and C. Yallop. Canberra: Aboriginal Studies Press.
———. 1995. Aboriginal Languages, Christian Missionaries, and Bible Translation. *Studies in the Humanities* 22:127–33.
Harvey, D. 1998. What's Green and Makes The Environment Go Round? Pages 327–55 in Jameson and Miyoshi 1998.
Harvey, J., and F. Houle. 1994. Sport, World Economy, Global Culture, and New Social Movements. *Sociology of Sport Journal* 11:337–55.
Hegel, G. W. F. 1977. *Phenomenology of Spirit*. Translated by A. V. Miller. Oxford: Clarendon.
Helleiner, E. 1994. *States and the Reemergence of Global Finance: From Bretton Woods to the 1990s*. Ithaca, N.Y.: Cornell University Press.

Hetata, S. 1998. Dollarization, Fragmentation, and God. Pages 273–90 in Jameson and Miyoshi 1998.
Hodge, B., and V. Mishra. 1990. *Dark Side of the Dream: Australian Literature and the Postcolonial Mind*. Sydney: Allen & Unwin.
Hoglund, Kenneth. 1992. *Achaemenid Imperial Administration in Syria-Palestine and the Missions of Ezra and Nehemiah*. Society of Biblical Literature Dissertation Series 125. Atlanta: Scholars Press.
Hoksbergen, R. 1994. Postmodernism and Institutionalism: Toward a Resolution of the Debate on Relativism. *Journal of Economic Issues* 28:679–713.
Hoogvelt, A. 1997. *Globalisation and the Postcolonial World: The New Political Economy of Development*. Houndmills: Macmillan.
Hope, A. D. 1973. *Selected Poems*. Sydney: Angus & Robertson.
Horsley, Richard. 1998. Submerged Biblical Histories and Imperial Biblical Studies. Pages 152–73 in Sugirtharajah 1998a.
———. 1999. *Bandits, Prophets and Messiahs: Popular Movements in the Time of Jesus*. Harrisburg, Pa.: Trinity Press International.
———. 2001. *Hearing the Whole Story: The Politics of Plot in Mark's Gospel*. Louisville: Westminster John Knox.
———. 2002. *Jesus and Empire: The Kingdom of God and the New World Disorder*. Minneapolis: Fortress.
Houlihan, B. 1994. Homogenization, Americanization, and Creolization of Sport: Varieties of Globalization. *Sociology of Sport Journal* 11:356–75.
Hughes, R. 1996. *The Fatal Shore: A History of the Transportation of Convicts to Australia, 1787–1868*. London: Harvill.
James, C. L. R. 1993. *Beyond a Boundary*. Durham, N.C.: Duke University Press.
Jameson, F. 1981. *The Political Unconscious: Narrative as a Socially Symbolic Act*. Ithaca, N.Y.: Cornell University Press.
———. 1991. *Postmodernism, Or, the Cultural Logic of Late Capitalism*. Durham, N.C.: Duke University Press.
———. 1988. Cognitive Mapping. Pages 347–57 in *Marxism and the Interpretation of Culture*. Edited by Cary Nelson and Lawrence Grossberg. Houndmills: Macmillan.
———. 1998a. Preface. Pages xi–xvii in Jameson and Miyoshi 1998.
———. 1998b. Notes on Globalization as a Philosophical Issue. Pages 54–77 in Jameson and Miyoshi 1998.
Jameson, F., and M. Miyoshi, eds. 1998. *The Cultures of Globalization*. Durham, N.C.: Duke University Press.
Jameson, Fredric, and Paik Nak-Chung, 1996. South Korea as Social Space. Pages 348–71 in Wilson and Dissanayake 1996a.
Jamieson-Drake, D. W. 1991. *Scribes and Schools in Monarchic Israel: A Socio-archaeological Approach*. Sheffield: Almond.

JanMohamed, A. 1992. Worldliness-without-World, Homelessness-as-Home: Toward a Definition of the Specular Border Intellectual. Pages 96–120 in *Edward Said: A Critical Reader*. Edited by M. Sprinker. Oxford: Blackwell.

JanMohamed, A., and D. Lloyd. 1997. Toward a Theory of Minority Discourse: What Is to Be Done? Pages 234–47 in *Postcolonial Criticism*. Edited by B. Moore-Gilbert, G. Stanton, and W. Maley. London: Longman.

Jobling, D. 1984. Lévi-Strauss and the Structural Analysis of the Hebrew Bible. Pages 192–211 in *Anthropology and the Study of Religion*. Edited by R. Moore and F. Reynolds. Chicago: Center for the Scientific Study of Religion.

———. 1991. Feminism and Mode of Production in Israel: Search for a Method. Pages 239–51 in *The Bible and the Politics of Exegesis*. Edited by David Jobling, Peggy L. Day, and Gerald T. Sheppard. Cleveland: Pilgrim.

———. 1992a. Forced Labor: Solomon's Golden Age and the Question of Literary. Representation. *Semeia* 54:57–76.

———. 1992b. Deconstruction and the Political Analysis of Biblical Texts: A Jamesonian Reading of Psalm 72. *Semeia* 59:95–127.

———. 1998. *1 Samuel*. Collegeville, Minn.: Liturgical Press.

Kaplan, Caren. 1996. *Questions of Travel: Postmodern Discourses of Displacement*. Durham, N.C.: Duke University Press.

Kapur, G. 1998. Globalization and Culture: Navigating the Void. Pages 191–217 in Jameson and Miyoshi 1998.

Kilham, C. A. 1990a. A Written Style for Oral Communicators? *Australian Review of Applied Linguistics* Series S 5:64–82.

———. 1990b. Translation and Training in Aboriginal and Islander Australia. *Australian Review of Applied Linguistics* Series S 5:83–99.

———. 1991. *Translation Time: An Introductory Course in Translation*. Preliminary edition. Darwin: Summer Institute of Linguistics.

Kirby, R. G. 1989. Whose Company Is It, Anyway? *Journal of Portfolio Management* 16:13–18.

Kitson, J. 1989. Towards Global Publishing. *Meanjin* 48:295–99.

Kolodny, A. 1975. *The Lay of the Land: Metaphor as Experience and History in American Life and Letters*. Chapel Hill: University of North Carolina Press.

Koolmatrie, W. (L. Carmen). 1995. *My Own Sweet Time*. Broome: Magabala Books.

Kwok Pui-Lan. 1995. *Discovering the Bible in the Non-biblical World*. Maryknoll, N.Y.: Orbis.

———. 2005. *Postcolonial Imagination and Feminist Theology*. Louisville: Westminster John Knox.

Laclau, E., and C. Mouffe. 1985. *Hegemony and Socialist Strategy: Towards a Radical Democratic Politics*. London: Verso

Lacocque, A. 1979. *The Book of Daniel*. Translated by D. Pellauer. Foreword by P. Ricoeur. Atlanta: John Knox.

Larsen, N. 1990. Postmodernism and Imperialism: Theory and Politics in Latin America. *Postmodern Culture* 1. Online: http://www3.iath.virginia.edu/pmc/text-only/issue.990/larsen.990.

Larson, M. L. 1984. *Meaning-Based Translation—A Guide to Cross-Language Equivalence*. Lanham, Md.: University Press of America.

Lattas, A. 1997. Aborigines and Contemporary Australian Nationalism: Primordiality and the Cultural Politics of Otherness. Pages 223–55 in *Race Matters: Indigenous Australians and "Our" Society*. Edited by G. Cowlishaw and B. Morris. Canberra: Aboriginal Studies Press.

Lawson, H. 1976. *Henry Lawson*. Edited by B. Kiernan. Brisbane: University of Queensland Press.

Lears, T. J. J. 1980. From Salvation to Self-Realization: Advertising and the Therapeutic Roots of the Consumer Culture, 1880–1930. Pages 1–38 in *The Culture of Consumption: Critical Essays in American History, 1880–1980*. Edited by R. W. Fox and T. J. J. Lears. New York: Pantheon.

Lefebvre, H. 1994. *The Production of Space*. Translated by D. Nicholson-Smith. Oxford: Basil Blackwell.

Leichhardt, L. 1847. *Journal of an Overland Expedition in Australia, from Moreton Bay to Port Essington, a Distance of Upwards 3000 Miles, During the Years 1844–1845*. London: Boone.

Lemche, N. P. 1985. *Early Israel: Anthropological and Historical Studies in the Israelite Society Before the Monarchy*. Leiden: Brill.

Lenin, V. I. 1950. *Imperialism, the Highest Stage of Capitalism*. Moscow: Foreign Languages Publishing House.

Longacre, R.E. 1985. Tagmemics. *Word* 6:137–77.

———. 1989. *Joseph: A Story of Divine Providence. A Text Theoretical and Textlinguistic Analysis of Genesis 37 and 39–48*. Winona Lake, Ind.: Eisenbrauns.

Loomba, A. 1998. *Colonialism-Postcolonialism*. London: Routledge.

Louw, J. P., and E. A. Nida. 1992. *Lexical Semantics of the Greek New Testament*. Society of Biblical Literature Resources for Biblical Study 25. Atlanta: Scholars Press.

Louw, J. P., et al., eds. 1989. *Greek-English Lexicon of the New Testament: Based on Semantic Domains*. New York: United Bible Societies.

Lukács, G. 1971. *History and Class Consciousness Studies in Marxist Dialectics*. Translated by R. Livingstone. Cambridge, Mass.: MIT Press.

———. 1993. *The Theory of the Novel: A Historico-Philosophical Essay on the Forms of Great Epic Literature*. Translated by A. Bostock. Cambridge, Mass.: MIT Press.

MacCannell, D. 1976. *The Tourist: A New Theory of the Leisure Class*. London: Methuen.

Maguire, J. 1994. Sport, Identity Politics, and Globalization: Diminishing Contrasts and Increasing Varieties. *Sociology of Sport Journal* 11:398–427.

Marx, K. 1973. *Grundrisse: Foundations of the Critique of Political Economy (Rough Draft)*. Translated by M. Nicolaus. Harmondsworth: Penguin, in Association with New Left Books.
———. 1976. *Capital: A Critique of Political Economy*. Translated by B. Fowkes. Introduction by E. Mandel. Harmondsworth: Penguin, in association with New Left Books.
Marx, K., and F. Engels. 1967. *The Communist Manifesto*. Harmondsworth: Penguin.
———. 1976. *The German Ideology*. Moscow: Progress.
Masters, F. 1982. The Pioneers. Pages 195–66 in *Arno Bay and District 1883–1983*. Edited by J. Clements and M. Smith. Arno Bay: Arno Bay Centenary Committee.
McClintock, A. The Angel of Progress: Pitfalls of the Term Post-colonialism. Pages 291–304 in Williams and Chrisman 1993a.
McCole, John. 1993. *Walter Benjamin and the Antinomies of Tradition*. Ithaca, N.Y.: Cornell University Press.
McKinlay, Judith. 1996. *Gendering Wisdom the Host: Biblical Invitations to Eat and Drink*. Sheffield: Sheffield Academic Press.
———. 2004. *Reframing Her: Biblical Women in Postcolonial Focus*. Sheffield: Sheffield Phoenix.
Mendenhall, G. E. 1962. The Hebrew Conquest of Palestine. *Biblical Archaeologist* 25:66–87.
Meschonnic, H. 1970–73. *Pour la Poetique*. Paris: Gallimard.
Miller, M. 1995. Where Is Globalization Taking Us—Why We Need a New Woods, Bretton. *Futures* 27/2:125–44.
Mishra, V., and B. Hodge. 1993. What is Post(-)Colonialism. Pages 30–46 in *Australian Cultural Studies: A Reader*. Edited by J. Frow and M. Morris. Sydney: Allen & Unwin.
Mitchell, K. 1996. In Whose Interest? Transnational Capital and the Production of Multiculturalism. Pages 219–51 in Wilson and Dissanayake 1996a.
Mitchell, T. L. 1839. *Three Expeditons into the Interior of Australia; with Descriptions of the Recently Explored Australia Felix, and of the Present Colony of New South Wales*. 2nd ed. 2 vols. London: Boone.
———. 1848. *Journal of an Expedition into the Interior of Tropical Australia: In Search of a Route from Sydney to the Gulf of Carpentaria*. London: Longmans.
Miyoshi, M. 1996. A Borderless World? From Colonialism to Transnationalism and the Decline of the Nation-State. Pages 78–106 in Wilson and Dissanayake 1996a.
Mohanty, C. T. 1994. Under Western Eyes: Feminist Scholarship and Colonial Discourses. Pages 196–97 in Williams and Chrisman 1993a.
Mongia, P., ed. 1996. *Contemporary Postcolonial Theory: A Reader*. London: Arnold

Montgomery, J. A. 1927. *A Critical and Exegetical Commentary on the Book of Daniel*. ICC. Edinburgh: T&T Clark.
Moore, Stephen D. 2006. *Empire and Apocalypse: Postcolonialism and the New Testament*. Sheffield: Sheffield Phoenix.
Moore-Gilbert, B. 1997. *Postcolonial Theory: Contexts, Practices, Politics*. London: Verso.
Moore-Gilbert, B., G. Stanton, and W. Maley. 1997. Introduction. Pages 1–72 in *Postcolonial Criticism*. Edited by B. Moore-Gilbert, G. Stanton, and W. Maley. London: Longman.
Moran, T. H. 1990. The Globalization of America's Defense Industries: Managing the Threat of Foreign Dependence. *International Security* 15:57–99.
Morris, J. 1991. Globalization and Global Localization: Explaining Trends in Japanese Foreign Manufacturing Investment. Pages 1–13 in *Japan and the Global Economy: Issues and Trends in the 1990s*. Edited by J. Morris. London: Routledge.
Morris, M. 1988. Tooth and Claw: Tales of Survival and Crocodile Dundee. Pages 105–27 in *Universal Abandon? The Politics of Postmodernism*. Edited by A. Ross. Minneapolis: University of Minnesota Press.
———. 1990a. Metamorphoses at Sydney Tower. *New Formations* 11:5–18.
———. 1990b. Banality in Cultural Studies. Pages 14–43 in *Logics of Television*. Edited by P. Mellencamp. Bloomington: Indiana University Press.
———. 1992. On the Beach. Pages 450–78 in *Cultural Studies*. Edited by L. Grossberg, C. Nelson, and P. Treichler. New York: Routledge.
Mosala, Itumeleng. 1992. The Implications of the Text of Esther for African Women's Struggle for Liberation in South Africa. *Semeia* 59:130–41.
Mouffe, C. 1988. Hegemony and New Political Subjects: Toward a New Concept of Democracy. Pages 89–101 in *Marxism and the Interpretation of Culture*. Edited by C. Nelson and L. Grossberg. London: Macmillan.
———. 1993. *The Return of the Political*. London: Verso.
Mountford, C. P. 1976. *Nomads of the Australian Desert*. Adelaide: Rigby.
Moylan, Tom. 1997. Bloch Against Bloch: The Theological Reception of *Das Prinzip Hoffnung* and the Liberation of the Utopian Function. Pages 96–121 in *Not Yet: Reconsidering Ernst Bloch*. Edited by Jamie Owen Daniel and Tom Moylan. London: Verso.
Mudrooroo Narogin Nyoongah (C. Johnson). 1979. *Wild Cat Falling*. Sydney: Angus & Robertson.
———. 1983. *Doctor Wooredy's Prescription for Enduring the Ending of the World*. Melbourne: Hyland House.
———. 1987. *Long Live Sandawarra*. Melbourne: Hyland House.
———. 1991. *The Garden of Gethsemane: Poems from the Lost Decade*. South Yarra, Victoria: Hyland House.
———. 1992. *Wild Cat Screaming*. Sydney: Angus & Robertson.
———. 1993. *The Kwinkan*. Pymble, New South Wales: Angus & Robertson.

Muecke, S. 1997. *No Road: Bitumen All the Way*. Freemantle: Freemantle Arts Press.
Naficy, A. 1996. Phobic Spaces and Liminal Panics: Independent Transnational Film Genre. Pages 119–44 in Wilson and Dissanayake 1996a.
Nida, E. A. 1947a. *Bible Translating: An Analysis of Principles and Procedures, with Special Reference to Aboriginal Languages*. New York: American Bible Society.
———. 1947b. *A Translator's Commentary on Selected Passages*. Glendale, Calif.: Summer Institute of Linguistics.
———. 1949. *Morphology: The Descriptive Analysis of Words*. 2nd edition. Ann Arbor: University of Michigan Press.
———. 1951. *An Outline of Descriptive Syntax*. Glendale, Calif.: Summer Institute of Linguistics.
———. 1952. *God's Word in Man's Language*. New York: Harper & Brothers.
———. 1954. *Customs and Cultures: Anthropology for Christian Missions*. New York: Harper.
———. 1957. *Learning a Foreign Language: A Handbook Prepared Especially for Missionaries*. 2nd edition. New York: Friendship Press for the Committee on Missionary Personnel, Division of Foreign Missions, National Council of the Churches of Christ in the U.S.A.
———. 1964. *Toward a Science of Translating, with Special Reference to Principles and Procedures Involved in Bible Translation*. Leiden: Brill.
———. 1966. *A Synopsis of English Syntax*. 2nd ed. The Hague: Mouton.
———. 1975a. *Componential Analysis of Meaning: An Introduction to Semantic Structures*. The Hague: Mouton.
———. 1975b. *Exploring Semantic Structures*. Munich: Fink.
Nida, E. A., and C. R. Taber. 1969. *The Theory and Practice of Translation*. Leiden: Brill.
Noth, M. 1953. *Josua*. Tübingen: Mohr Siebeck.
———. 1960. *The History of Israel*. 2nd edition. Translated by P. R. Ackroyd. London: Black.
O'Brien, R. 1992. *Global Financial Integration: The End of Geography*. New York: Council on Foreign Relations Press.
Ohmae, K. 1990. *The Borderless World: Power and Strategy in the Interlinked Economy*. New York: Harper Business.
Paik Nak-Chung. 1998. Nations and Literatures in the Age of Globalization. Pages 218–29 in Jameson and Miyoshi 1998.
Parpart, J. L. 1993. Who Is the "Other"? A Postmodern Feminist Critique of Women and Development Theory and Practice. *Development and Change* 24:439–64.
Parry, B. 1996. Resistance Theory/Theorising Resistance or Two Cheers for Nativism. Pages 84–109 in Mongia 1996.

Pattel-Gray, A. 1995. Not Yet Tiddas: An Aboriginal Womanist Critique of Australian Church Feminism. Pages 165–92 in *Freedom and Entrapment: Women Thinking Theology*. Edited by M. Confoy, D. A. Lee, and J. Nowotny. North Blackburn, Victoria: Dove.

Paxman, D. B. 1995. "Adam in a Strange Country": Locke's Language Theory and Travel Literature. *Modern Philology* 92:460–81.

Picciotto, S. 1990. The Internationalization of the State. *Review of Radical Political Economics* 22:28–44.

Pike, K. R. 1964. *Language in Relation to a Unified Theory of the Structure of Human Behavior*. The Hague: Mouton.

———. 1982. *Linguistic Concepts: An Introduction to Tagmemics*. Lincoln: University of Nebraska Press.

Pitjantjatjara Bible Translation Project. 1998. *Tjukurpa Palya Jesunyatjara*. Translated by a team headed by Paul and Ann Eckert. Ernabella, South Australia: The Pitjantjatjara Bible Translation Project.

Polan, D. 1995. Globalism's Localisms. Pages 255–64 in Wilson and Dissanayake 1996a.

Prato, P., and G. Trivero. 1985. The Spectacle of Travel. Translated by I. Chambers. *Australian Journal of Cultural Studies* 3:25–43.

Pullan, R. 1989–90. In Police Custody: 200 Pages of B. Wongar's Manhunt Novel. *The Australian Author* 21:11–12.

Punt, Jeremy. 2001. The New Testament, Theology and Imperialism: Some Postcolonial Remarks on *Beyond New Testament Theology*. *Neotestamentica* 35:120–45.

———. 2002a. From Rewriting to Rereading the Bible in Postcolonial Africa: Considering the Options and Implications. *Missionala* 30:410–42.

———. 2002b Towards a Postcolonial Reading of Freedom in Paul. Pages 125–39 in *Reading the Bible in the Global Village: Cape Town*. Edited by Justin S. Upkong et. al. Society of Biblical Literature Global Perspectives on Biblical Scholarship 3. Atlanta: Society of Biblical Literature.

———. 2003a. Postcolonial Biblical Criticism in South Africa: Some Mind and Road Mapping. *Neotestamentica* 37:59–85.

———. 2003b. Why Not Postcolonial Biblical Criticism in South Africa? Stating the Obvious or Looking for the Impossible. Pages 17–44 in *Society of Biblical Literature 2003 Seminar Papers*. Atlanta: Society of Biblical Literature.

Radice, H., et al., eds. 1990. *Beyond the Nation State: Global Perspectives on Capitalism*. Special issue of *Review of Radical Economics* 22

Rafael, V. L. 1993. *Contracting Colonialism: Translation and Christian Conversion in Tagalog Society under Early Spanish Rule*. Durham, N.C.: Duke University Press.

Rajan, G., and R. Mohanram. 1995a. Introduction: Locating Postcoloniality. Pages 1–25 in *Postcolonial Discourse and Changing Cultural Contexts: Theory and*

Criticism. Edited by G. Rajan and R. Mohanran. Westport, Conn.: Greenwood.

———. 1995b. Postcolonialism/Multiculturalism—Australia 1993: An Interview with Sneja Gunew. Pages 205–18 in *Postcolonial Discourse and Changing Cultural Contexts: Theory and Criticism*. Edited by G. Rajan and R. Mohanran. Westport, Conn.: Greenwood.

Regan, P. M. 1993. The Globalization of Privacy: Implications of Recent Changes in Europe. *The American Journal of Economics and Sociology* 52:257–74.

Reichart, K. 1996. It Is Time: The Buber-Rosenzweig Bible Translation in Context. Pages 169–85 in *The Translatability of Cultures: Figurations of the Space Between*. Edited by S. Budick and W. Iser. Stanford, Calif.: Stanford University Press.

Robbins, B. 1982–3. Feeling Global: Experience and John Berger. *Boundary 2: A Journal of Postmodern Literature and Culture* 11:292–308.

Robertson, R. 1987. Globalization and Societal Modernization: A Note on Japan and Japanese Religion. *Sociological Analysis* 47:35–42.

Roof, J., and R. Wiegman, eds. 1995. *Who Can Speak? Authority and Critical Identity*. Urbana: University of Illinois Press.

Rose, D. B. 1996. Rupture and the Ethics of Care in Colonized Space. Pages 190–215 in *Prehistory to Politics: John Mulvaney, the Humanities and the Public Intellectual*. Edited by T. Bonyhady and T. Griffiths. Melbourne: Melbourne University Press.

Rose, M. A. 1991. *The Post-modern and the Post-industrial: A Critical Analysis*. Cambridge: Cambridge University Press.

Ross, R. L. 1990. The Track to Armageddon in B. Wongar's Nuclear Trilogy. *World Literature Today* 64:34–38.

Roy, A. 1995. Postcoloniality and the Politics of Identity in the Diapora: Figuring Home, Locating Histories. Pages 101–16 in *Postcolonial Discourse and Changing Cultural Contexts: Theory and Criticism*. Edited by G. Rajan and R. Mohanran. Westport, Conn.: Greenwood.

Ruccio, D. F. 1991. Postmodernism and Economics. *Journal of Post Keynesian Economics* 13:495–510.

Ryan, S. 1996. *The Cartographic Eye: How Explorers Saw Australia*. Cambridge: Cambridge University Press.

Said, E. 1978. *Orientalism*. London: Routledge & Kegan Paul.

———. 1988. Michael Walzer's *Exodus and Revolution*: A Canaanite Reading. Pages 161–78 in *Blaming the Victims: Spurious Scholarship and the Palestinian Question*. Edited by E. Said and C. Hitchens. London: Verso.

———. 1990. Reflections in Exile. Pages 357–66 in *Out There: Marginalization and Contemporary Cultures*. Edited by R. Ferguson et al. New York: New Museum of Contemporary Art.

Salvatore, D. 1993. *International Economics*. 4th edition. New York: Macmillan.

Sampson, E. E. 1989. The Challenge of Social Change for Psychology: Globalization and Psychology's Theory of the Person. *American Psychologist* 44:914–21.
San Juan, E. 1998. *Beyond Postcolonial Theory.* New York: St. Martin's.
Sawhney, S. The Joke and the Hoax: Not Speaking as the Other. Pages 208–20 in Roof and Weigman.
Scholem, G. 1981. *Walter Benjamin: The Story of a Friendship.* Translated by H. Zohn. Philadelphia: Jewish Publication Society.
Schwartz, R. *The Curse of Cain: The Violent Legacy of Monotheism.* Chicago: University of Chicago Press.
———. 1997. An Interview with Regina M. Schwartz, Author of *The Curse of Cain: The Violent Legacy of Monotheism.* Interviewed by Homi Bhabha. Online: http://www.press.uchicago.edu/Misc/Chicago/741990.html.
Scott, Jamie. 1990. *Domination and the Arts of Resistance: Hidden Transcripts.* New Haven: Yale University Press.
Segovia, Fernando F. 2000. *Decolonizing Biblical Studies: A View from the Margins.* Maryknoll, N.Y.: Orbis.
———, ed. 2000. *Interpreting Beyond Borders* Sheffield: Sheffield Academic Press.
Segovia, Fernando F., and R. S. Sugirtharajah, eds. 2007. *The Postcolonial Commentary on the New Testament.* New York: T&T Clark.
Serle, G. 1973. *From Deserts the Prophets Come: The Creative Spirit in Australia 1788–1972.* Melbourne: Heinemann.
Sharpe, J. 1993. *Allegories of Empire: The Figure of Woman in the Colonial Text.* Minneapolis: University of Minnesota Press.
Shohat, E. 1992. Antinomies of Exile: Said at the Frontiers of National Narratives. Pages 121–43 in *Edward Said: A Critical Reader.* Edited by M. Sprinker. Oxford: Blackwell.
———. 1996. Notes on the Post-colonial. Pages 322–34 in Mongia 1996.
Shohat, E., and R. Stam. 1996. From the Imperial Family to the Transnational Imaginary: Media Spectatorship in the Age of Globalization. Pages 145–70 in Wilson and Dissanayake 1996a.
Simkins, Ron. 1999. Patronage and the Political Economy of Ancient Israel. *Semeia* 87:123–44
Simon, S. 1996. *Gender in Translation: Cultural Identity and the Politics of Transmission.* London: Routledge.
Sklair, L. 1991. *Sociology of the Global System.* Baltimore: Johns Hopkins University Press.
———. 1998. Social Movements and Global Capitalism. Pages 298–312 in Jameson and Miyoshi 1998.
Spivak, G. C. 1984. The Rani of Sirmur. Pages 128–51 in vol. 1 of *Europe and Its Others.* Edited by F. Barker et al. Colchester: University of Essex.
———. 1988a. *In Other Worlds: Essays in Cultural Studies.* New York Routledge.

———. 1988b. Can the Subaltern Speak? Pages 271–313 in *Marxism and the Interpretation of Culture*. Edited by C. Nelson and L. Grossberg. London: Macmillan.

———. 1990. *The Postcolonial Critic: Interviews, Strategies, Dialogues*. Edited by S. Harasym. New York: Routledge.

———. 1993. *Outside in the Teaching Machine*. New York: Routledge.

———. 1994. How to Read a Culturally Different Book. Pages 126–50 in *Colonial Discourse/Postcolonial Theory*. Edited by F. Barker, P. Hulme, and M. Iversen. Manchester: Manchester University Press.

———. 1996. *The Spivak Reader: Selected Works of Gayatri Chakravorty Spivak*. Edited by D. Landry and G. MacLean. New York: Routledge

———. 1999. *A Critique of Postcolonial Reason: Toward a History of the Vanishing Present*. Cambridge: Harvard University Press.

Spurr, D. 1993. *The Rhetoric of Empire: Colonial Discourse in Journalism, Travel Writing, and Imperial Administration*. Durham, N.C.: Duke University Press.

Stolcke, V. 1995. Talking Culture: New Boundaries, New Rhetorics of Exclusion in Europe. *Current Anthropology* 36:1–24.

Stone, L.G. 1991. Ethics and Apologetic Tendencies in the Redaction of the Book of Joshua. *Catholic Biblical Quarterly* 53:25–36.

Strehlow, T.G.H. 1961. *Nomads in No-Man's Land*. Adelaide: Aborigines Advancement League.

Stuart, J.M. 1865. *The Journals of John McDouall Stuart During the Years 1858, 1859, 1860, 1861, and 1862, When He Fixed the Centre of the Continent and Successfully Crossed It from Sea to Sea*. Edited by W. Hardman. 2nd ed. London: Saunders, Otley.

Sturt, C. 1833. *Two Expeditions into the Interior of Southern Australia, During the Years 1828, 1829, 1830, and 1831: With Observations on the Soil, Cilmate and General Resources of the Colony of New South Wales*. 2 vols. London: Smith, Elder.

———. 1849. *Narrative of an Expedition into Central Australia, Performed under the Authority of Her Majesty's Government, During the Years 1844, 5 and 6 Together with a Notice of the Province of South Australia, in 1847*. London: Boone.

———. 1984. *Journal of the Central Australian Expedition*. Edited by J. Waterhouse. London: Caliban.

Sugirtharajah, R. S. 1993. The Bible and Its Asian Readers. *Biblical Interpretation* 1:54–66.

———. 1998a, ed. *The Postcolonial Bible*. Sheffield: Sheffield Academic Press.

———. 1998b. Biblical Studies after the Empire: From a Colonial to a Postcolonial Mode of Interpretation. Pages 12–22 in Sugirtharajah 1998a.

———. 1998c. A Postcolonial Exploration of Collusion and Construction in Biblical Interpretation. Pages 91–116 in Sugirtharajah 1998a.

———. 1999. *Asian Biblical Hermeneutics and Postcolonialism: Contesting the Interpretations*. Maryknoll, N.Y.: Orbis.
———. 2001. *The Bible and the Third World: Precolonial, Colonial and Postcolonial Encounters*. Cambridge: Cambridge University Press.
———. 2002. *Postcolonial Criticism and Biblical Studies*. Oxford: Oxford University Press.
———. 2003. *Postcolonial Reconfigurations: An Alternative Way of Reading the Bible and Doing Theology*. St. Louis: Chalice.
———. 2005. *The Bible and Empire: Postcolonial Explorations*. Cambridge: Cambridge University Press.
———. ed. 2006. *The Postcolonial Biblical Reader*. Oxford: Blackwell, 2006.
Sutherland, R. K. 1992. Israelite Political Theories in Joshua 9. *Journal for the Study of the Old Testament* 53:65–74.
Thiong'o, Ngugi Wa. 1993. The Language of African Literature. Pages 435–55 in Williams and Chrisman 1993a.
Thompson, T. L. 1992. *The Early History of the Israelite People: From the Written and Archaeolological Sources*. Leiden: Brill.
Threlkeld, L.E. 1892. *An Australian Language, as Spoken by the Awabakal, The People of Awaba or Lake Macquarie (near Newcastle, New South Wales) Being an Account of Their Language, Traditions, and Customs; The Gospel by St. Luke Translated into The Language of the Awabakal*. Edited by J. Fraser. Sydney: Potter.
Urry, J. 1990. *The Tourist Gaze: Leisure and Travel in Contemporary Societies*. London: Sage.
Van den Abbeele, G. 1980. Sightseers: The Tourist as Theorist. *Diacritics* 10:2–14.
———. 1992. *Travel as Metaphor: Form Montaigne to Rousseau*. Minneapolis: University of Minnesota Press.
Van Liemt, G. 1992. Economic Globalization: Labour Options and Business Strategies in High Labour Cost Countries. *International Labour Review* 131:453–70.
Van Raaij, W. F. 1993. Postmodern Consumption. *Journal of Economic Psychology* 14:541–63.
Virilio, P. 1977. *Vitesse et Politique: Essai de Dromologie*. Paris: Éditions Galilée.
Vitiello, V. 1998. Desert, Ethos, Abandonment: Towards a Typology of the Religious. Pages 136–69 in *Religion*. Edited by J. Derrida and G. Vattimo. Stanford, Calif.: Stanford University Press.
Vološinov, V. N. 1986. *Marxism and the Philosophy of Language*. Translated by L. Matejka and I. R. Titunik. Cambridge: Harvard University Press.
Wallerstein, I. 1983. *Historical Capitalism*. London: Verso.
Walzer, M. 1984. *Exodus and Revolution*. New York: Basic Books.
Warf, B. 1989. Telecommunications and the Globalization of Financial Services. *The Professional Geographer* 41:257–71.

West, Gerald. 1999. *The Academy of the Poor: Towards a Dialogical Reading of the Bible*. Sheffield: Sheffield Academic Press.

Whitelam, K. W. 1996. *The Invention of Ancient Israel: The Silencing of Palestinian History*. London: Routledge.

White, R. 1981. *Inventing Australia: Images and Identity, 1688–1980*. Sydney: Allen & Unwin.

Willbanks, R. 1992. *Speaking Volumes: Australian Writers and Their Work*. Ringwood, Victoria: Penguin.

Williams, P., and L. Chrisman. 1993a. *Colonial Discourse and Post-colonial Theory*. Hemel Hempstead: Harvester Wheatsheaf.

———. 1993b. Introduction. Pages 1–14 in Williams and Chrisman 1993a.

Wilson, R. 1996. *Goodbye Paradise*: Global/Localism in the American Pacific. Pages 312–36 in Wilson and Dissanayake 1996a.

Wilson, R., and W. Dissanayake, eds. 1996a. *Global/Local: Cultural Production and the Transnational Imaginary*. Durham, N.C.: Duke University Press.

———. 1996b. Introduction: Tracking the Global/Local. Pages 1–18 in Wilson and Dissanayake 1996a.

Wongar, B. 1975. *The Trackers*. Collingwood, Victoria: Outback.

———. 1982. *Babaru*. Urbana: University of Illinois Press.

———. 1986a. *Walg*. Melbourne: Macmillan.

———. 1986b. *Karan*. Melbourne: Macmillan.

———. 1988. *Gabo Djara*. Melbourne: Macmillan.

———. 1992a. *Marngit*. North Ryde, New South Wales: Angus & Robertson.

———. 1992b. *The Track to Bralgu*. Pymble, New South Wales: Angus & Robertson.

———. 1993. *The Last Pack of Dingoes*. Pymble, New South Wales: Angus & Robertson.

———. 1994. *Raki*. Pymble, New South Wales: HarperCollins.

Wright, G. E. 1950. *The Old Testament against Its Environment*. London: SCM.

Yallop, C. 1982. *Australian Aboriginal Languages*. London: Andre Deutsch.

Yee, Gale A. 1999. Gender, Class and the Social Scientific Study of Genesis 2–3. *Semeia* 87:177–92.

———. 2003. *Poor Banished Children of Eve: Woman as Evil in the Hebrew Bible*. Louisville: Westminster John Knox.

———. 2007. Ideological Criticism: Judges 17–21 and the Dismembered Body. Pages 138–60 in *Judges and Method: New Approaches in Biblical Studies*. Edited by Gale A. Yee. Minneapolis: Fortress.

Ziegler, J., ed. 1968. *Septuaginta: Vetus Testamentum Graecum 16/2: Susanna, Daniel, Bel et Draco*. Göttingen: Vandenhoeck & Ruprecht.

Žižek, S. 1996. *The Indivisible Remainder: An Essay on Schelling and Related Matters*. London: Verso.

Zumthor, P. 1994. The Medieval Travel Narrative. Translated by C. Peebles. *New Literary History* 25:809–24.

Biblical Index

Genesis
1:1	156
1:10	105
1:12	105
1:18	105
1:21	105
1:25	105
1:28	85
2–3	43
3:17–19	105
28:18	64
30:11	66
31:46	63
37:12–36	100

Exodus
5:1	100
5:3	100
5:8	100
5:17	100
15:24	88
16:2	88
16:3	88
16:7	88
16:8	88
16:9	88
16:12	88
17:3	88
32	88

Leviticus
15:19	67
19:32	63

Numbers
11:1	88
11:4–6	88
12	88
12:14	65
13–14	88
14:2	88
14:27	88
14:34	88
14:36	88
16	88
16:11	88
16:41	88
17:5	88
17:10	88
17:20 [MT]	88
17:25 [MT]	88

Deuteronomy
26:5	82
32:10	102, 104

Joshua
2	131
2:9–11	127
6	90
7–8	90
7–9	89
9	8, 91, 109, 110, 125, 127, 130–32, 161
9:1	126
9:3	125, 126
9:4–5	127

Joshua (cont.)		Judges	
9:4–6	125	1	90
9:6	126		
9:7	125	**1 Samuel**	
9:8–10	125	21–30	65
9:9	126	26:8–9	65
9:9–10	126		
9:9–13	126	**2 Samuel**	
9:11–14	125	1:10	63
9:12	124, 126	16:13	65
9:12–13	126, 127		
9:15	125, 129	**1 Kings**	
9:16	125	13:2	62
9:17	126		
9:17–21	125	**2 Kings**	
9:18	129	23:16	62
9:18–20	130		
9:18–21	128, 129	**Nehemiah**	
9:19	129	8:15	64
9:20	129	9:19–25	88
9:21	128, 130		
9:22	126	**Psalms**	
9:22–23	129	68:7–8	88
9:22–27	125	72	43, 44
9:23	130	72:1–7	43
9:25	129	78:12–20	88
9:27	130	78:55	87
10	89		
10:2	90	**Proverbs**	
10:31–32	89	6:6	109
10:34–35	89	30:25	116
10:36–37	90		
10:38–39	89	**Isaiah**	
11	89	10:33–11:1	43
11:10–11	89	22:15–17	62
12:14	90	24:17	64
13–21	89	41:17	60
13:2–6	90	41:17–18	60
15:13–19	90	41:18	60
15:63	90	43:19	60
23:7–13	90	49:22	64
		64:3–4	63
		65:4	63

BIBLICAL INDEX

Jeremiah
2:2-7   89
6:1   63
9:17   62
9:18   62
48:37   62

Ezekiel
17   43
19:10-14   43
20:10-17   88
23:14   66
23:15   66
31   43

Daniel
1-6   42
4   8, 38, 42-49, 53, 161
4:7-9 [MT]   38
4:8   42
4:10-12   38
4:10-14 [MT]   46
4:11 [MT]   46
4:11-14 [MT]   48
4:12 [MT]   43
4:13 [MT]   47
4:13-14 [MT]   43
4:13-17   46
4:14   46
4:14 [MT]   48
4:14-17   48
4:15   43
4:15-24 [MT]   43
4:16   47
4:16-17   43
4:17   48
4:19-27   43
7-12   42

Hosea
2:21-25   89

Mark
1:1   157
4:10   157
4:13   157
4:14   157

John
1   157
1:1   156, 157

Acts
22:23   65

Subject Index

Aborigines, Aboriginal   7-9, 13-16, 19, 32, 57, 60-67, 74-76, 79-80, 84, 86, 102-3, 105-6, 109-12, 117-22, 124, 135, 137, 141-43, 146-59, 161, 163-65, 167-71
agency   4, 27, 30-1, 135, 143-7
anticapitalism   168-71
anti-essentialism   19, 94, 112-16, 124, 131-33
antipodality (as politics)   17-22
Asiatic mode of production   44-45, 47, 52-53, 90, 95, 127
Awabakal (language and people)   86, 142, 151, 155
Bible Society (in Australia)   137, 141, 143, 155-57
British and Foreign Bible Society in Australia   156
Canaan   82-93, 130
capitalism   5-6, 17-22, 24, 29, 39-42, 45, 49, 51-53, 55, 70, 73, 75, 87, 94, 99-101, 133, 143-44, 162, 166, 168-71
church   11-12, 15-16, 32, 35, 37, 146, 162-66
   Anglican   61, 78, 123, 162, 164
   Congregationalist   164
   Dissenting   86, 151, 162-64
   Methodist   162-64
   Presbyterian   11, 15, 154, 162-64
   Roman Catholic   12, 37, 155, 162-64, 166
   Uniting   146
class   10-11, 16, 19-20, 22, 25-26, 32-35, 41, 52-54, 70-71, 73, 98-100, 130-31, 147, 165
colonialism   2-14, 16-17, 19-20, 23-31, 40, 68, 73, 75-76, 78, 81, 100, 109-10, 113, 116, 120, 122, 128, 130, 144-47, 151-53, 161-71
colonized   2, 7, 21, 30, 110, 113, 116, 121-23, 135, 145, 169-70
colonizer   7-8, 27, 30, 110, 121-22, 135, 145, 154
cultural cringe   9-10
cultural hierarchy   9
decolonization   5-7, 116, 154
deconstruction   3, 26-27, 30-31, 112, 115
desert   10, 57, 59-61, 74, 76, 79, 88, 94-96, 102-6, 117-18, 150, 154; *see also* wilderness
diaspora   2, 30, 93-94, 96-98, 100-101
disintegration   5, 13, 37, 40, 46, 52-55; *see also* reification
DuBois, W. E. B.   4, 24-25
dynamic equivalence   137-41, 156
emulation (in biblical scholarship)   12-13
Ernabella   74, 142, 146, 149-50, 154, 165
essentialism, 3-4, 8, 109-17, 121, 123-24, 127, 131-33, 146, 161; *see also* anti-essentialism
ethics   52-55
exile   3, 8, 81, 83, 91-103, 105, 110, 161
exodus   8, 34, 81-93, 95-96, 98, 102, 109-10, 161, 166, 168

SUBJECT INDEX

explorers (of Australia)   8, 57–80, 87, 99, 104, 109–10, 136, 144, 149, 161
Fanon, Frantz   3, 9, 24–25, 27, 98, 169
feminism   3, 16, 26, 30, 48, 78, 111, 112, 123
Gibeonites   124–32
globalization   2–5, 8, 13–14, 16, 37–42, 44–55, 161–62
hegemony   4, 18–19, 22, 24–26, 138
hybridity   3, 27, 31, 101, 144–47
identity   2, 3, 8–9, 14, 16, 27–28, 30, 46, 51–53, 83, 85, 91, 93–94, 96–98, 101, 109–11, 113–14, 116–17, 121–25, 131, 135, 143, 161, 167
ideology   2, 11–12, 15, 18–22, 25–28, 35–38, 42–46, 48, 51, 54–55, 59, 73, 75, 82–83, 87, 90–98, 101–2, 112, 127, 130, 139, 156, 162, 164, 167–69
Israel   8, 31, 34, 44, 53, 58–67, 82–92, 95, 98, 101, 104, 109, 125–32, 161, 166–67
Israelites (Aborigines as implicit)   58–67
Korah   34
Lacan, Jacques   4, 27, 30–31, 111, 132
Marx, Karl   3–4, 20–29, 32–33, 40–41, 50, 55, 69, 83, 95–96, 112, 133, 166, 170–71
Marxism   3–5, 15, 17–20, 22–30, 32–34, 39–41, 49, 54, 82–83, 90, 96, 112, 130, 132, 147, 164, 168–69, 171
method   1–2, 15, 23, 26–28, 30, 31, 33, 37–39, 72, 109–10, 147; *see also* postcolonial criticism and postcolonial theory
hunting methods   63–64
mimicry   3, 15–16, 27, 122, 144–45
missionaries   71, 86, 99, 142–51, 153–55, 163–64, 166, 170
missions   61, 137, 151–52, 154, 156, 162–64
nationalism   3, 10, 12–15, 22, 32, 51, 54, 83, 98

nomad, nomadism, nomadology   3, 8, 82, 90–98, 100–102
nominalism—*see* essentialism
panopticism   67–78
Philippines   144, 155, 163
Pitjantjatjara (language and people)   137, 143–44, 148–50, 153–57
positive unoriginality   14–17
postcolonial criticism   1–4, 6, 17, 23–24, 27–29, 68, 81, 110, 168–70
postcolonial theory   1, 3–4, 8, 23–28, 30–31, 49, 81, 101, 109, 115–16, 161–62, 169
postmodernism   3, 5, 8, 12, 17–19, 21, 31, 37–38, 51, 53–54, 81, 94, 96–98, 100–101, 111–12, 114–15, 124, 132, 143, 169, 171
providence   58–61, 69–78, 87
psychoanalysis   27, 30, 95–96
queer readings   78–80
reification   49–55, 168; *see also* disintegration
subaltern, subalternity   3, 112–13, 121
subject, the   2, 30–31, 48, 72, 112–13, 132
colonial subject   2, 7, 116
subject position   109, 111, 132
subject-effect   117, 121, 124–25
Summer Institute of Linguistics   136–37, 143, 155; *see also* Wycliffe Bible Translators
Tagalog   144, 146, 148
tagmemics   136, 139
Tjukurpa   152–58
translation (Bible)   2–3, 8, 39, 133, 135–59, 161, 164, 166
tyranny of distance   10–12
wilderness   74, 81–82, 85, 87–88, 91–99, 102–7; *see also* desert
world tree   42–7
Wycliffe Bible Translators   136, 141, 143, 152; *see also* Summer Institute of Linguistics

Author Index

Achebe, C. 154
Adam, I. 3
Adorno, T. W. 97
Afshar, F. 39
Ahlström, G. W. 91
Ahmad, A. 3-4, 12, 20-22
Albright, W. F. 89-90
Alt, A. 89
Amin, S. 49
Appadurai, A. 52
Appiah, K. A. 171
Aronson, J. D. 39
Ashcroft, B. 4, 6, 14, 99
Assmann, J. 140, 158
Bakhtin, M. 23, 27-28, 30-34
Barnstone, W. 135, 139-40, 158
Barnwell, K. 143
Baudrillard, J. 100
Beekman, J. 138-39
Behdad, A. 99-100
Belasco, W. J. 99
Bell, S. 39
Bello, W. 39
Benjamin, W. 94, 139-41, 152, 155, 158-59
Benterrak, K. 102
Bentham, J. 68-72, 76, 78, 102
Berquist, Jon L. ix
Beyer, P. 39, 41, 49
Bhabha, H. K. 3-4, 6, 8, 15, 24, 26-28, 31-34, 81, 93, 97-98, 122, 125, 135, 144-46, 161, 169
Blainey, G. 10, 102
Blake, B. J. 150
Bloch, Ernst 23, 33-35, 88, 164, 166, 168
Boehmer, E. 3, 122
Boer, R. 28, 30, 127
Bośovič, M. 71-72
Boyer, Robert 29
Bowe, H. J. 150
Boyarin, D. 93-96, 101-2, 161
Boyarin, J. 93-96, 101-2, 161
Brett, Mark 28, 31-35
Brewster, A. 5, 8
Bright, J. 89
Brown, D. 49
Buckley, K. 18
Callaghan, D. 123-24
Callow, J. 138-39
Cathcart, M. 78-79
Cerny, P. G. 39
Chakrabarty, D. 3
Chaseling, W. S. 102
Chrisman, L. 40
Collins, J. J. 42-43, 45
Confoy, M. 16
Connor, M. 16, 120
Cooke, M. 143, 157
Coombes, A. E. 3
Coote, R.B. 91
Copleston, F. 115
Cowan, G. M. 141, 154
Cowhey, P. F. 39
Coxon, P. W. 42
Croatto, J. S. 82
Curthoys, A. 84-85
Dandeker, C. 39

AUTHOR INDEX

Darby, P. 3
Davies, M. R. 39
Davies, P. 91, 131
Deleuze, G. 94–96, 100, 102, 112, 161
Derrida, Jacques 4, 26, 38, 112, 115, 124, 132
Devi, M. 3
Dicken, P. 39
Dirlik, A. 4–5, 21, 28–29, 48, 53–54, 93, 101, 169
Dissanayake, W. 49, 51, 52, 135
Dixon, R. M. W. 150–51
Dobrez, L. 119
Docker, J. 9, 85
Donaldson, Laura E. ix
Douglas, Mary 31
Douglas, W. H. 150
Drewe, R. 117
Dube, Musa x
Duff, A. 114
Dussell, E. 3, 21
Eades, D. 149
Eckert, A. 142–44, 153
Eckert, P. 143–4, 153, 156
Elliott, B. 104–5
Engels, F. 41
Eyre, E. J. 57–58, 60, 65, 67, 74, 77, 99, 161
Featherstone, M. 52
Feuer, L. S. 83
Fitzgerald, R. 18
Foucault, M. 4, 26, 68–73, 82, 125, 132
Frampton, K. 17
Freud, S. 68, 78, 88, 98, 127, 129
Fuery, P. 7
Fuss, D. 113–14, 132,
Gandhi, L. 3
George, R. M. 20
Giddens, A. 40
Giles, E. 57–61, 74, 76, 79–80, 87, 89, 99, 103–5
Gill, S. 39
Ginibi, R. L. 121
Glass, A. 137
Goddard, C. 150, 155
Goldingay, J. E. 42
Gottwald, N. K. 28, 89–90
Gourgouris, S. 100, 145
Gramsci, Antonio 4, 17, 19, 25–28
Gray, J. 125
Greenwood, J. 39
Grey, G. 57–60, 66–67, 74–75, 78, 99, 103, 148
Griffiths, G. 4, 6, 14, 99, 113
Guattari, F. 94–96, 100, 102, 112, 161
Guha, R. 3
Gunew, S. 7–9
Gwin, M. 100
Hackett, D. 137
Hall, S. 41, 114
Haraway, D. 112, 125
Hardt, Michael 29
Harris, J. 151, 153
Harvey, D. 45
Harvey, J. 39
Head, B. 39
Hegel, G. W. F. 1, 49, 50, 94,
Helleiner, E. 39
Hetata, S. 52
Hodge, B. 6, 100, 103
Hoglund, Kenneth 31
Hoksbergen, R. 49
Hoogvelt, A. 3, 39
Hope, A. D. 104, 106
Horsley, Richard 28
Houle, F. 39
Houlihan, B. 39
Hughes, R. 18
James, C. L. R. 3, 25,
Jameson, F. 3, 5–6, 19, 22–3, 37–38, 40, 49–51, 53–54, 70, 87, 96, 115, 169
Jamieson-Drake, D. W. 91
JanMohamed, A. 53
Jobling, D. 28, 43–44
Kaplan, Caren 81–82, 98–99

Kapur, G.	3, 51	Montgomery, J. A.	42–45
Kilham, C. A.	137–39, 141–43, 152–53	Moore, Stephen D.	ix–x
Kirby, R. G.	39	Moore-Gilbert, B.	3, 20, 25, 168–69
Kitson, J.	40	Moran, T. H.	39
Kolodny, A.	79	Morris, J.	49
Koolmatrie, W. (L. Carmen)	122	Morris, M.	7, 10, 15–16, 144
Kwok Pui-Lan	10	Mosala, Itumeleng	29
Laclau, E.	18–19, 115, 125	Mouffe, C.	18–19, 115–16, 125
Lacocque, A.	42–43, 47–48	Mountford, C. P.	102
Larsen, N.	114	Moylan, Tom	33
Larson, M. L.	138	Mudrooroo Narogin Nyoongah (C. Johnson)	15–16, 121–22
Lattas, A.	84		
Law, D.	39	Muecke, S.	102–3
Lawson, H.	104–5	Naficy, A.	51
Lears, T. J. J.	55	Negri, A.	29
Lee, D.A.	16	Nida, E. A.	136–41, 155–56
Lefebvre, H.	52	Noth, M.	89–90, 125
Leichhardt, L.	57, 61, 67, 74–75	Nowotny, J.	16
Lemche, N. P.	91	O'Brien, R.	39
Lenin, V. I.	24	Ohmae, K.	39
Lloyd, D.	53	Paik Nak-Chung	3, 22, 40, 51
Longacre, R. E.	136, 139	Parpart, J. L.	49
Loomba, A.	3, 110, 113	Parry, B.	113
Louw, J. P.	137	Pattel-Gray, A.	16
Lukács, G.	50, 97	Paxman, D. B.	100
MacCannell, D.	99–100	Picciotto, S.	39
Maguire, J.	39	Pike, K. R.	31, 136, 139
Maley, W.	3	Polan, D.	53
Marx, K.	41, 50, 69	Prato, P.	99
Masters, F.	85	Pullan, R.	119
Matthews, D.	16, 120	Punt, Jeremy	x
McClintock, A.	5	Radice, H.	39
McKinlay, Judith	x	Rafael, V. L.	144–48, 152, 155–56
Mendenhall, G. E.	90	Rajan, G.	3, 8–9, 13
Meschonnic, H.	139	Regan, P. M.	49
Miller, M.	39	Reichart, K.	141, 159
Mishra, V.	6, 100, 103	Robbins, B.	40
Mitchell, K.	53, 101	Robertson, R.	39
Mitchell, T. L.	57, 62–66, 69, 74–75, 87, 99, 104, 106, 161	Robins, L.	39
		Roe, P.	102
Miyoshi, M.	39, 49, 53	Roof, J.	123
Mohanram, R.	3, 8–9, 13	Rose, D. B.	84–85
Mohanty, C. T.	78	Rose, M. A.	41

AUTHOR INDEX

Ross, R. L. 118
Roy, A. 97
Ruccio, D. F. 49
Ryan, S. 17, 68–69, 72–74, 76, 78, 144
Said, E. 3–4, 6, 8, 20, 24–26, 28, 82–85, 92–93, 97–98, 125, 161, 169
Salvatore, D. 39
Sampson, E. E. 39
San Juan, E. 3, 20
Sawhney, S. 112, 123–24, 132
Schwartz, R. 83–85
Scott, J. 31
Segovia, Fernando ix–x
Serle, G. 81
Sharpe, J. 113
Shohat, E. 5, 28, 41, 52, 83–85, 93–94, 97
Simkins, Ron 28
Simon, S. 139
Sklair, L. 29, 39, 54
Spivak, G. C. 3–4, 6, 17, 24, 26, 28, 31, 101, 112–13, 115, 117, 121, 123, 125, 136, 152, 169, 171
Spurr, D. 19, 68–69, 75
Stam, R. 41, 52
Stanton, G. 3
Stolcke, V. 39
Stone, L. G. 125
Strehlow, T. G. H. 102, 142, 151
Stuart, J. M. 57, 61–62, 75, 99, 114, 161
Sturt, C. 57, 61, 67, 74–79, 99, 103
Sugirtharajah, R. S. ix, xiv, 16, 28–31
Sutherland, R. K. 125, 127

Taber, C. R. 137–38, 140
Thiong'o, Ngugi Wa 154
Thompson, T. L. 91
Threlkeld, L. E. 86–87, 89, 142–43, 151–53, 155, 164
Tiffin, H. 3–4, 6, 14, 99, 113
Trivero, G. 99
Urry, J. 99
Van den Abbeele, G. 99–100
Van Liemt, G. 39
Van Raaij, W. F. 49
Virilio, P. 41
Vitiello, V. 94
Vološinov, V. N. 32, 147–48
Wallerstein, I. 40–41
Walzer, M. 82–83
Warf, B. 39
West, Gerald 28
Wheelwright, T. 18
White, R. 81, 106
Whitelam, K. W. 91–92, 131
Wiegman, R. 123
Willbanks, R. 118
Williams, P. 40
Wilson, R. 49, 51, 52, 53, 135
Wongar, B. 7, 16, 109–10, 116–25, 132
Wright, G. E. 89
Yallop, C. 149–50
Yee, G. 28
Ziegler, J. 42
Zumthor, P. 99
Žižek, S. 32, 43, 51, 70, 111

www.ingramcontent.com/pod-product-compliance
Lightning Source LLC
Chambersburg PA
CBHW031312150426
43191CB00005B/202